Christian-Jewish Dialogue

–

Exploring Our Commonalities
and Our Differences

HEBRAIC HERITAGE CHRISTIAN CENTER

Hebraic Heritage Christian Center is an institution of higher education that is dedicated to the vision of restoring a Hebraic model for Christian education. A consortium of scholars, spiritual leaders, and business persons, the Center features a continually developing curriculum in which each course of study is firmly anchored in the Hebrew foundations of the Christian faith.

The Hebraic Heritage Christian Center vision combines both the ancient and the most modern in an educational program that conveys knowledge, understanding, and wisdom to a world-wide student population. The Center seeks to restore the foundations of original Christianity in order to equip its students with historically accurate, theologically sound understanding of the biblical faith that Jesus and the apostles instituted and practiced. At the same time the Center endeavors to implement the finest in innovative, cutting-edge technology in a distance-learning program that delivers its user-friendly courses by the Internet.

Among the wide range of services and products that Hebraic Heritage Christian Center offers are the publications of Hebraic Heritage Press. These are delivered both in traditional print media as well as in electronic media to serve both the Center's student population and the general public with inspiring and challenging materials that have been developed by the Center's team of scholars.

Among the additional resources of the Hebraic Heritage Christian Center is its journal, *The Christian Hebraist*, which offers periodical scholarly insights into ongoing research from the field of Hebraic-Christian theological restoration and spiritual renewal.

Those who are interested in sharing in the development of Hebraic Heritage Christian Center and its commitment to restoring the Jewish roots of the Christian faith are invited to join the Founders' Club, people who support this team of scholars and leaders by becoming co-founders of this institution. Many opportunities for endowments are also available to those who wish to create a lasting memorial to the cause of Christian renewal and Christian-Jewish rapprochement.

HEBRAIC HERITAGE CHRISTIAN CENTER

P. O. Box 450848
Atlanta, GA 31145-0848
www.hebraiccenter.org

Christian-Jewish Dialogue

–

Exploring Our Commonalities and Our Differences

By Isaac C. Rottenberg

PRESS
Hebraic Heritage Press
P. O. Box 450848
Atlanta, GA 31145-0848
www.hebraiccenter.org

*This book is dedicated to
the memory of*

SRUL TABAKSBLAT

*Disciple of Yeshua and
Teacher of Torah*

TABLE OF CONTENTS

FOREWORD

By the dawn of the second century of the common era, the faith community that had been birthed and nurtured by Jesus and his apostles had begun to drift away from its moorings in the safe harbor of the Judaism in which the founders of the Christian faith had lived their lives and had expressed their devotion to God. Because they had understood their prophetic mission to be a light to the nations, the leaders of the nascent church had opened the door of faith to the Gentiles around them. Ever increasing numbers of former aliens from the Commonwealth of Israel had been grafted into God's family tree of salvation and covenant relationship.

In order to fulfill the Great Commission, the final commandment of Jesus himself, the church adopted strategies for mission that they had learned from the Pharisees and other Jewish leaders who had become witnesses to the nations of God and his Word. They made one mistake, however: they crossed the line between a healthy contextualization of their faith for the masses and an insidious syncretism that brought pagan philosophy and tradition into the church. Thus began the process of Hellenization and Latinization that severed the church's connection with its Jewish roots and created an ever-widening breach with the Christians' co-religionists, the Jews.

Because of the church's increasing infatuation with other worldviews and philosophies, what began as a rift within the family of God began to grow into an ever widening and deepening chasm. Christianity eventually came to define itself as being "not Jewish," something that Jesus himself would never have understood, much less have condoned. Christianity forsook its patrimony, renounced its citizenship, and abandoned its heritage. God's family became increasingly dysfunctional and exploded in domestic violence: child against parent, brother against brother in ever mounting internecine strife. When the church finally gained political acceptance, the scene was set for unspeakable horrors.

The sad tragedy of ecclesiastical history's ever-unfolding foment of division, conflict, and violence–both emotional and physical–found its foundation in the proto-schism that parted the ways between Christianity and Judaism. What had been birthed in the transcendent love of Jesus was perverted into a culture of hate that for centuries was focused upon the Jewish people. The resulting trail of human suffering is virtually incomprehensible. The Jewish people were subjected to unrelenting and systematic caricature and slander, violence and mayhem, torture and murder that finally culminated in the Holocaust of the twentieth century and the murder of six million Jews, including over one million children.

With an honest view of ecclesiastical history, how could anyone expect that any relationship could be possible between the perpetrators and the victims of this seemingly unending terror and violence? In what can only be described as amazing grace, however, the Jewish people have opened their hearts to Christian repentance to God for the atrocities of the past, and they have opened their minds to dialogue with individual Christians and with Christian faith communities!

Breaking with nineteen centuries of contempt for Jews and Judaism, Christians by the thousands, perhaps millions, have come to recognize the error of past ignorance, arrogance, and triumphalism. Light from the Jewish lamp that the church had exhausted all efforts to extinguish has begun to shine into Christian hearts. Faith communions both large and small have come face to face with the truth of Jesus' declaration that "salvation is from the Jews."

Rapprochement is the spirit of the day, a time when Christians have begun to recognize that the biblical foundations of their faith are Jewish foundations. In ever-increasing numbers, they are seeking interaction with their Jewish brothers and sisters. The initially tentative dialogue has become more healthy and robust as respect has been earned by action as well as by word.

Many pioneers led the way in early post-Holocaust dialogue efforts. Some were mavericks, inflaming their own and others' passions with challenging rhetoric. Others were careful and methodical proponents of the need for and methods of individual and group interaction. Together, they opened a door that decades before would have seemed impossibly sealed. Hearts were made bare and were unashamed. Words were exchanged. Meeting began.

Among the pious men and women whom God used in the formative stages of the Christian-Jewish dialogue was Rev. Isaac C. Rottenberg, a pastor and theologian who accepted the call to play a leading role as a catalyst for dialogue. The son of a Jewish father and a Christian mother, he had unique insights into both Judaism and Christianity and their relationship with each other. Indeed, Isaac has been able to discuss from experience the perspectives of at least four communities: the traditional Jewish community, mainline denominational Christianity, evangelical Christianity, and the Messianic Jewish community.

An open and honest broker of transparent integrity, Isaac helped lead the fledgling dialogue movement through minefields of potential disaster. Even when he was personally victimized by the drama of bureaucratic intrigue, he stood resolutely for the principles on which he had ordered his life. He became a dialoguer *par excellence*, daring to open doors and explore with grace and dignity areas where others feared to go.

For more than 40 years, Isaac Rottenberg has poured his life into the effort to build bridges between Christians and Jews and between Christianity and Judaism. He has paid a dear price for his passion and his devotion to this quest. The hand of the Lord of Israel has been upon him, however, leading him and sustaining him.

Isaac has contributed significantly to the dialogue both in his careful analysis of difficult and sensitive issues and in his promotion of the need for and the means of achieving true dialogue. His writings have been published in numerous journals and in book form, inspiring untold numbers of people with knowledge about the subject matter and wisdom to implement it.

Christian-Jewish Dialogue: Exploring Our Commonalities and Our Differences is the result of an effort to bring together Rottenberg treasures both old and new and to publish them in a form that can be a virtual textbook on Christian-Jewish dialogue. The fact that this book is being produced at this time, on the occasion of Isaac's 80th birthday, is a testimony to the longevity of his commitment to the dialogue and to the track record of integrity that has made such a long-standing commitment possible and successful.

Isaac Rottenberg has both preached and practiced his insights into dialogue. He is both a hearer and a doer of the work, and his practical experience makes his theory all the more powerful. These are ideas that have been tested in the crucible of the active dialogue movement over several decades, and they are trustworthy.

This is a book that you will want to reread, perhaps many times. The information and observations are so profound and the outpouring of the heart is so eloquent that you will be enriched each time you return to this fountain of inspiration and insight. Through Isaac Rottenberg's eyes you will see the wisdom of a wide range of scholars, and you will hear their heartbeat as well. You will gain the wisdom of one who has lived the book.

The range of insights in this volume is very comprehensive. Things that every Christian believer needs to know about Christian-Jewish relations are clearly and unequivocally set forth in eloquent and challenging style. All the essentials are here. Implementation of these ideas in the spirit in which they are proposed will do nothing but move the Christian-Jewish dialogue along toward a better and brighter future in which the covenant peoples of God can stand alongside one another in mutual affirmation.

Great opportunities await those who are bold enough to lay hold on the vision for Christian-Jewish rapprochement and to actualize that vision through concrete actions of the grace that is born only in the *chesed* of God himself. Christians can ensure that the church will never again be complicit in either overt actions against the Jewish people or in conspiracies of silence in the face of mounting global anti-Semitism. They can echo the anguished cry of the Jewish heart, "Never again!" They can join one of Jesus' maternal ancestors, who also happened to be a Gentile, in an exclamation of the soul to their Jewish family: "Your God shall be my God; your people shall be my people; where you live I will live; and where you die, I will die." Nothing less than this level of total commitment will suffice in a day when human hearts are increasingly and desperately wicked.

Rev. Isaac Rottenberg's life is a testimony to commitment on this level. It has been freely and uncompromisingly offered to the God he has revered, to the Christian church that he has served, and to the Jewish community that he has honored and supported.

I pray that this volume will inspire you and will move you to action to join the growing numbers of Christians and Jews who understand the need for building strong relationships of mutual respect and support that will stand the test of time.

John D. Garr
Chancellor
Hebraic Heritage Christian Center

PREFACE

Dialogue has become a popular concept in recent decades, not only in religious circles but in the realms of education and business as well. Through excessive and careless usage, however, the word may face the danger of being devalued to buzzword status. TV commentator Edwin Newman, apparently tired of hearing the term, has called it "one of the most boring words to come along in years . . . a word that is bunk." After all, he added, it just means that people are talking.

True dialogue, however, means more than "just talk." It is talk of a special quality, talk that involves conversation of the deeper kind. It has been said that when two people talk with each other, six "parties" may be involved: what each person said–two parties; what each person heard the other person say–two more; and finally, what each person really meant to say–a total of six perspectives.

Talk without genuine listening does not constitute dialogue. True listening seeks to hear what is behind the words, or even behind the unsaid. Martin Buber, author of the classic "I-thou," tells the story about an evening when he was engaged in deep thought and a student called saying that he urgently needed to talk. Buber arranged for an appointment the next day. That night the student committed suicide. Reflecting on this tragic event, the great philosopher confessed that he had failed to hear the "unuttered." He had heard, but not listened with love.

Dialogue enables people to talk about things that really matter. This is particularly true of interfaith dialogue, when we deal with issues of ultimate concern. We move beyond abstractions and enter into the sphere where mind and heart meet. David Bohm, a distinguished physicist who wrote extensively on the subject, referred to dialogue as "a process of awakening." Buber also spoke about sparks flying back and forth from heart to heart in true dialogue. Such experiences continue an ancient tradition, as Plato already used similar language when he wrote: "Suddenly a light, as it were, is kindled in one soul by a flame that leaps to it from another, and thereafter sustains itself" (see *The Seeker,* by Daniel J. Boorstin, p. 34). At its best, dialogue will be a transforming force.

In this volume we focus on Christian-Jewish dialogue. After centuries of estrangement and hostility, particularly on the part of Christians against Jews, the two communities have now been in conversation for about fifty years. Much has been achieved, but many obstacles to reconciliation remain. So much bad history needs to be overcome! It is our hope that this volume will be of some help in the urgent cause of bridging what some perceive to be an impassable chasm.

The essays gathered here have grown out of the author's personal participation in many dialogue events. As is indicated, most of the chapters have been published before in various journals and periodicals. We are grateful for permission to reproduce them in this collection.

Over the years my son, Dr. John A. M. Rottenberg, has faithfully served as my editorial critic. For this I owe him a debt of gratitude. He deserves credit for some of the positive features the reader may find in this volume. The blame for any shortcomings belongs entirely to me.

Isaac C. Rottenberg

DYNAMICS OF DIALOGUE

CHAPTER 1

The Risk Factor in Interreligious Relations

"The most important prerequisite of interfaith is faith"
Abraham Joshua Heschel

The interchurch dialogue movement has evolved out of the (at first predominantly Protestant) ecumenical movement with its search for greater unity. The ecumenical movement itself evolved out of the missionary movement as the people involved in church missions increasingly experienced the export of Western denominational divisions to other continents as an embarrassment, if not a scandal. Major Ecumenical Missionary Conferences (Edinburgh, 1910; Jerusalem, 1928; Tambaran, India, 1938) laid the foundation for the World Council of Churches, which was born in 1948, after a delay of some years because of World War II.

The post-World War II period brought about a number of radical changes on both the world and church scenes.

• The era of Western colonialism came to an end. The spirit of anti-colonialism led to a critical assessment of the elements of cultural imperialism that had become embedded in Christian missionary practice. The establishment of independent nations led to the development of indigenous churches, with leadership increasingly in the hands of local Christians free to cast the gospel message in the cultural forms of their society.

• The conciliar ecumenical movement and the Roman Catholic Church felt increasingly compelled to face the implications of the split between them that had existed since the 16th century. Ironically, the war which had caused so much separation and breakdown of communication also brought together Protestant and Catholic missionaries stranded in various part of the world, as well as Protestant and Catholic church leaders imprisoned in Nazi camps, under conditions that engendered conversations between them on a depth level most of these people had not known before. Finally, the Second Vatican Council (1963-1965) would prove to be an ecumenical event of world-historic significance.

• Among the greatest horrors of World War II must be counted the Nazi war against the Jewish people. The post-Holocaust era saw some Christian leaders ready to confront the long history of ecclesiastical anti-

Judaism, including the role Christian attitudes toward Jews had played in cultivating the soil in which Hitler's "Final Solution" was able to flourish.

• Recognition of the powerful impact which cultural and religious pluralism is having on the contemporary world led to a re-evaluation of certain policies and doctrinal positions within the Christian community. What about the relationship of the churches to other major religions and ideologies? Is it time to abandon the church's missionary outreach and turn to dialogue instead? Since Christianity and Judaism share a unique (albeit mostly unhappy) history, the question arose as to where Christian-Jewish relations would fit into the overall scheme of things. The World Council of Churches (WCC) established a separate Consultation on the Church and the Jewish People within the Division of Dialogue with People of Living Faiths and Ideologies. From time to time suggestions have been made that this relationship be treated as an ecumenical rather than an interfaith issue (for instance, as part of the Faith and Order Commission), but that idea has not met with positive responses from Jewish leaders. Vatican II originally dealt with the non-Christian religions within the schema of the Decree on Ecumenism, but eventually issued the Declaration on the Relationship of the Church to the Non-Christian Religions (*Nostra Aetate*) as a separate document with a rather lengthy section on the church's relationship to the Jewish people. "Since the spiritual patrimony common to Christians and Jews is ... so great," declared the delegates, "this sacred Synod wishes to foster and recommend that mutual understanding and respect which is the fruit above all of biblical and theological studies, and of brotherly dialogues." One by one, churches have abandoned the supersessionist theologies which for centuries had taught that the church has replaced a rejected Jewish people in the divine covenant.

Today, debates and occasional controversies are raging on such issues as pluralism, Christian mission, the religion/culture dynamic in various societies, and the further need to revise certain doctrinal positions, particularly with respect to Christology. We have already referred to the question of mission or dialogue. In many ecclesiastical and ecumenical documents, mission and dialogue are treated as activities that go on simultaneously. For some theologians, however, the reality of pluralism makes it increasingly an either-or issue.

Diana Eck, who for years has been active in interfaith dialogues under sponsorship of the WCC, sees interreligious dialogue as a major factor in the pursuit of world peace.[1] Her view of authentic religious pluralism leaves little room for Christian witness in the traditional sense of proclaiming confessional truth (*kerygma*), as distinguished from involvement in projects of social concern (*diakonia*). "Those of us who are Christians," she writes, "speak of the uniqueness and centrality of Christ, and yet at the same time we know that our Muslim brothers and sisters affirm the uniqueness and centrality, indeed the finality, of God's revelation in the Holy Qur'an."[2] Hence, in order for constructive and peace-promoting dialogue to take place, the parties should accept "the parity of religious claims." In the words of John Hick: ". . . we have as much reason to think that the other great world religions are true and salvific as to think this of Christianity,"[3] Thus, in the name of peaceful coexistence, a voluntary moratorium is recommended on the things that really matter. It reminds one of the observation attributed to Edward Gibbon to the effect that, in Roman society, all religions were to the people equally true, to the philosophers equally false, and to the government equally useful.[4] More on this later, but at this point the question may be raised whether any of our mullah partners have agreed to such dialogue concessions.

Jürgen Moltmann, also a frequent participant in WCC-sponsored interfaith events, notes serious "imbalances" in the give-and-take of those dialogues, as well as a general lack of interest on the part of Muslims, Hindus, and Buddhists. He does, however, call for "a new concept of mission" which he describes as "an invitation to God's future." As we Christians give that future "present force in the gospel of hope and in the service of love," we invite others to work with us to give the vision of a recreated world embodiment in history. In this approach the biblical message about the kingdom of God as revealed in Christ remains central.[5]

One thing has become quite clear over the past decades: interreligious dialogue involves risks. In the words of Harvey Cox, "To expose one's tradition to dialogue is willy-nilly to open it to change, ferment, and internal debate. I believe God can and does speak to us through people of other faiths. And as people of faith we have always known, when God speaks mountains melt and the seas roar."[6] But, even among those who agree with such a statement in general, the question still arises as to who proposes what kind of risk. Or, what level of risk and how radical a change in doctrine is an individual believer, but especially a faith-community, prepared to accept?

The WCC published a book by M. M. Thomas, entitled *Risking Christ for Christ's Sake: Toward an Ecumenical Theology of Pluralism*. He looks at pluralism "from the standpoint of our ultimate commitment to Jesus Christ as the revelation of God."[7] Rather than abandoning the historic Christian belief in the centrality of Christ, he suggests that we broaden the revelatory impact of Jesus through such notions as the "ontic Christ" or the "cosmic Christ," who is present *incognito* in other religions. Instead of focusing on the so-called uniqueness of Christ, he emphasizes the universality of the divine revelatory presence, a view that is somewhat akin to what has often been referred to as "general revelation." The point to be made here, however, is that, according to some pluralists, Thomas' very starting point in the centrality of God's revelation in Christ precludes a genuine interfaith dialogue. His approach is considered as essentially too risk-averse.

In the following sections I shall discuss four levels of dialogical risk. My argument will revolve around these key terms: *information, collaboration, transformation,* and *creative confrontation.* The focus will be mainly, but not exclusively, on Christian-Jewish relations.

INFORMATION

Some occasions referred to as dialogues are basically *information-sharing* events. This is by far the safest and most nearly risk-free form of dialogue. A church youth group or adult fellowship visits a synagogue and are taught the most elementary facts about Jewish symbols and worship practices. Or a class of Christian theological seminarians pays a two-hour visit to a Buddhist center where the monks present a lecture on basic Buddhist beliefs and ceremonies, followed perhaps by a question-and-answer period–usually focused on comparing the two traditions.

Large seminars, national workshops on interfaith dialogue, or interreligious congresses tend to be strong on the reading of academic papers and weak on extended periods of face-to-face and faith-to-faith encounters. The Third Parliament on the World's Religions, meeting in Cape Town, South Africa during December, 1999, attracted 6000 delegates from 200 different religious groups. In order to cope with scheduling pressures, seminars were being conducted while plenary meetings were in session.

I recall the Protestant-Catholic "Living Room Dialogues" of the early 1960s. It was very exciting, especially because of the novelty of it all. The element of repeatedly gathering in a small group made mutual acquaintanceship possible and enhanced the potentials of "I-thou" encounters (i.e., conversations on a deep and personal level). Resources for similar meetings between Jews and Christians have been developed in recent years.

I do not wish to minimize the value of such events. In order to truly understand one another, let alone love each other, we must first meet and learn about the others in all their "otherness." Still, although such meetings may lead to some changes of mind, they are rarely life-transforming in the sense that we feel existentially challenged to re-evaluate some of our long-held beliefs. In the latter case, our pleasant get-togethers may sometimes turn into painful experiences.

COLLABORATION

Some Orthodox rabbis, like the late Rabbi Joseph Soloveitchik, avoid dialogue on matters of faith because they see it as an endangerment of people's fidelity to Jewish traditions, or because they judge it to be a futile exercise in light of the fact that the language of one faith is allegedly incomprehensible to members of another faith community. On the latter point, I would grant that it would be extremely difficult, if not impossible, for me to enter fully into Rabbi Soloveitchik's belief-world. It would not only require years of study in the sources, but also a long experience of the daily realities of his faith. Still, I do not believe that we are therefore totally incomprehensible to each other. Nevertheless, it should be kept in mind that avoidance of theological exchanges does not mean that those who hold such views are always averse to conversations on matters of common social concerns. I have witnessed Orthodox Jews and evangelical Christians in New York City engage in dialogue about possible cooperative efforts in such areas as abortion and pornography.

One can also find collaborative ventures between synagogues and churches on the local level. The United Church of Christ in Denver, where I occasionally worship, and nearby Temple Sinai are engaged in a wonderful joint program to assist homeless families. These congregations are large enough to have the resources in terms of volunteers, facilities, and finances to host a number of families for a set period of time, providing them not only with food and shelter, but also with counsel and assistance in the search for jobs and housing. I suspect that similar projects are being undertaken in many localities.

Information-sharing and cooperative efforts certainly have their place in the search for better interfaith relationships even though, in many cases, they are of a pre-dialogical nature. While not unrelated to faith issues, they do not generally tend to focus on such issues in an articulated way.

TRANSFORMATION

Transformative dialogue, involving what is sometimes referred to as "transformational learning," seeks to move beyond the information-sharing phase and hence to a higher level of risk-taking. One of the best examples of such an approach that has come to my attention is "The Catholic-Jewish Colloquium," a project supported by a Lilly Endowment grant and conducted by Mary C. Boys and Sara S. Lee, both educators with sound credentials. An entire issue of the journal *Religious Education* was devoted to articles on this particular "experiment in interreligious learning." The following points are worth noting:

• The focus is on transformation through "study in the presence of the other." The emphasis is not just on learning *about* the other, but *with* the other, and that over an extended period of time. State Boys and Lee: ". . . we explicitly set about designing a curriculum that would engender new understandings of the other. Further, we hypothesized that participants' changed perceptions of the other would alter their own self-understanding."[8]

• The project designers assumed that "Jews don't so much have to change their theology as they do their self-understanding based on history," while "Christians have to reconstitute their theology because so much of it is grounded in an inadequate understanding of Judaism."[9] In other words, the transformations the designers thought the participants would undergo were not symmetrical. Which side assumed the greater risk depends, one suspects, on each individual.

• The project was undertaken in the hope that it would "further a genuinely pluralistic society."[10] "Interreligious learning," we read, "offers a way of deepening one's particularity while simultaneously providing a ground for pluralism."[11] A pluralistic society requires "education for paradox," i.e., it involves "a delicate and necessary tension between fostering 'responsible ambiguity' and 'responsible identity.' "[12] In short, we want people to question, or even critique, their own faith-tradition while at the same time holding on to, or even strengthening, their commitment to that tradition.

• The participants were carefully selected and were all religious educators who had achieved a certain stature in their field. "Too often, in our view," state Boys and Lee, "dialogue is reduced to a sharing of opinions and uninformed perspectives, or it is largely a passive meeting in which people listen to a speaker for whom they have neither proper preparation nor subsequent opportunity to pursue the presentation in one another's presence."[13]

Dialogue, declared Abraham Joshua Heschel in his famous "No Religion Is an Island" lecture at Union Theological Seminary, "is not an enterprise for those who are half learned or spiritually immature." That same year, Eliezer Berkovits published his scathing article, entitled "Judaism in the Post-Christian Era," in the journal *Judaism,* accusing some dialogue devotees of being "Jews without memories, or Jews for whom Judaism is exclusively a matter of public relations, or confused or spineless Jews unable to appreciate the meaning of confrontation in full freedom." More recently, David Novak also has lamented that "American Jews, contrary to the tendency of all of previous Jewish history, have hardly looked for piety, learning, or Jewish insight in our leaders."[14] Quality dialogue, these scholars clearly believe, requires intellectual and spiritual maturity.

I also hear their remarks as a warning against the "bureaucratization" of the dialogue. As a former church executive, I must admit that I empathize with such a concern. Major organizations and church councils usually have the resources (budgets, staff, etc.) to organize events; but as employees of such establishments, staff members can never totally detach themselves from organizational agendas that may seek to use the dialogue for their own purposes. To deny that is, it seems to me, like living in fantasyland. At any rate, the point to be made here is that the participants in the "Catholic-Jewish Colloquium" were for the most part well-informed and committed members of their respective religious communities, without undue attachment to organizational interests.

What have been the results of this experiment? Judging from the testimonies found in *Religious Education,* one would have to conclude that learning in the presence of the other over an eighteen-month period has indeed had a transformative impact on most participants. Cynthia Reich, teacher in a Talmud Torah Day School, opens her evaluation with the sentence "Jesus changed my life," and closes with these words: ". . . Jesus could change my life–by helping me break out of a limited perspective, by broadening my vision, by drawing me closer to God and by sending me back to my Jewish life and work with renewed commitment."[15]

A Catholic participant responded as follows: "I did not anticipate that the *major* insights I would take from the Colloquium would pertain to Catholicism . . . I am now clearer about my beliefs, more enamored of my own religious tradition, and more concerned about educating others in the Catholic faith tradition than before."[16] In short, each of those participants deepened their awareness of their religious "particularity." There was conversation and transformation, but–just as the designers had fervently hoped–no conversions.

The Jewish participants were understandably appreciative of Catholic confessions of past Christian sins against the Jewish people. Some Catholics were moved by the suggested readings to question the historic Christian views on Jesus and Christology. One gains the impression that there were some intellectual/spiritual struggles on both sides but that there was a minimum of confrontation concerning core beliefs. Most of the participants, one gathers from the reactions, were initiated into the Christian-Jewish dialogue through assigned readings and the subsequent exchanges in person.

When a person has once been introduced to the dialogue on that level, is there perhaps a next and possibly more risky level of dialogue that one might want to pursue? Dialogue "veteran" Michael Kogan has introduced the idea of "total dialogue" into the conversation.[17] He wants to move beyond mutual respect to mutual influence and mutual enrichment. In doing so, he wants people to talk about core faith issues. For instance, Jews might take a new look at the Christian doctrine of incarnation or the Christian concept of sin. Rabbi A. James Rudin of the American Jewish Committee called the proposal a "bad bargain for both Jews and Christians," but many Christian scholars responded quite positively to Kogan's suggestions. He advocates a "particularism without exclusivism," i.e., no one makes exclusivist truth claims, any element of disputation is carefully avoided, and the idea that a dialogue partner may be moved to change his or her religious affiliation should be regarded as a derailment of the desired process.

Yet, in the real world it is simply a fact of life that Protestants become Catholics and vice versa; Jews become Christians and vice versa; people raised in Jewish or Christian families turn to Buddhism or Hinduism; large numbers of African-Americans have converted to Islam; and when people of different faiths meet in conversation, their core beliefs are, in fact, often incompatible. Is there any room for an occasional dispute as part of a contest for truth?

CREATIVE CONFRONTATION

Once more we pose the question: What can we talk about and how do we talk about it without violating the spirit of genuine dialogue? In what ways does a growing awareness of the pluralistic nature of our society, and indeed the world, affect our answer to this question?

As mentioned earlier, because of the past, Jewish-Christian relations pose sensitivities all their own. Let me return for a moment to the articles by Eliezer Berkovits and Abraham Joshua Heschel. Berkovits, filled with an understandable fury about the atrocious treatment the Jewish people have suffered at the hands of Christians, notes with satisfaction that "the Christian era has come to an end."[18] For the first time since the 4th century, there may be a confrontation between Judaism and Christianity in full freedom as Jews encounter a morally bankrupt Christian civilization and a spiritually bankrupt Christian religion. The article makes perfectly clear that, as far as Berkovits is concerned, this confrontation takes the form of disputation without dialogue; confrontation without reconciliation. "In a hundred years, perhaps, depending on Christian deeds toward Jews, we may be emotionally ready for the dialogue."[19] But even then, a *theological* dialogue would be totally fruitless and pointless: theologically, we have nothing to discuss, Berkovits noted.

Abraham Joshua Heschel wrote in a very different spirit and from a different perspective on what a de-Christianized world might mean. He had escaped Hitler's ovens in Europe and understood the dangers of an emerging neopaganism and nihilism. Instead of writing gleefully about "the end of the Christian era," he asks the question, "What religious alternative do we envisage for the Christian world?"[20] As to recent history, he observes, "Realizing that it was Christianity that implanted attachment to the God of Abraham and involvement with the Hebrew Bible in the hearts of Western man, Nazism resolved that it must both exterminate the Jews and eliminate Christianity, and bring about instead a revival of Teutonic paganism."[21] Sociologically speaking, many Western societies must still be regarded as Christian, in a broadly cultural sense, because no other integrated belief system has as yet been able to take the place of the Judeo-Christian worldview that has shaped those societies. However, as Heschel puts it, "we stand at the brink of the abyss together." Hence, it is imperative that we talk.

It was Heschel's hope that, across the chasm, Jews and Christians would extend a hand to one another, carry on a controversy without acrimony and criticism without loss of respect; in short, that participants would not allow dialogue to degenerate into bitter dispute. Now, it must be kept in mind that, to the Jewish ear, the word "dispute" has a very distinct connotation. It is a reminder of the infamous and coercive disputations in the Middle Ages when Christians did all the talking and Jews were forced to listen to the vilification of their faith. So, Heschel did not advocate a dialogue without any mutual critique, but rather he proposed a confrontation without that pernicious impulse to conquer and debase the other's faith.

In addition to acrimonious disputes, Heschel mentions the matter of conversion. We must converse without entertaining even "a silent hope" that the partner might adopt our faith, because that would be an offense to the other's religion and human dignity. To be sure, dialogues are not to be abused as opportunities for evangelistic appeals. On the other hand, it is hard to conceive of a devout believer who delights in the richness of inner peace and life's fulfillment found in faith–whether he or she be a Hindu, a Buddhist, a Jew, a Muslim or a Christian–who would not entertain even the slightest inner hope that partners in conversation too might experience this spiritual treasure. Of course, Heschel spoke from the point of view of a profound historical memory which does not allow Jews to forget the forced conversions and baptisms their people had to endure during certain periods of Christian history. Furthermore, before they triumphantly hope that Jews will become just like us, Christians ought to ponder the destructive consequences for the church's life and theology of the systematic de-Judaization of the faith that took place early in its history. Many among the so-called "Messianic Jews" struggle with this question: How can one be a follower of Jesus without accepting all the wrappings Western theology has packaged him in? It is a complex issue, because their very attempts to answer this question in practice has become a matter of profound controversy in the dialogue movement.

The issues of conversion, exclusivism, and disputation have also become hot topics of debate in the broader interreligious dialogue. One of the most wide-ranging discussions among Christian scholars on these controversial matters can be found in the aforementioned book, *The Uniqueness of Jesus: A Dialogue with Paul F. Knitter*. A few years ago, Knitter had offered an article entitled "Five Theses on the Uniqueness of Jesus" for publication in the *Journal of Ecumenical Studies*. The editors then suggested that those theses become the basis for a dialogue with other scholars to be issued in book form. It is an example of a dialogue intermixed with sharp and sometimes harsh disputes. One wonders whether such public soul-searching about central issues of faith for the sake of interfaith relationships is going on within other religious traditions, or whether, at present, this is a uniquely Christian phenomenon. In that case, it would not really be part of a dialogical dynamic, but fall more under the category of unilateral spiritual disarmament.

Christian pluralists have argued that one may not enter the arena of dialogue with exclusivist claims, e.g., claims about a unique or once-for-all redemptive event in Jesus Christ. Why not? Because, some would say, we have no reason to assume that other religions are not equally salvific; while others would hold that possibly, or even probably, God has not limited redemptive revelation to one faith. Furthermore, most of them would agree that making unique claims simply isn't fair. Christians would, in essence, try to enter the dialogue with an advantage while, it is argued, genuine dialogue requires a "level playing field."

It seems to me, however, that the condition of the playing field is not really at issue; certainly not if it is assumed that all parties have equal rights to present whatever claims their religious tradition prescribes. Rather, what is at stake is the way some players may want to keep score. They want conquest: win the game above anything else. But, at least in the Judeo-Christian tradition, dialogues don't lead to final scores. That is left to the *eschaton*, the divine future when we shall know as we are known by the Almighty. No victory parades in the present dialogical dispensation! The ancient confession, "Jesus is Lord and none other!" expresses a triumphant faith which is dear to millions of Christians, but that confession does not give one a license to act in a triumphalistic fashion when dealing with people of other faiths.

Does this then mean that, in the meantime, I must constantly wonder what I can talk about in encounters with dialogue partners? Great scholars and solemn assemblies have repeatedly assured us that, in an honest-to-God dialogue, each party should be free to express his/her faith even to its deepest existential core. Decades ago, Paul Tillich taught that dialogue with representatives of different religions ought to be a serious confrontation in which each participant is able to represent his or her faith with conviction. In 1988, the Lambeth Conference declared that "genuine dialogue demands that each partner brings to it the fullness of themselves and the tradition in which they stand." One could cite many other sources making the same point. But what, then, if the fullness of me and my tradition include a confession about a decisive ("once-for-all") revelatory act of God in the life, death, and resurrection of Jesus who, therefore, I believe played *the* central role in the divine plan for the re-creation of the world and the coming of God's kingdom? Surely, I ought to watch my language; but can I talk about it, perhaps even argue about it? What did Martin Buber mean when he said that, in genuine "I-thou" encounters, sparks are bound to fly back and forth from heart to heart? That does not usually happen when we exchange cautiously crafted intellectual positions about our faith. Of course, such a dialogue also implies that we open our hearts to the others and our minds to what they might teach us.

Still, argument always involves some risk, even if one aims it to be a creative confrontation and wishes to hear the other person out. The argument all too easily takes on the sound of anger. There are moments in interreligious relations, of course, when anger is called for. That was the case in Germany when the signers of the Barmen Declaration of 1934 opposed the position of the *"Deutsche Christen"* as idolatry. It is always the case when, for instance, injustices are justified in the name of religion. "Be angry, but do not sin," say the Scriptures; and we are bound to sin when, in a dialogue situation, we quickly take offense when our own tradition comes under critical scrutiny from the perspective of someone who holds a very different view.

Let me illustrate this point with an example from ecumenical dialogue. In his encyclical *Ut Unum Sint,* Pope John Paul II described dialogue in terms of mutual gift-giving and a dialogue of love. At the same time, when discussing other ecclesial bodies as the "separated churches," he stated that they "suffer from defects," a remark Protestants may take as a hurtful blow to their devout egos. By the same token, most of us Protestants are not reluctant to critique the Roman Catholic view of papal authority. So, in the midst of a sincere mutual reaching out to each other, there is some pain on both sides. That, I would submit, is inherent in an honest dialogue, and such moments of painful discomfort can actually become the basis of mutual growth and respect. Catholic-Protestant relations have matured considerably over the past decades.

Do the same principles apply to interfaith relationships? This brings us back to Paul Knitter, who started his book by pointing out what we cannot say in a genuine interfaith dialogue. The argument goes like this: Love of neighbor is a divine imperative. So is dialogue, because love calls us to a mutuality of dialogue. We cannot love our neighbors unless we are ready to dialogue with them. The spirit of charity and openness also requires that we do not come to the table claiming that we possess the "fullness" of revelation and the norm of all truth, thereby implying that our partners and their faith are somehow inferior. Hence, the need to reinterpret the uniqueness of Jesus in a non-exclusivist fashion.

Still, what Knitter considers permissible to be said is quite significant. One can affirm that Jesus is *truly* the mediator of God's saving grace without necessarily insisting that he is the *only* mediator. While Knitter thus avoids being accused of "salvific monism," he goes on to say that we proclaim the truth made known in Jesus as *indispensable*;

i.e., to know Christ is to feel that Buddhists and Hindus and Muslims need to know him too. "In a qualified but still real sense, persons of other religious paths are 'unfulfilled' without Christ."[22] This view quite naturally raises the issues of mission and conversion.

Respondent John Hick maintains that we cannot have a dialogical level playing field as long as one partner claims that other religions are only possibly or probably true and salvific. Monika Hellwig, on the other hand, affirms that, in her many years of dialogue experience, she has never found that others held back because she professed faith in Christ as universal savior. Quite the contrary, they expected that she represent her tradition as it really is.[23] Other respondents, too, wonder why, in a heart-to-heart dialogue, people should not be able to speak their mind as well as witness to their faith experience.

In his final reply, Knitter grants that "normative" claims can be made as long as "I speak my mind in such a way that you can do the same." He comes to the conclusion that the term *correlational* dialogue is to be preferred over the adjective "pluralistic." "Thus," he writes, "each participant in the conversation will assert his or her convictions in a clear, affirmative, yes, 'normative' manner: 'I hold these truths.' This is part of maintaining one's identity. But at the same time, each will also allow and encourage the other to do likewise, recognizing that the other's truth claims might turn out to be normative also for oneself. This is part of respecting the other as partner. For me such a model can best be described as *correlational*."[24]

Finally, while he wishes to understand and practice mission mainly in terms of dialogue, Knitter affirms that "insofar as it is an inherently universal religion, Christianity must remain a 'missionary religion,'"[25] and does not want entirely to preclude proclamation of the gospel and potential conversions. John Macquarrie makes the interesting observation that the "old fashioned type of missionary proclamation" may be especially appropriate in the secularized nations of Europe and North America.[26]

As it turns out, correlational dialogue in a pluralistic setting is not entirely without its elements of confrontation. Mature dialogue requires honesty, and the greater the honesty with which issues are approached, the higher will be the risk factor. In order for the confrontation to be creative, however, it helps if honesty is intermixed with a dose of humor. So we conclude with a few reflections on that topic.

Humor, when it bears a relationship to faith, hope, and love, can have a touch of holiness about it. If God is sovereign Lord, I can let go of some of my hyper-seriousness. It is not that we should take religion lightly, but rather that we should learn to laugh a little at ourselves; not to think too highly of ourselves or our theological expertise. Christian theology is in its very nature a *theologia viatorum*, a journey under the critical guidance of the Spirit. Dietrich Bonhoeffer has reminded us in one of his letters from prison that "absolute seriousness is not without a dose of humor."

Christian faith involves confession and, like humor, it has a good deal to do with the removal of façades. Humor pricks the bubble of self-conceit, deflates the overblown ego, but without the intention of destroying the other person's selfhood. It is meant to be humbling without being humiliating. Late night TV hosts poke fun, not so much at the sinners, but the pompous "saints" and the foibles of people who do not practice what they preach. Faith involves trust in the grace of God; it knows of forgiveness, and thus fosters a sense of humor that saves me from engaging in dialogue with people of other faiths as if it were a holy war.

The Brazilian theologian Rubem Alves wrote in his book, *Tomorrow's Child*, that "humor keeps hope alive."[27] The converse is also true: Hope keeps humor alive. And hopeful humor has often kept people alive, even in the darkest moments of history. Jewish humor and black humor testify to that. It has been said that humor is a "humanizing agent." It helps us maintain a sense of our own humanity in a world of cruelty and conflict, as well as the humanity of those whom we encounter along life's dialogical way. Hope, says the apostle Paul does not disappoint us, because God's love has been poured into our hearts (Romans 5:5).

Love becomes the greatest (1 Corinthians 13) when it is inspired by the love God has shown not only for us and our spiritual fraternity, but for the *world*. Love helps us know the difference between humor and sarcasm. The former soothes; the latter stings. The great teachers of dialogue from different religious backgrounds have been people of good humor and loving hearts. To love is to risk vulnerability. Dialogue is about equal rights of religious expression as well as equal risks to have our faith challenged; and that, in the words of Eric Hoffer, may force us to face "the ordeal of change." A healthy dose of fear and trembling may be in order, as long as we don't forget that, in the final analysis, love *does* cast out fear (1 John 4:18).

---

[1] Diana Eck, *Encountering God: A Spiritual Journey from Bozeman to Banaras* (Beacon Press, 1993).

[2] *Ibid.*, p. 14.

[3] John Hick, quoted in Leonard Swidler and Paul Mojzes, eds., *The Uniqueness of Jesus: A Dialogue with Paul F. Knitter* (Maryknoll, NY: Orbis Books, 1997) p. 80.

[4] Lesslie Newbiggin, *A Word in Season* (Grand Rapids MI: Eerdmans, 1994).

[5] Jürgen Moltmann, *God for a Secular Society* (Minneapolis: Fortress Press, 1999), p. 233ff.)

[6] James H. Charlesworth, ed., *Jesus' Jewishness: Exploring the Place of Jesus within Early Judaism* (New York: Crossroad, 1991) p. 61.

[7] M. M. Thomas, *Risking Christ for Christ's Sake: Toward an Ecumenical Theology of Pluralism* (Geneva: WCC Publications, 1987) p. 3.

[8] Mary C. Boys and Sara S. Lee, *Religious Education*, Fall 1996, p. 425.

[9] *Ibid.*

[10] *Ibid.*, p. 417.

[11] *Ibid.*, p. 455.

[12] *Ibid.*

[13] *Ibid.*, p. 435.

[14] Richard John Neuhaus, ed., *Jews in Unsecular America* (Grand Rapids MI: Eerdmans, 1987) p. 60.

[15] Boys and Lee, *Religious Education*, pp. 555, 561.

[16] *Ibid.*, p. 562.

[17] Michael Kogan, "Toward Total Dialogue," *National Dialogue Newsletter*, Winter 1990/1991.

[18] Eliezer Berkovits, "Judaism in the Post-Christian Era," *Judaism*, 1966.

[19] *Ibid.*

[20] Abraham Joshua Heschel, "No Religion Is an Island," lecture at Union Theological Seminary, 1966.

[21] *Ibid.*

[22] Swidler and Mojzes, *The Uniqueness of Jesus*, p. 10.

[23] *Ibid.*, p. 77.

[24] *Ibid.*, p. 154.

[25] *Ibid.*, p. 174.

[26] *Ibid.*, p. 97.

[27] Rubem A. Alves, *Tomorrow's Child* (New York: Harper & Row, 1972).

CHAPTER 2

Jewish Voices in Christian-Jewish Dialogue

After decades of Christian-Jewish dialogue and a sizable body of literature on the subject, questions are still being raised about the basis, scope, purpose, value, and even the possibility of such a dialogue. Doubts about this approach to interfaith relationships are being expressed in both Christian and Jewish circles, especially among those who fear that basic tenets of faith will be relativized and compromised.

It seems fair to say that the most frequent and articulate criticisms come from the Jewish side and often from people who are personally involved in the dialogue or, at least, identified with the movement because of their writings. In contrast, Christian critics of the enterprise in most cases speak from a position of detachment and tend to belong to the more conservative, evangelical wing of the church. Mainline Protestants and Roman Catholics are usually the most enthusiastic defenders of the dialogue approach and the most optimistic about its potential results.

Jewish ambiguity and hesitation are quite understandable, especially in view of a long history during which constructive Christian-Jewish encounters were rare and destructive Christian attitudes toward Jews and Judaism very common. Furthermore, outside the State of Israel, most Jews still live as small minorities in predominantly "Christian" societies.

THE BASIS OF DIALOGUE

As to the basis of dialogue, one could argue that, in principle, a spirit of openness is all that is required for a genuine encounter to take place. Such openness would imply a willingness to listen, as well as the ability to deal with a diversity of views, and to show mutual respect. Some emphasize that an important element in the art of listening is to let members of the various faith communities define themselves.

For most participants genuine dialogue takes place at a level deeper than that of a mere intellectual exchange of views. It has an existential-relational dimension to it, the quality of an "I-thou" encounter in the Buberian sense. Hence, the true basis for dialogue is sought in our com-

mon humanity. Dialogue is then seen as taking place from Jewish existence to Christian existence and vice versa, rather than from one academic or dogmatic position to another. In short, the meeting of faiths is
very different from an academic exchange.

As a general theory such views about the basis of dialogue will find
widespread approval. But, in practice, things are not always that simple.
For instance, one can hear it said that there is no sense engaging in dialogue with people who believe in evangelizing adherents of other faiths,
and Jews in particular. The issue then is not so much the person's behavior in an actual dialogue situation, but the individual's theological stance.
It is simply assumed that anyone committed to evangelism is an un-
suited candidate for open dialogue, even though such a person may well
agree that that kind of encounter is not the proper occasion for evangelistic appeals, and confirm that conviction by his or her conduct. The
issue becomes particularly controversial in the case of Jewish followers of Jesus who feel compelled by their faith to witness to their
brothers and sisters.

Other illustrations could be given where it appears that the basis
for dialogue is shifted from attitudes to views. For instance, some years
ago Rabbi Henry Siegman proposed the much-debated thesis that "the
starting point of Christian-Jewish dialogue must be a mutual acceptance
of the ultimate incommensurability of Judaism and Christianity. . . ."[1]
While the previous position would seem to exclude millions of evangelically oriented Christians from dialogue, this thesis would eliminate quite
a few non-evangelical candidates for whom such an "ultimate incommensurability" is simply not acceptable.

Fortunately, proposals delimiting the basis for dialogue are often
made in the context of an ongoing dialogue and, in practice, do not
really turn out to be preconditions. Evangelicals and Jews do engage in
dialogue and published volumes of the proceedings show the world what
they talked about. Rabbi Siegman, in fact, remained very open to recon-
sider his thesis in view of counter arguments presented.

THE SCOPE OF THE DIALOGUE

Questions surrounding the scope of dialogue tend to deal mostly
with the issue of theology. For the majority of Christians, interfaith
dialogue is, at heart, a theological matter because they are inclined to
express their faith in confessional terms. In Judaism, with its *halachic*
tradition, doctrinal formulations tend to play less of a role.

Orthodox Jews, particularly, while being open to exchanges on
common concerns of a social or cultural nature, do not generally approve of dialogue on matters of faith. Some see it as an endangerment of
people's fidelity to Jewish traditions. Others hold that religious beliefs
are so personal and private that communicating them to outsiders is

impossible. In the words of the late Rabbi Soloveitchik, "[t]he language of faith of a particular community is totally incomprehensible to the man of a different faith community. Hence the confrontation should occur not at a theological, but at a mundane human level . . . the great encounter between man and God is a holy, personal and private affair, incomprehensible to the outsider. . . ."[2]

Others again point not so much to the lack of a common language, but to the antithetical relationship between the two faiths. Eliezer Berkovits, who sees neither reason nor need for Jewish-Christian dialogue, has stated this position quite bluntly when he wrote that "Judaism is Judaism because it rejects Christianity, and Christianity is Christianity because it rejects Judaism."[3] When groups define themselves in opposition to each other, meeting grounds are usually turned into battlefields, which is not what dialogue is all about. There are other nuances of this position to which we shall return later.

Rabbi Leon Klenicki, for whom dialogue is a profession in the dual sense of that word, seeks to maintain at least a minimum of theological content by using phrases like "understanding the other as a person of God" and "acknowledging a common ground of being, that is God." Dialogue then becomes a "tool" to recognize each other as distinct in faith and spirituality but with a common humanity, "two peoples with valid religious commitments, vocations called by God."[4] The goal of this process seems to be a respectful relationship in which confrontation is carefully avoided. Fervor is allowed as long as it is mindful of different vocations. Truly an "I'm OK, You're OK" situation.

THE PURPOSE OF THE DIALOGUE

This all sounds rather charming, even enchanting, but is that really the purpose of dialogue? Should dialogue be considered a "tool" to arrange for polite meetings in nice hotels? The literature shows that different participants also have different purposes in mind for the dialogue. There are those who seek deeper mutual understanding. Others are looking for an encounter of equals which, in turn, can lead to a "theology of equality." Then there are people who say that dialogue has achieved its goal if Jews end up being better Jews and Christians better Christians. Others again (to the chagrin of some of their co-religionists) speak about mutual influence and fertilization, while some advocates of dialogue seek to establish a common faith against the forces of secularism and/or the paganization of society. Frequently, people hope for a number of these as well as other purposes to be achieved.

But every once in a while a specific purpose is offered as the true validation of dialogue. For instance, in his contribution to the book, *Overcoming Fear between Jews and Christians*, Alan Segal states that "to be valid, the purpose of dialogue must be the converse of conversion; it must affirm Judaism as an equally valid response to the promises of the Old Testament God."[5] In other words, it is not enough when Christians agree that the purpose of a dialogue meeting is not to evangelize the other party; there must be a further affirmation about equal validity, an assumption that runs counter to the basic self-understanding of many Christians as well as Jews. Again, for a Jewish follower of Jesus, such a position would make his or her often-agonizing participation seem totally meaningless.

THE VALUE OF THE DIALOGUE

The value of dialogue is most likely to be questioned by participants who have been disappointed with the results. All the effort and expenses have simply not paid off. Jewish leaders who have reached out in friendship to the Christian community have repeatedly found that, in moments of crisis, support from their partners is not always forthcoming. Biased attacks on the State of Israel by some Christian leaders have been especially painful to Jews who had hoped for a more sympathetic understanding. So has been the silence in the past of most churches at moments when the survival of Israel seemed to be at stake.

THE POSSIBILITY OF THE DIALOGUE

Finally, challenges to the very possibility of dialogue between Jews and Christians seem the most striking of all, particularly when they come from people who have been involved in the process. Dialogue, as is the case with all relationships, is based on a positive recognition of the otherness of the other. But what if the other claims to be wholly other, so different that we not only deal with some irreconcilable differences, but with two irreconcilable or even antithetical faiths? In that case, the devout desire of those who wish to avoid confrontation will be disappointed. For others, the encounter may become more interesting, because it has to struggle with convictions concerning perceived truths.

THE CONTINUITY/DISCONTINUITY DEBATE

Are Jews and Christians speaking to each other as spiritual relatives? The imagery often used is that of mother-and-daughter religions, or an older-and-younger-brother relationship. Most commentators acknowledge both continuity and discontinuity between the two faiths, elements of commonality and elements of more or less radical differences. However, some scholars are inclined to accentuate the distinctions to such a degree that little or no room is left to establish a common ground. On the other hand, there are also well-known scholars who affirm such a close affinity between the two faiths that they feel comfortable declaring them to be essentially one faith.

To the question, "What have you and we in common?" Martin

Buber gave the answer: "a book and an expectation."[6] True, we interpret the Scriptures that we hold in common differently, but still, "in this place we can dwell together, and together listen to the voice that speaks here."[7] Furthermore, although our expectation is founded on different views of God's action in history, there are still moments when we can cooperate in preparing the way for the coming kingdom. [8]

POLARIZED VIEWS OF JUDAISM AND CHRISTIANITY

In discussing the scope of dialogue, we have already mentioned the position of Eliezer Berkovits, that a theological dialogue between Jews and Christians is futile, particularly since it tends to be based on the "fantasy" of a Judeo-Christian tradition, while in truth they confront each other in antithetical terms. Finally, says Berkovits, the very idea of interreligious understanding "is ethically objectionable because it makes respect for the other man dependent on whether I am able to appreciate his religion or his theology."[9]

We also noticed Rabbi Henry Siegman's statement about "the ultimate incommensurability of Judaism and Christianity." Sinai and Calvary are simply mutually exclusive. However, for Siegman, such contrasts have never precluded dialogue; rather, mutual acceptance of such radical differences is regarded as a good starting point for a constructive interfaith exploration. As a matter of fact, he has shown a willingness to put his own thesis up for debate and for possible reconsideration on his part. So, as distinct from Berkovits' "let's go it alone attitude," Siegman leaves the lines of communication wide open.

Levi Olan has presented a position somewhere in between Berkovits and Siegman. He could find very few Christian theologians with whom a modern Jew could "comfortably dialogue," since, in order to qualify, one must "unmistakably reject the proposition that Jews must or will become part of a united community with Christians to form the one Israel of God."[10] So even an eschatological vision of Jews and Christians united as one people of God would seem to be an obstacle to dialogue.

But there is more. No dialogue with Jews is possible today, "unless Christians are prepared to understand Judaism as a self-contained religious community wholly unrelated to Christianity."[11] Virtually all church declarations on Jews and Judaism issued over the past decades fail Olan's test. Furthermore, the question must be asked whether dialogue should be conducted on the basis of each participant's comfort level.

Gershon Mamlak emerged as a passionate advocate of an antithetical relationship between Judaism and Christianity. He contested "the claim of Christianity to be the offspring and heir of Judaism," arguing that Christianity belonged "within the syncretistic orbit of Hellas."[12] A good deal of Mamlak's ire is directed at the "Jesus-a-true-Jew historical school" and Jewish intellectuals, whom he accuses of having become "the vanguard of the myth about a Judeo-Christian civilization . . . the greatest hoax of modern times," which undermines the uniqueness of Judaism and the Election of Israel.[13] Writes he: "It is precisely in the religious differences between the two religions that the essential uniqueness of Judaism is anchored."[14]

He finds this uniqueness in Judaism's recognition of man's dependence on God and God's dependence on man and human activity in a partnership aimed at the perfection of creation. Jesus and the later Jesus-fellowship, on the other hand, are said to have rejected the law as a vehicle to redemption and, as a consequence, have turned a this-worldly religion into a totally otherworldly faith. Hence, Christianity must be considered the most comprehensive refutation of the Judaic idea, which holds to the decisive importance of deeds, and the notion of Judaism being the "Mother faith" to Christianity is a pernicious fiction.[15] If there are Jewish elements in nascent Christianity, these are not due to the Jewishness of Jesus, but simply reflect the syncretizing spirit of the entire Greco-Roman world.

Professor Jacob Neusner, following in the footsteps of Arthur Cohen, is today a leading critic of the idea of continuity. "The only authentic Judeo-Christian tradition," according to Cohen, "is that God bears both communities down to the end of time unreconciled. The Judeo-Christian tradition is that from a common source there should have issued such profound and shattering disagreement."[16] We must confront each other in a contest of truth, honestly facing the enmity that is there, while at the same time laying the groundwork for a "Judeo-Christian humanism" that will allow us "to work within history to make the way smooth for the Kingdom."[17]

Cohen does not deny a certain confluence in doctrine, but sees it as the product of an artificial philosophical construct detached from the realities of fideist passions. At heart, the two faiths are utterly different, and those differences are irreducible and irreconcilable. Hence, a Jew who becomes a disciple of Jesus is considered to have severed all ties with his/her Hebraic heritage.

Professor Neusner, too, concedes that Christianity and Judaism episodically reach conclusions that coincide, but still holds that "in general the two religions share no common agenda and have conducted no genuine dialogue."[18] Judaism and Christianity have developed into two entirely different religions; the abyss between the New Testament and the tradition of oral Torah is immense. Spiritually, we literally live worlds apart, even though we can affirm one God–the same God. Historical developments, however, have produced two faiths which–as religions–have little to say to each other. Hence, we are now, and always have been, basically engaged in monologues, even though at times on the same topics.

Christianity must reaffirm itself as "an absolute and autonomous religion on its own," wholly distinct from Judaism. At the same time the uniqueness of Judaism must be recognized. "This program," writes Neusner, "aims at allowing Christianity to be absolute, Judaism to be unique, and the two to define for the 21st century a shared range of genuinely religious discourse, one to which the facts of history are not critical, but the confrontation with God central."[19] In short, what we need is "a theological theory of the other,"[20] which leads us beyond mutual toleration and enables us to treat as legitimate and authentic a religion other than our own.

Reading Neusner certainly reinforces one's skepticism about claims in dialogue newsletters of how members of small group discussions during a conference were enabled to enter into the inner world of each other's faith. Just to begin to gain an insight into one another's authoritative writings is incredibly complicated and requires more time and effort than a thirty-minute buzz session will allow. On the other hand, the idea of reclaiming Christianity's absoluteness along the lines of the church fathers, namely, as totally unrelated to Judaism, while avoiding conflict by means of "a theological theory of the other," is simply not an acceptable option for most Christians. To return to a past, so rightly rejected by most theologians today, which detached the faith of the church from its roots in Judaism, would seem a dismal prospect indeed, and not one likely to improve interfaith relationships. Furthermore, as important as a recognition of the rights of other religions is, mutual declarations of "authenticity" do not seem to be the answer. Jim Jones and David Koresh also desired to be declared authentic expressions of religious beliefs.

A "CONSTRUCTIVE CONTRAST OF HARMONY"

In the face of antithetical portrayals of the relationship between Judaism and Christianity, some dialogue advocates plead for the acknowledgment of at least a "family resemblance."[21] Others go much further than that. For instance, some years ago Pinchas Lapide expressed his belief "that Judaism and Christianity stand in a constructive contrast of harmony to one another, and that their inner tension can lead not to hatred but to a mutual spiritual fertilization."[22] He further asserted that "the dialogue between church and Judaism can . . . remove much one-sidedness in our understanding of the saving realities, deepen our acknowledgment of God as ruler of world history, and reconcile apparent opposition in the world pictures of the two religions.[23]

One of the major voices against polarized views of Judaism and Christianity was the Hebrew University scholar, David Flusser, who had few equals when it came to familiarity with both Jewish and early

Christian sources. Many of his conclusions about Jesus, the early Jesus-fellowship, and the impact of Judaism on Christianity ran counter to those reached by some of the scholars mentioned above.

During a theological seminar held in Jerusalem on the theme, "Jews and Christians between past and future," Flusser presented 58 theses on "The Emergence of Christianity from Judaism." Thesis No. 56 is stated, "Christianity and Judaism are really one faith." In the published proceedings of the conference, Flusser is reported to have made the following comments during the discussion period: "When both Judaism and Christianity acknowledge that it is fundamentally one religion, one faith, and do not deny it, as still happens so much–either out of ignorance or out of dogmatic prejudices–then they really can debate with each other."[24]

Almost half a century ago, the novelist Sholem Asch also wrote about "the Jewish-Christian idea,"[25] which makes the two religions part of a single whole, in his booklet *One Destiny*. He was more of a romantic than David Flusser, writing as a poet rather than a critical textual scholar. But neither author pulled punches when delivering their critiques of Christian history. Their views were based on a common vision regarding revelation, faith, the future–a vision that transcends theological diversity or even doctrinal incompatibility. In short, the search is not for a syncretistic mix that obscures sharp differences nor for an accommodation in order to facilitate friendliness in dialogue.

The internal debates within Judaism guarantee that Jewish-Christian dialogue takes place on various levels, each with their own dynamics. Valuable contributions are made by people who reject any "establishment" dialogue agenda and who may not frequent interfaith meetings and conferences. The same is true for Christian-Jewish dialogue.

---

[1] Rabbi Henry Siegman, "Jesus and Christians–Beyond Brotherhood Week," *Worldview*, December, 1975, p. 35.

[2] Cited in Marcus Braybrooke, *Time to Meet: Towards a Deeper Relationship between Jews and Christians* (Philadelphia: Trinity Press International, 1990), p. 15.

[3] Eliezer Berkovits, in *Disputation and Dialogue: Readings in the Jewish-Christian Encounter*, F. E. Talmage, ed., (New York: Ktav Publishing House, 1975), p. 291.

[4] Rabbi Leon Klenicki, "On Christianity, Toward a Process of Spiritual and Historical Healing: Understanding the Other as a Person of God," *Dialogue*, Vol. 1, No. 1, Spring, 1993, pp. 21-36.

[5] James H. Charlesworth, ed., *Overcoming Fear between Jews and Christians*, (New York: Crossroad, 1992), p. 96.

[6] Martin Buber, "The Two Foci of the Jewish Soul," *Disputation and Dialogue*, p. 282.

[7] *Ibid.*

[8] *Ibid.*

[9] Berkovits, *Disputation*, p. 293.

[10] Levi Olan, "Christian-Jewish Dialogue: A Dissenting Opinion," *Religion in Life*, Summer, 1972. Vol. XLI, No. 2, p. 164f.

[11] *Ibid.*, p. 176f.

[12] Gershon Mamlak, "How Jewish Was Early Christianity?–A Symposium,"

Midstream, December, 1982, p. 41. The original essay, "Was Christianity a Jewish Sect?" appeared in the June/July 1981 issue of the same periodical. Hyam Maccoby II presented a similar argument by blaming the decisive break between Judaism and Christianity on "Pauline Gnosticism" and Christianity's adoption of a dualistic mystery-cult religion. See "Christianity's Break with Judaism" in *Commentary*, August, 1984, pp. 38-42. For letters and responses, see the November, 1984, issue.

[13] Mamlak, "The Ineluctable Uniqueness of Judaism" *Midstream*, August/September, 1986, pp. 17, 19.

[14] *Ibid.*

[15] Mamlak, "A Pernicious Fiction: Judaism as the 'Mother of Religions,' " *Midstream*, May, 1987, pp. 20-24.

[16] Arthur A. Cohen, *The Myth of the Judeo-Christian Tradition*, (New York: Harper & Row, 1970), p. 217.

[17] *Ibid.*, p. 221.

[18] Jacob Neusner, *Jews and Christians: The Myth of a Common Tradition* (Philadelphia: Trinity Press International, 1991), p. IX.

[19] *Ibid.*, p. 22.

[20] *Ibid.*, p. 110.

[21] Rabbi Allan Mittleman in response to Hyam Maccoby's article: "Christianity's Break with Judaism" *Commentary*, November, 1984, Vol. 78, No. 5, p. 5.

[22] Pinchas Lapide, *Journal of Ecumenical Studies*, Fall, 1975, Vol. 12, No. 4, p. 491.

[23] *Ibid.*, p. 492.

[24] See *Jews and Christians between Past and Present* (Baam, Holland: Instituut voor Internationale Excursies, 1975), pp. 19, 30, 26.

[25] Cf. Scholem Asch, *One Destiny: An Epistle to the Christians* (New York: Putnam & Sons, 1945), p. 83ff.

CHAPTER 3

Toward Total Dialogue!

Over the years, a growing sense of restlessness has developed in Christian-Jewish dialogue circles. One could see it reflected in issues of the *National Dialogue Newsletter*, which for some time was an important forum for advocates of improved Christian-Jewish relations. Both then and now, there have been repeated suggestions that we need to enter a new stage in the dialogue or find new directions. In one form or another, the question "Where do we go from here?" has been raised with growing frequency and urgency. Some have even talked of a crisis.

As might be expected, the solutions that have been proposed depend very much on how the crisis is perceived. There are those who suggest that so much progress has been made in our efforts toward mutual clarifications, understandings, and trust, that we can now move on to total mutual acceptance as equals in faith. Conversions from one faith to the other do occur but should not be sought or even desired, nor should the idea of affecting each other's theological positions be entertained.

Rabbi Leon Klenicki viewed the present situation in terms of a time of transition.[1] We have come a long way, but now we must face the challenge of "the next step." He found the answer in a recognition of each other "as two different ways, two covenants of peace, two 'ways' to bring the Kingdom." Sometimes it is emphasized that the aim of dialogue is not a process of mutual influence but, rather, to make each side gain a deeper appreciation for the best values in their own faith. Such a laudable goal is hard to argue with, but one cannot help but wonder whether the dynamics of life and faith commitments can be contained within the confines of such neatly designed dialogue agendas. The ferment that is evident in current debates does not suggest that the dialogue can come to rest in what some have called a "theology of equality."

As far as the Christian side is concerned, dialogue literature has clearly been aimed at more than mutual clarification and deeper appreciation for tradition. It has called for radical change, not only in behavior, but in crucial theological positions as well. One denomination after another has responded with confessions of past sins against the Jewish people, as well as changes in credal statements and educational materials.

Progress has been made, but profound concerns still remain about what some have referred to as the "ecumenical plumbing problem," namely, that new insights gained at the loftier heights of dialogue meetings are very slow to flow down to the local level. Hence, not much has changed in the preaching, teaching, and practice in local congregations, not to mention theological seminaries. Perhaps not that much has changed, either, in the general view among Jews about Christianity. That raises the issue of better communication of results thus far achieved. However, some people are not satisfied with that, for they wish to raise deeper questions about the current dialogue process itself, including some of its theological dimensions. There are probings both on how to expand the theological agenda and how to determine the limits of radical theological reconstruction.

Father Edward H. Flannery, who played such a central role in bringing about changes in the churches, referred to "a state of at least mild crisis." He wondered whether the source of some tensions might lie in the fact that we have tended to emphasize "mutualities, especially theological, that manifest a certain unity of Judaism and Christianity," while failing "to confront basic differences, which are also numerous, profound, and permanent."[2] He then warned against raising false expectations about the extent to which churches may be prepared to modify their doctrinal positions, pointing out that faith commitment involved "a basic minimum of doctrinal and moral tenets that are non-negotiable."[3] Earlier that same year, Michael McGarry had sounded a similar warning, citing as a specific illustration the position of Alice L. and A. Roy Eckardt with regard to the resurrection of Jesus, which, he felt, was "going too far" in dismantling basic Christian doctrine.[4] Both sides of that particular debate have had their defenders and opponents.

There is general agreement among participants that dialogue cannot live by conventional theology alone. Traditional views have to be challenged: christological interpretations that turned the cross into a symbol of hatred, ecclesiologies that were not only supersessionist but virtually identified the church with the kingdom of God, soteriological theories that told lies about the role of Torah in Judaism, etc. Maverick positions can also create misunderstandings if, to quote Flannery again, dialogue participants do not make clear "whether they speak, on any particular topic, from within the mainstream of their faith-tradition, a branch or off-shoot of it, or for themselves."[5]

What about debates within the Jewish community? Rabbi Henry Siegman pointed out that Jews and Christians come to the dialogue with disparate agendas, the former focusing more on historical issues, the latter on theological questions. Of course, history does have an impact on theology. As Siegman himself pointed out: "A genuine confrontation with history, and most particularly with Auschwitz, demands of Christians the submission of their tradition to a searching critique."[6] He also posed questions as "to what extent Jews are able to attend to the Christian agenda," adding that, "Taking full advantage of the perquisites of the injured party, Jews have successfully managed the dialogue so that it has focused entirely on what we consider to be Christian failings." In short, to what extent should Jews now also reexamine their "own theology and traditions . . . within the context of the dialogue?"[7] In the same article, Siegman reported his lack of enthusiasm for a "theology of equality" and about Christian mission as part of most Christians' self-identity, which must not be violated in the name of dialogue.[8]

A later illustration of the search for new directions on the Jewish side can be found in Michael Kogan's much-debated proposal that we move "Toward Total Dialogue." Once a mutual enrichment process has been achieved, he suggested that the next step would be one from mutual respect to mutual influence. "Let nothing be held back," wrote Kogan.[9] Christians should study the Holocaust and the experience of modern Israel "with the same attention and openness" they bring to the study of ancient "biblical" Israel, while Jews should examine the gospels, open to the possibility of hearing the divine voice in the teaching of one who may come to be viewed as the last of the great Jewish prophets."[10] It can fairly be said that Kogan's suggestion that we broaden and deepen the dialogue agenda, including such topics as incarnation and our different concepts of sin, has been received more warmly in Christian than in Jewish circles. Particularly, participants who represent national Jewish organizations have expressed deep concerns about his proposals.

In the meantime, a number of major Jewish scholars have already accepted "mutual influence" as a dialogical fact of life and seem to have chosen it over a "theology of equality." Three Orthodox Jewish scholars might be mentioned in this connection, calling particular attention to their perspectives on incarnational theology, a subject traditionally so central in the Christian faith.

Rabbi Irving Greenberg viewed the recognition of the profound interrelationship between the two faiths as the unfinished agenda of the Jewish-Christian dialogue. Jewish theologians, he said, need to be more open to Christian self-understanding, including belief in the incarnation and resurrection. For instance, from a Jewish perspective, one may well argue that incarnation is improbable, but one can hardly rule out the possibility of such a divine act of revelation.[11]

Michael Wyschogrod went further, stating that, once he had freed himself from the need to be as different from Christians as possible, he was able to recognize incarnational motifs in Judaism.[12] Judaism's understanding of Christian theologies on incarnation, according to

Wyschogrod, caused it to recoil "to the other extreme and (make) the absolute incorporeality of God essential."[13]

Finally, Prof. David Flusser stated that "Jewish presuppositions for faith in Christ have not yet been sufficiently and creatively enough drawn upon"[14] and that "the significant influence on Christology of a Jewish theology on the hypostasis of God"[15] are not as well known as they ought to be. In other words, Christians have assigned to the Messiah/Christ the hypostatic titles of God's immanence, which were borrowed from Judaism.

Pursuing such a line of inquiry, we might overcome some distortions in the way we portray each other's tradition and also remove some facile and false contrasts, not for the purpose of artificially harmonizing real and fundamental differences but, rather, to focus more clearly on those differences.

Historically, the question "Is Jesus the Messiah?" has been at the heart of the Christian-Jewish dynamic with all its manifold and often tragic aspects. From the very start this issue has been dealt with in the spirit of polemics and, eventually, once the church gained the upper hand as an imperial power, in terms of coercive force. The compulsory disputations of medieval times had nothing to do with dialogue, because the cards were clearly stacked against the advocates of Judaism. While vitriolic language and specious arguments could be used in an attempt to refute Judaism, the veracity of positions on the Christian side could be impugned only at risk of severe punishment.

Not too long ago Jesus was still one of the most despised figures in Judaism, because he was seen through the eyes of people who suffered persecution at the hands of Christians. Once Jews were in a position to research the sources in freedom, the view of Jesus changed. Increasingly, Jesus was no longer seen as the figure that divides us but, rather, the church's interpretation of Jesus as Christ/Messiah. In the words of Schalom Ben-Chorin: "The belief of Jesus unites us . . . but the belief in Jesus separates us." True, but there is still considerable room for discussion on the nuances in various positions, and perhaps issues can be defined less in terms of long-held dichotomies. Christian proof texts and prophetic interpretations have consistently been met with the argument that Judaism's expectations were simply not fulfilled in the person of Jesus. What precisely were and are Jewish messianic expectations? On that point, there never has been a uniformity of view among the Jewish people, while the very concept of "messiahship" has been in constant flux over the centuries.

Joseph Klausner's view–contrasting the Jewish King-Messiah, whose rule is definitely "of this world," with the Christian allegedly spiritualized version of the Redeemer-Christ–has had considerable influence on subsequent theological developments. For Klausner there was no doubt that Jewish messianic faith had been the "seed of progress," which, he believed, has flowered throughout the world.[16] This has led many Jewish scholars to interpret messianic expectations primarily in this-worldly and sociopolitical terms. However, someone like Flusser does not follow them. In his above-mentioned foreword to Thoma's book, he wrote about "an overhasty consensus among Jews and Christians, as if Jewish messianic faith was merely this-worldly and political."[17] He did not deny the political dimension, so often neglected in Christian theology, but wanted to eschew premature conclusions and one-sided interpretations of a complex concept that has been in process of development over many centuries. Recent debates surrounding the Dead Sea Scrolls have raised similar questions.

Some Christian theologians, following in the footsteps of such scholars as Rosemary Radford Ruether and the Eckardts, no longer see a legitimate basis for referring to Jesus as Messiah. Hence, we are left with the man Jesus, not a risen Lord, but a Jew who lived in expectation of the messianic age and died hoping for its arrival–a Jew who is asleep, together with multitudes of his martyred brothers and sisters, awaiting the resurrection of the dead. For the vast majority of Christians, such a radical theological reconstruction is unacceptable; neither do they see much promise for further rapprochement with the Jewish community along those lines. This, however, does not mean that they are unwilling to explore new directions in the dialogue, both through a change of agenda items and by being open to the possibility of a broadened perspective and common theological framework from which issues under discussion might be probed, perhaps leading to a reconsideration of perceived dichotomies that are sometimes based on misinterpretations of each other's tradition.

For instance, during past years, the christological debates within the dialogue movement have focused very much on the relationship between Christology and eschatology. Since we live in an unredeemed world, how can one say that redemption has come in Christ? Eschatology inevitably confronts us with questions pertaining to the idea of the kingdom of God, a concept that, in our earlier quote from Klenicki, was offered as a common Jewish-Christian vision. A theology of the kingdom of God may well offer us perspectives that move us beyond some of our sterile either-or positions on many issues, including christological questions. Thoma put it concisely when he wrote: "In the last resort neither in Judaism nor in Christianity is it a question of the messiah but of the Kingdom of God."[18]

It is my contention that, despite fundamental differences that should never be ignored or glossed over, Judaism and Christianity share a basic vision of faith and history. Within that theological framework, we can look for common ground and clarify differences, remembering

Flusser's dictum that "[p]olarization as a method of clarification must lead to over-simplification."[19]

Herewith, I offer a very brief outline of themes we might explore, clustering the discussion around four key terms: the kingdom of God, incarnation, covenant partnership, and expectation.[20]

THE KINGDOM OF GOD

The gospels state that Jesus came proclaiming the kingdom of God. Many of his parables are to be characterized as parables of the kingdom. In his ministry the power of the kingdom was declared to be manifested: ". . . if it is by the finger of God that I cast out the demons, then the kingdom of God has come to you" (Luke 11:20, NRSV). This concept of the kingdom was current and very much alive in the spiritual-cultural climate of that day. It has roots in the visions of Israel's prophets and seers and has cosmic-historical dimensions, encompassing not only individuals and the covenant community, but also nature and the destiny of nations. Torah has been given for the sake of the kingdom of God, as has the Christian *kerygma*. This motif thus constitutes a unifying theme in the Hebrew and Christian Scriptures, making both faiths essentially futuristic. "All living is living into the future," Wyschogrod wrote,[21] echoing the words of Pierre Teilhard de Chardin, "The only thing that really interests me now is the universe of the future."[22]

In some Christian circles it has become fashionable to say that only in the cosmic end-time will the messiahship be fully seen and fully realized. Paul claimed the exact opposite: it is then that the messiahship will end, because the mission of the kingdom's mediator will have been completed. Christ will surrender the kingdom to the Creator. In short, the present rule of Christ brings with it manifestations of the power of the kingdom but is not the final consummation of the kingdom. Says Paul, God will be "all in all" (1 Corinthians 15:28). Confusion on this point among both Christians and Jews has often plagued the dialogue.

INCARNATION

All biblical theology is at heart a theology of the presence of God. The God of Abraham, Isaac, and Jacob is the God of the covenant, the One who comes and dwells among God's people and is faithful to the divine promises. The divine "yes" once pronounced over creation cannot be annulled by the "no" of human sin and rebellion, nor will God break the covenant once made with God's people Israel.

This God, according to Christian confession, has been revealed in Jesus. Eventually, Christian incarnational faith, through a process of fierce debates and many conflicts, was developed into a trinitarian theology that drew heavily on the concept of *hypostasis*. Traditional Judaism has tended to interpret these developments as a departure from the basic monotheistic faith of Israel. Christians have always denied this, but some of the church's terminology used in its doctrinal development leading up to the Council of Chalcedon has not helped to lend credibility to these Christian denials. Speculative Christian theology, with its dependence on Greek philosophical categories, often made it extremely difficult to recognize the Hebrew roots of the New Testament message. As Christians, we must ask whether orthodoxy is inextricably tied up with those philosophical/theological categories.

However, as Flusser has already reminded us, Christians have assigned to the Messiah/Christ the hypostatic titles of God's immanence, which were borrowed from Judaism. We might discuss such concepts as *Metatron*, *Memra*, *Shekhinah*, *Ruach ha Kodesh*, and *Bat-Kol*–all seemingly having something to do with the presence and activity of God in the world: the living Word, the sanctifying Spirit, the divine power. Thoma has pointed out that followers of Jewish mysticism, while emphatically denying Christian trinitarian thought, admit–together with Christians–"a rich life within the Deity, various manners of God's efficacy outside of himself, and unfathomable dialectical and dialogic movements between the infinity of God and his efficacy in the world."[23] The fundamental difference in our understanding of Jesus is not changed by such probing thoughts, but the spirit of polarization in which such issues are often discussed could be affected, and the dialogue could perhaps be moved into more fruitful directions.

COVENANT PARTNERS

Christianity is often portrayed by our Jewish dialogue partners as an otherworldly faith. It is claimed that Christian views of redemption lead to a denial of the significance of history post-*Christum* and implicitly undercut human responsibility for the social, economic, and political realities that each generation must face. It is true that the idea of covenant partnership has been more strongly stressed in Judaism than in Christianity. Hence, the Jewish community has tended to be more oriented toward human activism and the promotion of society's welfare. On this score, Christians could learn a good deal from their Jewish dialogue partners, even while maintaining what many Christians consider to be their less optimistic but more realistic view of human nature.

Christians have at times spiritualized the message of the kingdom of God, or totally internalized it, or transcendentalized it to the point that it seemed to have everything to do with heaven and nothing to do with earth. So, we have had our apolitical pietists and our antisocial spiritualists. By the same token, however, we have also had our world-transforming revivalists (such as John and Charles Wesley) and our this-worldly social-gospel protagonists, some of whom have so politicized the gospel that it took on the appearance of a party platform. Judaism, too, has known its messianic mystics, its political quietists, its religious anti-Zionists, and all sorts of fervent believers who could hardly be considered devotees of Klausner's idea of an "ardent progressivism."[24] To declare specific movements or schools of thought–which often serve a corrective purpose in their respective religious communities–normative for either Judaism or Christianity does not, it seems to me, advance the cause of dialogue.

Dialogue must encourage each of us to return constantly to the sources of our faith. The New Testament message as a whole, although strongly eschatological, is not world-escapist. The call to justice may not be sounded there as insistently as in the pronouncements of Israel's prophets, but that is precisely why the Hebrew Scriptures must be studied and heard by the churches with much greater diligence than they usually are. Still, the New Testament contains plenty of calls for people to be transformed, to do good works, to be perfect. Discipleship is always portrayed as involving *diakonia*, service to the world modeled after the ministry of Jesus. As a matter of fact, according to Matthew 25:45, in the final judgment the love shown to the least of God's children will be a decisive factor as to who enters the kingdom. Some Bible versions translate Luke 17:21 as saying that the kingdom of God (that is, the power of transformation) is "in your midst" (New American Standard Version) or "among you" (New Revised Standard Version), which, of course, does not preclude the inner mystical experience–the kingdom that is "within you" of other translations (King James Version, New International Version).

EXPECTATION

Both Jews and Christians find the foundation for their future hope in what they believe God has done and is doing in history. Christianity expresses God's dealings with the world predominantly in terms of Christ and the Holy Spirit. Because of New Testament "fulfillment" language, it is hard for Jews (and many Christians as well) to understand that an experience of "fulfillment" has nothing to do with historicizing the eschatological, but involves a rebirth to hope (1 Peter 1:3). As a matter of fact, Paul describes the whole creation post-*Christum* as pregnant with expectation, waiting with eager longing (Romans 8:18ff.) So life, rather than coming to rest in a presumed "realized eschatology," becomes a "straining forward to what lies ahead" (Philippians 3:13).

Even as balanced an observer of Christianity as Wyschogrod declares that "Christianity deals with a completed salvation history."[25] It is a misunderstanding that we must continue to deal with in our dialogue. Yes, we believe that Christ has "realized" a unique and decisive redemptive-messianic act, which, while not being the realization of the eschaton, gives us a foretaste of the age to come. It is more than a promise, more than a new understanding; it is *presentia realis* in the sense of sacramental theology, and precisely for that reason it is the source of our expectation. This is the dialectic of the Christian confession of "fulfillment."

There is then a *fait accompli* aspect to our understanding of redemption in Christ, and therein lies, in the words of Martin Buber, the "gulf which no human power can bridge."[26] To some, the preceding remarks will sound like the words of an unregenerate supersessionist. So be it. A dialogue that moves on reductionist impulses is, in my opinion, on a dead-end track. One Jewish scholar claimed that the theologies of Paul van Buren and John Pawlikowski are still tainted by remnants of supersessionism.[27] When supersessionism becomes defined in maximalist fashion–as any confession of any element of "newness" in the Christian understanding of redemption in Christ–the price for dialogue becomes too high. Is it not better to live with Buber's "gulf which no human power can bridge," while keeping in mind that he also added, "But we can wait for the advent of the One together, and there are moments when we may prepare the way before him together."[28]

The above reflections are very fragmentary and quite preliminary. There must be a variety of ways in which the dialogue might be refocused, revised, and possibly revitalized. The subject can be changed; the composition of the participants can be diversified and perhaps become less compartmentalized (why must we have separate Jewish-"mainline" and Jewish-"evangelical" dialogues?). However, in the end, it is the spirit of the dialogue that really counts. It does not wait for bureaucratic decisions to be made about the direction of dialogue. The spirit of dialogue is ever restless, ever risking, ever reaching out to others–funny and strange, and frightening as they often may seem in their "otherness."

MORE EXPLORATIONS AND RESPONSES

Michael Kogan's proposals concerning "total dialogue" provoked a good deal of debate–and deservedly so. His later follow-up was equally striking in its title, "Toward a Jewish Theology of Christianity," and equally challenging in the ideas presented.[29] Christian-Jewish dialogue desperately needs some real debates!

I would offer here an appreciative but critical response to some of the issues Kogan is raising. His central thesis is that the time has come for Jews to respond theologically to New Testament affirmations and some basic doctrines the church has derived from them. Kogan specifically mentions the incarnation, vicarious atonement, and the resurrection.

It seems to me that Kogan is seeking to bring some spark to a dialogue that, some would say, is in danger of burning out (while others would claim that a true dialogue between the two faith communities has not even started yet). Martin Buber's "I-thou" philosophy used the imagery of sparks flying back and forth from heart to heart. Few dialogue meetings, with their usually heavy agenda of academic lectures, display that kind of excitement. I suspect that the problem is not just one of form but also one of substance and of subjects avoided.

At any rate, I welcome Kogan's challenge to explore new directions and dig more deeply into each other's traditions. By the same token, it seems to me that he tends to underestimate the obstacles that stand in the way of pursuing that course. On the Christian side, I would say that there is much greater complexity, ambivalence, and disagreement on certain positions than his essay suggests. I am referring specifically to the so-called mainline churches.

First, however, let me make an historical observation. Kogan's point that we have entered a wholly new era in Christian-Jewish relations seems to me to be beyond dispute. However, to say, as he and many others do, that this new era has been "opened up" by Vatican II strikes me as a somewhat provincial North American perspective that ignores developments on the European Protestant scene during the two decades preceding Vatican II. The *Encyclopedia Judaica* portrays things more accurately by pointing out that the Reformed Church in the Netherlands was "the first to mold a more positive theological approach to Judaism . . . and to advocate the adoption of a dialogue in place of missionary activities."[30]

We also ought to keep in mind colloquia held under the auspices of the WCC. At the Bossey Consultation in 1949, for instance, scholars (among them James Parkes) delivered papers that made what *Nostra Aetate* had to say on the subject of anti-Semitism seem quite timid by comparison. However, on that subject and other related issues the Roman Catholic Church has come a long way since then, and in Christian history (if not world history) Vatican II remains an event of supreme significance.

More consequential than the above historical observations are the definitive conclusions Kogan draws from the pronouncements on Jews and Judaism by various churches and ecumenical bodies. Most of those statements have been unequivocal in rejecting supersessionism and traditional church triumphalism, but they have been quite ambivalent on the question of Christian witness to Jews. The ambiguity embodied in these ecclesiastical documents can easily be misunderstood as meaning that the churches have adopted a sort of "theology of equality" or a "two-covenant theology" *a la* Franz Rosenzweig: the way of Torah is fully valid for Jews; the way of Jesus, for Gentiles.

I fear that Kogan has indeed drawn such an implication when he repeatedly declares that all those churches now agree with the central proposition of the Jewish faith, encompassing not only the eternal covenant with Israel but also a recognition of the full validity of the Torah-centered way of life. If this is interpreted to mean that the churches have reached a clear conclusion that the Christ-centered *kerygma* of the church has no relevance for Jews, it would not accurately represent the position of ecclesiastical and ecumenical bodies. The language of public pronouncements is purposely ambiguous, expressing perhaps an appreciation (even admiration) for Jewish faithfulness to Torah, but at the same time presupposing the universal nature of the church's apostolate. Attempts in mainline church assemblies to articulate an opposite position have, to the best of my knowledge, always failed.

In sum, theologically, the churches want to hold on to the missionary mandate, encompassing all peoples and nations, while also recognizing that Jews, as the people of a covenant that has never been revoked and through whom Torah has come to the world, are *sui generis*. Practically, however, most churches no longer engage in mission to Jews, because, historically, such mission has become increasingly complicated, if not questionable. In light of the horrors of Christian history, and the unique position of the Jewish people in the history of redemption, how does the church witness to them? Hence, Gentile missions to Jews have been in decline over the past decades.

At the same time, it should be mentioned (certainly in a total dialogue without taboos) that a whole new historical dynamic is emerging that gives the question of mission to Jews an entirely new dimension and that affects the dialogue in various ways. I am referring to the highly charged issue of so-called "Messianic Jews." We can argue about that designation (a misnomer in my judgment) and/or about the scope and significance of that movement, but the fact that it is a dynamic reality in a number of countries, including Israel, can hardly be denied. I shall not further discuss this phenomenon yet, except to say that this could turn out to be one of the great divine ironies in history: on the one hand, a new encounter between Jews and Gentile Christians for the purpose of rapprochement and mutual edification and, on the other hand, a New Testament-type family debate between Jews who do and those who do not believe in Jesus' messiahship. When, according to Acts 17, Paul dialogued (Greek: *dialegomai*, a word used only for encounters with his kinsfolk) on three successive Sabbaths in the synagogue in Thessalonica, Buberian-type sparks were probably flying back and forth from heart to heart.

The second point I want to address about Kogan's essay deals with the need to be sensitive to the self-definition of one's dialogue partners. This argument has commonly been directed at Christians who have had a penchant for describing Judaism in terms of preconceived notions of "biblical Judaism," ignoring rabbinic developments. Now, Kogan applies the same principle to his own community, urging his co-believers to abandon the notion that they can deal adequately with Christianity in terms of the Noahide Law. To do so, he writes, would be evidence that Jews "continue to ignore Christianity as a distinct movement. No Christian can recognize herself or himself in this limited list of minimal requirements for civilized life."[31]

The dialogue "from faith to faith," rather than from individual opinion to individual opinion, would certainly gain depth if both parties took more time and effort to understand each other's traditions. This would also introduce more controversy and more elements of disputation into the dialogue, and a few sparks might fly. However, dealt with maturely and in full freedom, this would be preferable to avoiding anything that might evoke passion out of fear that a fragile dialogue could disintegrate.

The third theme in Kogan's essay that caught my attention has to do with his view that Christianity, rather than being a threat to Judaism, is "a Jewish outreach into the world."[32] Hence, he raises the important issue of the "missionary" calling of Israel, rooted in God's call to Abraham with its promise of a universal blessing for the nations. Israel is indeed "a witness-people ever en route to the Kingdom"–God's original missionary people *par excellence.*[33]

However, we face the historical reality that it was through the agency of Christianity that the God of Israel became known among the nations, or in Kogan's words, ". . . Jesus of Nazareth appeared, and through him and his interpreters God's covenant with Israel was dramatically broken open to include the Gentile peoples."[34] Conceivably, history could have moved differently. Gentiles could have converted to Judaism in large numbers, which Kogan assures us, would have been welcomed by Jews. Or, as others might speculate, a large number of Jews could have followed the path of the Jesus movement. However, neither of those developments occurred. As a result, we have this dual thrust of the one *Missio Dei* to the nations: Israel and the church, both called to be instruments of God for the sake of the coming of the kingdom of God.

A good deal could be said about how this has worked out historically on both sides, both positively and negatively. Now, however, I am particularly interested in the growing number of Christians who recognize the tremendous need for the churches to pay heed to the witness of Judaism. The source of so much sickness in the churches can be traced back to the long process of the de-Judaization of the Christian faith. The more I engage in Christian-Jewish dialogue, the stronger has become my sense of calling, particularly to call the churches to conversion. How can the encounter with Judaism help the churches find healing as well as a new vision about their life and mission in the world? That, I believe, is one of the crucial questions for the church in our day.

Kogan has a way of confronting us with issues that we are not always eager to face. That makes him somewhat of a "troubler" (1 Kings 18:17) in Christian-Jewish dialogue. My own view is that he is still too willing to divide the field of faith into sovereign spheres of truth. Occasional tensions are inevitable, both between the two communities and within them. The question, it seems to me, is how we handle our differences and whether they lead to creative confrontation or to destructive and divisive conflicts.

Radical voices are heard, some of them questioning central tenets of faith. I earlier referred to the Reformed Church in the Netherlands as probably the first denomination in history to affirm God's eternal covenant with Israel as an article of confession. Now I must also mention that that same church has since become embroiled in a heated dispute about the agenda of Christian-Jewish dialogue. What happened? As this denomination engaged in union negotiations with two other churches, a commission was appointed to draft a new constitution for the uniting bodies. The proposed draft included an article that stated that "the church seeks dialogue [with the synagogue] concerning the kingdom of God and the confession of Jesus as the Christ." Others, including Jewish scholars (Schalom Ben-Chorin comes to mind), have stated that the messiahship of Jesus is the central issue in Christian-Jewish dialogue. However, the formulation in this draft document had an "I dare you" tone about it, which led to anger and threats on the part of Jewish leaders to leave the cooperative council through which much of the dialogue was being conducted in the Netherlands.

From personal conversations with various parties involved in this dispute, I concluded that there was an element of church leaders striking back, as it were, at individuals within their own circles, who, they believed, were prepared to undermine the christological foundation of the faith in the name of antisupersessionism and the need for radical post-*Shoah* theological revisions.

This raises the question of a consensus *fidelium*.[35] There must be room in dialogue for individual and sometimes adventurous positions. The voices of mavericks must be heard. But, if the dialogue is going to be conducted between communities of faith, beliefs historically confessed and still held by the vast majority of members should not be dealt with in a cavalier fashion. Doctrinal revision should occur until the dawning of the Day of the Lord, but it should be a process in which the community is involved through representative councils and synods, even though insightful individuals may give the first impetus to change. Kogan also emphasized this point in his essay.

At the same time, he speculated about what might have happened had Jesus been a bit more circumspect in his teachings and had his followers made more modest claims. In that case, "Jesus would probably have been incorporated into Jewish faith as at least a noted rabbi, or at most an eloquent prophet of a compassionate God."[36] Today, one wonders how much more modest are we Christians supposed to become in our claims? Specifically, what are the christological implications of the "nonexclusivist" Christianity Kogan and others wish to have as a dialogue partner? These are issues that must be discussed. They are also questions that threaten churches with divisiveness, a result hardly to be desired from interfaith relations.

On the question of Jesus' messiahship, Kogan, supported by a number of church theologians, would really prefer that Christians drop the term *messiah* from their confessional vocabulary, but he is realistic enough to recognize that this is not about to happen. Nonetheless, he would like us at least to make it clear that we "are defining it in an internalized and spiritualized way unknown to mainstream Judaism."[37] To that I say, "God forbid!" To surrender to the myth of a totally internalized and spiritualized Christian messianic faith would be suicidal for the churches. It would mean the loss of the incarnational core of our faith, the abandonment of the gospel of the kingdom of God, and an atrophied and eventually totally irrelevant witness to the world of politics, culture, economics–the world of people's daily lives.

To be sure, Christians have at times succumbed to such distortions of the *kerygma*, but after decades of dialogue it should be time that we stop perpetuating, through constant repetition, the myth of a wholly internalized and spiritualized Christian message. Repeating that myth does not make it any more true than the oft-repeated myth of a totally legalistic Judaism, even though there have obviously been legalistic strains within it. As readers might surmise, I have warmed up to the dialogical challenges posed by my good friend Michael Kogan. I hope that his challenge will not be met with silence and that he will succeed in unleashing a few sparks in the Christian-Jewish dialogue. May his tribe increase!

The original, unedited form of this chapter was first published in the Winter, 1992, and the Spring, 1996, issues of the Journal of Ecumenical Studies. Reprinted by permission.

[1] Rabbi Leon Klenicki, "Dialogue: From Crisis to Recognition," *National Dialogue Newsletter* 4, Spring/Summer, 1989, p. 3.

[2] Father Edward H. Flannery, "A New Stage of Dialogue?", *National Dialogue Newsletter* 4, Fall, 1988, p. 3.

[3] *Ibid.*

[4] See Michael McGarry, "Emil Fackenheim and Christianity after the Holocaust," *American Journal of Theology and Philosophy* 9, January-May, 1988, pp. 117-135.

[5] Edward H. Flannery, "A New Stage," *National Dialogue Newsletter* 4, Fall, 1988, p. 3.

[6] Henry Siegman, "A Decade of Catholic-Jewish Relations–A Reassessment," *Journal of Ecumenical Studies* 15, Spring, 1978, 248-249.

[7] *Ibid.*, pp. 253-254.

[8] *Ibid.*, pp. 255ff.

[9] *National Dialogue Newsletter* 6, Winter, 1990-91, p. 6.

[10] *Ibid.*

[11] See *Quarterly Review*, Rabbi Irving Greenberg, "The Relationship of Judaism and Christianity: Toward a New Organic Model," Vol. 4, No. 4, Winter, 1984, reissued in the *Perspectives* series by the National Jewish Center for Learning and Leadership.

[12] Michael Wyschogrod, *The Body of Faith: Judaism as Corporeal Election* (New York: Seabury Press, 1983), p. xv.

[13] *Ibid.*, p. xv.

[14] David Flusser, quoted in Clemens Thoma, *A Christian Theology of Judaism*, (tr. and ed. Helga Croner), *Studies in Judaism and Christianity, A Stimulus Book* (New York and Ramsey, NJ: Paulist Press, 1980), p. 13.

[15] *Ibid.*, p. 12.

[16] See Joseph Klausner, "The Jewish and the Christian Messiah," in Frank Ephraim Talmage, ed., *Disputation and Dialogue: Readings in the Jewish-Christian Encounter* (New York: Ktav Publishing House and the Anti-Defamation League of B'nai B'rith, 1975), p. 69.

[17] Thoma, *A Christian Theology of Judaism*, p. 13.

[18] *Ibid.*, p. 135.

[19] David Flusser, "A New Sensitivity in Judaism and the Christian Message," *Harvard Theological Review* 61, April, 1968, p. 107.

[20] I have developed these themes more fully elsewhere; see, especially my *Redemption and Historical Reality* (Philadelphia: Westminster Press, 1964), and *The Promise and the Presence: Toward a Theology of the Kingdom of God* (Grand, Rapids, MI: Wm. B. Eerdmans, 1980).

[21] Wyschogrod, *Body of Faith*, p. 224.

[22] Pierre Teilhard de Chardin, *Letters from a Traveller*, ed. Bernard Wall (London: William Collins Sons and Co., Ltd.; New York: Harper & Brothers Publishers, 1962), p. 105.

[23] Thoma, *A Christian Theology*, p. 127.

[24] Klausner, "The Jewish and the Christian Messiah," p. 64.

[25] Wyschogrod, *Body of Faith*, p. 80.

[26] Martin Buber, "The Two Foci of the Jewish Soul," in Talmage, *Disputation and Dialogue*, p. 282.

[27] Peter Haas, "Toward a Post-Holocaust Christian View of Judaism," a paper presented at the October, 1990, meeting of the Christian Study Group on Judaism and the Jewish people.

[28] Buber, "The Two Foci," p. 282.

[29] See Michael S. Kogan, "Toward a Jewish Theology of Christianity," *Journal of Ecumenical Studies*, 32, Winter, 1995, pp. 89-106, 152.

[30] Yona Malachy, "Protestants," in *Encyclopedia Judaica*, vol. 13 (Jerusalem: Keter Publishing House, Ltd.; New York: Macmillan Co., 1971), col. 1252. In 1994 the Dutch scholar Jacobus Bastiaanse received his doctorate on the basis of a massive two-volume dissertation in which he presented a wealth of historical data on developments in the Netherlands and beyond between 1925 and 1965 (*De Jodenzending en de eerste Decennia van de Hervormide Road voor Kerk en Israel–1925-1965–een generatie in dienst van de foods-Christelke Toenadering* ['s-Gravenhage: Boekencentrum, 1995]).

[31] Kogan, "Toward a Jewish Theology," p. 92.

[32] *Ibid.*, p. 98.

[33] After the second World Mission Conference in Jerusalem (1930) had called the churches to pay more attention to the Jewish people, the Dutch delegate J. H. Grolle wrote in the *International Review of Missions* about a potential part the Jew-

ish people might play in world mission because of the continuing calling of Israel to be a witness to the nations (Bastiaanse, *De Jodenzending*, Vol. 1, p. 104).

[34] Kogan, "Toward a Jewish Theology," p. 96.

[35] Richard Mouw deals with this topic in his delightful little book, *Consulting the Faithful: What Christian Intellectuals Can Learn from Popular Religion* (Grand Rapids, MI: William B. Eerdmans Publishing Co., 1994).

[36] Kogan, "Toward a Jewish Theology," p. 97.

[37] *Ibid.*, p. 98.

CHAPTER 4

Danger Signs Along the Dialogue Road

I am a mainline Protestant cleric who, ever since his earliest years in the pastorate, has been active in ecumenical and interfaith endeavors. I have done my share of ecumenical jet-set traveling, attending interfaith assemblies on four continents. The challenges of living in a world of religious pluralism and a multicultural society are very real to me. As a pastor, I had the privilege of teaching and preaching every week in a church with a racially and ethnically diverse membership.

My theological position is one in which the centrality of biblical revelation is affirmed, as is the confession of Christ's atoning death on the cross. I do not, however, specialize in speculations about the *massa perditionis*–all those heathen Buddhists, Muslims, and others who presumably are going to hell. My major involvements have been in Christian-Jewish dialogue. For both theological and historical reasons I consider the relationship between Judaism and Christianity to be in a class by itself. My writings on that subject have been consistently anti-supersessionist, rejecting the idea that the church has replaced the Jewish people in God's convenantal economy of redemption.

In terms of today's much-favored typology, I would probably be considered an inclusivist of a kind, as distinguished from an exclusivist or a pluralist. On the contemporary "mainstream" ecumenical/interfaith scene, let us say, in the counsels of the councils of churches, my kind of "inclusivist fulfillment theology," with its emphasis on the uniqueness of Jesus' ministry of world reconciliation, is not particularly popular. I sense a definite pluralist pull among my one-time colleagues in the National and World Council of Churches.

This is not an Elijah-type complaint that I have become a lonely traveler along the road of historic Christianity. I know that I share the stigma of "not really being with it" with a large company of mainline denominational brothers and sisters, as well as evangelicals and Roman Catholics, including the "holy father" in Rome. The late Pope John Paul II showed a greater openness to other religions and their leaders, and a greater appreciation for the positive values they represent than any of his predecessors. At the same time, he spoke unhesitatingly about the centrality and uniqueness of Jesus Christ in God's dealings with the world.

Papal pronouncements have not always been cast in the most felicitous language, which occasionally has led to criticism, not only from devoted pluralists, but also from dialogue participants who have shared the Pope John Paul II's basic theological stance. Such criticism, I believe, is to be expected as part of the dialogical process, since we are all on a journey that at times leads into *terra incognita,* where few guideposts from the past are to be found and occasional missteps are virtually inevitable.

It should be kept in mind that the dialogue/interfaith movements are quite young. In a number of respects, we are still in the experimentation stage. The attempt to engage people with profound faith commitments and often opposing views in an open, no-holds-barred conversation is an historic novelty. Can this be done without preconditions? Or is genuine dialogue possible only if we presuppose a sort of "theology of equality," as some participants in Christian-Jewish dialogue have claimed, or a universal religious parity, as more and more pluralists are claiming today? These are some of the questions that are simmering, not only between religious communities, but also within them.

One of my concerns is that the dialogue movement, particularly as it has become embodied in conciliar forms, is taking on the characteristics of an establishment with all the elements of rigid entrenchments that tend to accompany establishmentarianism. The latter are usually not so much doctrinal as organizational or ideological.

I remember that, when I was still a pre-teenage youth in Holland, my father introduced me to his colleague, Dr. Visser 't Hooft, a well-known churchman, scholar, and ecumenical pioneer. When out of sight, he and his ecumenical associates were usually discussed with considerable respect, an almost disbelieving admiration. Looking back, it seems to me that these people were respected the way the Don Quixotes of this world are respected, those who dare dream impossible dreams. They were people with a vision of unity rooted deeply in the biblical witness during decades when ecclesiastical divisions–particularly between Protestants and Catholics, but also among the various Protestant denominations–seemed insuperable.

By the time I entered the world of the denominational-ecumenical bureaucracy in the late 1960s, the churches had come a long way in breaking down walls of ecclesiastical hostility. On the ecumenical front, in the meantime, few of the original visionaries were still actively involved, and a growing number of functionaries had taken their place. This was not due to some diabolical scheme. It simply is the way things tend to develop in the world of institutions. In order for dreams to be translated into reality, organizational structures are necessary. Dreamers are often not very good administrators. On the other hand, establishments tend to become increasingly resistant to the voices of new Don Quixotes who battle against the ever-rotating windmills of organizational busyness, preoccupation with budgets, and the accompanying power plays.

My reading of history suggests that movements, born in the hearts and minds of visionaries and mavericks, are perennially in danger of dying at the hands of functionaries. Surely, the ecumenical/interfaith movement has not been immune to the virus of bureaucratization that is infecting life on a worldwide scale. The founders of the movement, focused as they were on a central biblical vision, as well as on the threat of a Nazi neo-pagan totalitarianism, were not easily distracted by ideological and party-line thinking.

That changed, however, when the issue of a Soviet-style socialist totalitarianism arose. Already during the first WCC Assembly in 1948, the confrontation between Joseph Hromadka and Reinhold Niebuhr (with some input from Karl Barth) foreshadowed disputations of an ideological nature that were to follow. Only after the breakdown of the Soviet system would the WCC come to recognize clearly how ideological blinders had affected some of its actions and pronouncements.

Soon "Israel politics" began to interfere with calm theological deliberations, as dialogue was often replaced by diatribe. It started at the Evanston Assembly in 1954, had heated up by the time delegates arrived in Uppsala (one year after the Six-Day War in 1967!), and was feared to become a divisive force during the 1975 Nairobi Assembly. The general secretary considered the threat of a United Nations-like Zionism/Racism resolution serious enough to summon a group of us to Geneva for a damage-control strategy session.

Eventually, ideological party lines were drawn on a number of other socio-political issues as well. I recall a worship service in the Interchurch Center chapel in New York where the preacher proclaimed with impassioned rhetoric that, in the face of racism and the oppression of the poor, the time of reconciliation talk was long past. While, to our 475 Riverside Drive "God Box" environment, the singing of "Onward Christian Soldiers" was definitely taboo, the spirit of uncompromising militancy and revolutionary rhetoric were alive and well in that center of ecumenism.

One would hope that, once the *Sturm-und-Drang* (storm-and-stress) phase of the ecumenical maturing process had run its course, a new openness toward theological issues would become possible. But I am not overly optimistic because dialogue, praised widely as an idea and ideal, has proven rather difficult to pull off in practice. Everyone claims to favor openness but, because of the unavoidable influence of personal and group agendas, certain perspectives have a tendency to become predominant, while invisible boundaries to dialogue are erected, if only by careful selection of the voices that will be heard at meetings and conferences. My experience as a church bureaucrat has taught me all too well how easily one can affect the outcome of assembly meetings through one's influence on the agenda process. Again, there is no need to introduce the idea of a demonology into the picture; most of these dynamics work almost subconsciously and are usually set in motion with the best of intentions.

For example, many meetings with interfaith agendas are not really dialogues at all. They tend to be heavily loaded with academic lectures delivered to mostly passive listeners. I see this as a side-product of the bureaucratization of the dialogue and of a mentality that prefers safe agendas over controversy. But real dialogue involves more than meetings about interfaith topics; it is an encounter. As we have observed, sparks can–and often will–fly in a true Buberian "I-thou" dialogue. Do we seek to protect ourselves against such sparks because we fear that our dialogue climate will inevitably ignite the fires of hostility and conflict? If so, then the quality of true dialogue has been lost already.

In the Christian-Jewish dialogue, some significant trust relationships have been developed. That does not mean, however, that there are no taboo subjects or no sometimes subtle and sometimes not-so-subtle attempts to keep the focus on a limited agenda of favored topics. Let me mention one issue for illustrative purposes. Admittedly, I have selected an emotional and controversial one: namely, Jewish converts to Christianity. The controversy is as old as the Christian church, although it has assumed various forms throughout the troubled history of Christian-Jewish relations. Today, I believe, the issue is taking on a renewed theological and historical urgency because of a growing and dynamic "Messianic Jewish movement."

I first raised the question in an almost postscript fashion during an interfaith forum at Temple Emanu-El in New York, where Dr. Michael Wyschogrod and I led a discussion on Jewish and Christian understandings of "witness."[1] During the following years, my work as executive director of the National Christian Leadership Conference for Israel curtailed my writing activities, certainly on that particular topic. In recent years, I have been pushing the subject a bit more aggressively. More recently, an entire issue of *Modern Theology* was devoted to a dialogue between Michael Wyschogrod and various scholars on precisely this subject, which should speak for itself. But, in most dialogue circles, ours are clearly the voices of a minute minority.

This is a subject of extreme sensitivity, especially for Jews, but also for many Christians. It is, however, precisely such questions that call, not for silence, but for conversation. Otherwise, instead of addressing the issues or people involved, we will merely talk about them and that in mostly derogatory terms.

Why, one might wonder, do so many Christians seem to have such difficulty with Jewish converts to Christianity, especially when they openly show their enthusiasm for the newfound faith in demonstrative ways and yet insist on holding fast to elements from their Jewish heritage? The fact that they are seen as a disturbing element in burgeoning Jewish-Christian relations cannot be the full answer. My own suspicion is that those people are visible reminders of historic concepts of revelation, salvation in Christ, and mission that have become somewhat of an embarrassment and scandal in the spiritual-cultural climate of our day. This leads us to the subject of pluralism.

Most of my remarks will be centered around Diana Eck's well-written book, *Encountering God.*[3] The work reads like a long and richly illustrated sermon. With almost evangelical zeal she pleads for pluralism in order to save a crisis-ridden world. All we need to create a new world system, said Karl Marx, is a new kind of person. He pursued the goal along the path of economic materialism. Eck wants to change people and prepare the way for world peace by radically changing people's religious beliefs and behavior. For Christians (as well as for Jews) this means fundamental change in their view of revelation.

In the beginning of the book, it all sounds rather benign. "Pluralist theologians insist," states Eck, "that Christians must also listen to the voices of people of other faiths and not pretend that we can do our theological and ethical thinking in a vacuum, without engaging in energetic interreligious exchange."[4] For a moment I thought that I, too, might qualify as a pluralist, but I soon learned that, at best, I could be counted among the inclusivists. Christian pluralism demands a concept of revelation unconfined to any particular religion; i.e., the end to confessions that imply belief in a unique revelation, and the acceptance instead of the parity of religious positions. In the dramatic imagery of pioneer pluralist thinker John Hick, such a "Copernican revolution" in contemporary theology will mean that we view God as "the sun, the originative source of light and life, whom all the religions reflect in their own different ways."[5]

Historically, Christian theologians, while taking their starting point in a particular divine revelation (God's revelation in Israel and through Jesus), have usually not had great problems also accepting a "general revelation." None other than the apostle Paul claimed in Romans 1:20 that, ever since the creation of the world, God's "eternal power and divine nature, invisible though they are, have been understood and seen through the things he has made."

Eck's problem with inclusivists is, however, precisely that they view world religions and social issues from a specific frame of reference (i.e., a view of revelation) that is not broad enough to validate other religions on the basis of the parity principle. The root cause of this deficiency is then found in a lack of ability to listen to dissenting voices.[6] Why, I wonder, can't she accept the fact that we have, in fact, listened carefully and then have rejected the conclusions she and other pluralists have put forth? Eck reminds inclusivists that they will be challenged by the independent voices of other people of faith, including other inclusivists. To that I can only reply, "Fine! That is what dialogue is supposed to be all about, an encounter from faith to faith in full freedom."

Encountering God bears as its subtitle "A Spiritual Journey from Bozeman to Banaras." Peter Berger has described what "the dialogue between Jerusalem and Banaras" means to him in an essay entitled "God in a World of Gods."[7] These two scholars raise similar questions and, yet, come up with very different answers. However, Berger's highly dialectical approach to interreligious dialogue can hardly be accused of an unwillingness to hear dissenting voices.

We are being told that Christian pluralism does not imply a "nihilist relativism." By all means, people should stand fast in their faith commitments–except if that commitment has anything to do with what historically has been known as the "Great Commission." Any form of a prophetic-apostolic witness to the nations is, *ipso facto*, religious imperialism.

In a remarkable *tour de force*, Eck points to (of all people!) the apostle Paul as an exemplary pluralist. Didn't he, during that famous sermon in Athens, say that the people in that god-saturated city were not only searching and groping for God, but were actually finding him (Acts 17:27-28)? According to Eck, Paul's experience was similar to that of missionaries who go to Africa only to discover that what they are bringing is already there. Poor souls indeed, so dedicated to carrying corn to Iowa only to find that Iowans can tell them a thing or two about corn.

This strikes me as one of the neatest pieces of eisegesis appearing in print in a long time. Surely, it does not take a Ph.D. in Greek to see that this text speaks about the universal human desire and search for the divine. They grope in the hope of finding God. As a collateral text, one can turn to the apocryphal book Wisdom of Solomon 13:6, where people are also described as "seeking God and desiring to find him," and in the process they end up with idols. If Paul were really such a pluralist, why in the world did he keep on crossing land and sea from Athens to Rome and beyond to proclaim Christ crucified and risen?

Historically, the ecumenical movement emerged from the missionary movement. Therefore, it speaks volumes about developments in the WCC that, after the 1983 Vancouver Assembly, had rejected the idea of Paul's certainty concerning the universal discovery of the God he preached, a 1990 WCC consultation incorporated such language in their final document. I wonder and worry about an ecumenical movement that has so little to say of a distinctive nature to the nations of the world. Movements that have lost any real sense of "reaching out" have a tendency to seek survival through a perpetual process of reorganization. That is exactly what has been happening to denominations and ecumenical bodies that have surrendered to the relativistic spirit of our age.

Diana Eck mentions an apartment building in the Elmhurst section of Queens, New York, where people of eleven countries dwell on a single floor, all living in isolation and fear. In a way, that floor can be regarded as a miniature version of our global village, with all the potentials for social friction and eventual violence. In a sort of fantasy fashion, one might ask what would happen if that floor were to be turned into an experimental laboratory with two research teams, each working with half of the residents. One team would consist of pluralist theologians trying to get those people to study and then incorporate some of the best elements of their very diverse religio-cultural traditions into their personal lives as a basis for a new style of community. The other team would consist of an ecumenical, interracial, and cross-cultural group of evangelically oriented Christians doing their thing. Which approach would produce the most powerful impetus toward positive change?

No knowledgeable person would claim that Christian missions have been an unmixed blessing for the world. Far from it! Therefore, all our dialogue involvements need to be approached with penitent hearts and contrite spirits. This is especially true in the case of Judaism. It is, therefore, appropriate that Jewish-Christian dialogue has over the past decades been marked by sharp attacks on the sins of Christianity, sometimes deeply rooted in historic doctrinal positions. Many churches have felt compelled to change long-held views. Still, the irreconcilable differences between the way of Torah and the way of the Cross have not been resolved, and perhaps never will be on this side of history. Yet the dialogue and moves toward reconciliation are continuing.

Judaism is called to be a light to the nations, not as one of the numerous reflectors of a universal divine sunburst, but as a prophetic witness to the revelation of the God of Israel. Christianity finds its source of life in Christ who, according to apostolic witness, represents a specific way of salvation. A "principled pluralism," which, according to Rabbi Greenberg, moves beyond absolutism and relativism, is not afraid to articulate the particular while at the same time being profoundly aware that even the highest heavens cannot contain the Holy One.

Any religious belief in particularity involves the dangers of pride, prejudice, and missionary imperialism. On the other hand, as someone has observed, there is also the danger that theologians, seeking to excise a cancer, end up removing the heart. Harvey Cox's contribution to the volume *Jesus' Jewishness* contains a wonderful discussion on "the most nettlesome dilemma hindering interreligious dialogue," namely, how to balance the universal and the particular. Toward the end of his essay he states his belief that "the critically important conversation among people of diverse faiths could founder and fail if we–the dialoguers–lose touch with our fellow believers who cluster on the particularistic side. We may not admit it, but we do need each other. They remind us that, without the radical particularity of the original revelation, we would have no faith to share."[8] Eck's book has a lot to teach us, but this is one lesson she herself does not seem to have learned yet.

My good friend, Richard Rhem, has cautiously suggested that genuine dialogue can begin when we as Christians become more open to the view that the gospel of Christ may be one of many ways to salvation.[9] I am not so sure. I see a more than even chance that such a dialogue, in the words of Cox, could "deteriorate into a repetitious exchange of vacuities" and "end with a whimper."[10] Such a dialogue can also become embroiled in endless religio-philosophical profundities. In both cases we cease to speak to each other from faith to faith.

There is a danger, it seems to me, that certain dialogue trends, while seeking to promote interreligious harmony, may end up contributing to internal discord. There are, of course, always the inevitable growing pains that go with the maturing process. But then there are also the avoidable pains caused by our lack of maturity in dealing with true encounters, found among exclusivists, inclusivists, and pluralists alike. May God grant us the grace to know the difference.

The original, unedited form of this chapter was first published in the May, 1996, issue of Perspectives. Reprinted by permission.

[1] My contribution appeared in print in the June 1978 issue of *Reformed World*, published in Geneva.

[2] *Modern Theology*, April 1995.

[3] Diana Eck, *Encountering God: A Spiritual Journey from Bozeman to Banaras*, (Boston: Beacon Press, 1993).

[4] *Ibid.* pp. 17-18.

[5] *Ibid.*, p. 190.

[6] *Ibid.*, p. 185.

[7] Peter Berger, *First Things*, August/September, 1993.

[8] Harvey Cox in *Jesus' Jewishness: Exploring the Place of Jesus Within Early Judaism*, James H. Charlesworth, ed., (Philadelphia: New York: American Interfaith Institute; Crossroad, 1991), p. 49, 6a.

[9] Richard Rhem, "Interreligious Dialogue: What Is Required of Us?" *Perspectives*, May 1995, p. 51.

[10] Cox, *Jesus' Jewishness*, p. 51.

CHAPTER 5

A Protestant Comments on a Jewish-Catholic Exchange

Interfaith Focus, a publication of the Anti-Defamation League, once devoted an issue to a discussion of the Catechism of the Catholic Church. In a mildly critical evaluation of the Catechism, Rabbi Leon Klenicki mentioned two New Testament writings as worthy candidates for a joint study between Christians and Jews: Paul's letter to the Romans and the epistle to the Hebrews. Such a study, he believed, could "enrich both spiritualities despite past history."

What a superb choice that is: two writings, very diverse in a number of ways and yet posing a common challenge for Jewish-Christian dialogue! Furthermore, both letters have often played an important role in Catholic-Protestant encounters as well. But are we really prepared for the rough-and-tumble discussion these controversial epistles invite? After participating in numerous dialogue sessions, I am not so sure, and reading the aforementioned issue of *Interfaith Focus* hasn't helped. I pose a few questions:

WHY ARE ROMANS AND HEBREWS SUCH EXCELLENT CHOICES?

Precisely because they take such a radical approach to the issues. Both authors hold passionately to the central perspective of faith. Their words don't lend themselves very well to an exchange of waffling niceties. In describing redemptive realities pre- and post-*Christum* their language takes on a radical tone.

To be precise, both Paul and the author of Hebrews believe that the God of Israel has done a new, unique, and decisive thing in Jesus. The Lord of history, the Holy One who is truly free and sovereign, who does new things all the time, even though we may not perceive it (Isaiah 43:19), has invaded existence with saving power in the life and ministry, death and resurrection, of this son of Israel named Jesus. The radical break, the miraculous rupture, and the new beginning have always been fundamental notions in the faith of Israel. But in the New Testament in general, and in Romans and Hebrews in particular, we find the claim that the divine invasion in and through the incarnation has become, not just a stage, but the central chapter in the drama that leads from creation to the new creation and the promised kingdom of God. This is truly a "new age" faith.

For Paul, it means that the righteousness of God has been revealed (Romans 1:17). To speak about the righteousness of God in biblical context means that one comes face to face with the Torah, the revealed will of God in the midst of Israel. Something very radical has happened in Jesus, and it involves the law. In short, Jesus has done what humans have not been able to do: fulfill the law in holy love. According to the Christian *kerygma,* the implications of this are immense, affecting the human heart, world history, and even the cosmos.

The author of Hebrews describes the new thing the God of Israel has done in cultic terms, using the imagery of the Day of Atonement. The One who has spoken (and acted) in many and various ways in the covenant history of Israel, has "in these last days" spoken through the Son (Hebrews 1:1ff.). Thus, the sovereign Lord has created a new order–from Aaron to Melchizedek. But note that the only way to describe the new order is in terms of the old one, which continues to have an impact. The old order may be in the process of disappearing (Hebrews 8:13), but then, from the perspective of the promised "new thing" in the eschaton, that is true of the church as well. In the meantime, far from declaring the old order *passé,* the author of Hebrews portrays both the land of Israel and the Sabbath as signs of future glory and eternal life.

When the Lord Almighty acts, history moves in leaps. There are radical "shifts" (Jeremiah 31) and "turns," rather than a smooth ascending line, as in some philosophies of progress. How does one express a faith like that, and particularly, how does one talk about the "once-for-all" dimension of the new, while maintaining the dialectical tie-in with the old, a connection rooted in nothing less than the eternal covenant faithfulness of God? After all, the law is still "holy, just, and good" (Romans 7:12) and is still being fulfilled in us through the Holy Spirit (Romans 8:4). "All Israel will be saved" (Romans 11:26), and living in hope remains an essential element of the Jewish and Christian experience. Christian realities, just like Jewish realities, are like signs and shadows of the "good things to come" (Hebrews 10:1).

This problem with language, which in Christian history has all too often been "resolved" in a boastful and sinful triumphalism, remains very much part of an honest dialogue. The language of Romans and Hebrews, as well as the principles of faith expressed therein, are bound to pose some obstacles at times, but they also offer opportunities for a joint study that is searching and unafraid of sharply conflicting views. This leads to the next question:

WHAT KIND OF A DIALOGUE ARE WE LOOKING FOR?

People who are involved in interfaith work almost full-time tend to develop a fuzzy vocabulary which is non-confrontational to such a degree that it appears designed to avoid healthy debate about real differences. For instance, we earlier quoted Rabbi Klenicki who referred to Judaism and Christianity as two "spiritualities." That sounds so benign and so un-Hebraic. The Word of the Lord is like a two-edged sword, but in dialogue we talk about "spiritualities." That's not a key well suited to unlocking the message within writings like Romans and Hebrews.

We don't dialogue as representatives of "spiritualities," but as adherents to faiths that believe in historical revelation, as witnesses to the presence of the God of Israel, and as people who find their inspirations in the prophets who addressed kings and nations, societies and cultures. Klenicki defines dialogue as "a respectful interchange of equals sharing God's faith and recognizing the uniqueness of the faith commitment of the other person in dialogue." Again, I sense the coziness here of an inner circle of people who have found a high level of comfort with each other. Klenicki claims that he wants to move beyond the niceties of the "tea and sympathy" days to in-depth discussions, but this kind of language just won't do it.

Take the phrase "sharing God's faith." I thought that, in a more modest vein, dialogue had to do with our common struggle to understand and interpret divine revelation and to do so together, despite our often mutually conflicting views. But when do those respectful interchanges of equals end up in a "theology of equality," which will challenge the other party's position only if it is seen as failing to recognize the equal validity of both faiths? On those assumptions a joint study of Romans and Hebrews can only be successful if Christians end up renouncing most of what those writers have to say. There is no "theology of equality" there–nor "tea and sympathy." And there are numerous believers today, both Jewish and Christian (and Muslim), who seek a dialogue in which each party presents its core beliefs with conviction and without pressure to adapt to someone else's preferences. Which leads to yet another question:

WHO SHOULD DIALOGUE WITH WHOM?

The issue of *Interfaith Focus* that we have noted presented the contributions of three Catholic respondents: Dr. Eugene Fisher, who represents the Catholic Bishops on matters of Christian-Jewish relations, and professors Padraic O'Hare and Mary Boys. The latter two display a definitely critical mindset, but mostly *vis-a-vis* their own church.

O'Hare leaves little doubt about his theological agenda which, it seems to me, is quite different from that of the Catechism. As an educator, he seeks "the formation of noble human beings," or, in the words of Zen Buddhist Suzuki, he seeks lives that are "inimitable masterpieces." "There must be a way," he writes, "to form a religious people who confess the *Shema*, proclaim the lordship of Jesus, affirm no God but Allah, practice Buddha mind." As he sees it, one major obstacle standing in the way of this goal is "the prevailing Christology of popular Christianity." A Christology that allows for such universal syncretism is not the faith of historic Christianity and can certainly not be found in the Catechism.

Mary Boys rejected the affirmation: "The New Testament fulfills the Old Testament," but she approved of this one: "Both the Jews and the church are faithful witnesses to the one God." What is meant by such statements, and what did Jesus mean when he said that he had come specifically not to abolish the law and the prophets, but to fulfill them (Matthew 5:17)? There is such a hopeless confusion in dialogue circles about the biblical notion of fulfillment! The concept comes much closer to saying that what went before has been validated (confirmed) and newly empowered, than that it has been done away with. Let me just say about the presumed faithful witness of the Jews and the church that such a view reflects a romantic reading of history quite contrary to the prophetic and apostolic witness. A key idea in the Bible is that the kingdom will come despite the failures and repeated unfaithfulness of Jews and Christians alike.

It seems to me that there is little real dialogue left between Rabbi Klenicki and Professors O'Hare and Boys. They have become like a mutual-affirmation society. They still can meet for mutually enlightening and respectful interchanges, which obviously have their value, but it will little reflect a conversation between communities of faith that have deep differences.

My argument is not that *Interfaith Focus* failed to raise important issues, but rather that the approach taken did not seem conducive to confronting our differences in a way that challenged both Judaism and Christianity to share, not "God's faith," but devoutly held theological truths that sometimes are in conflict with each other. So, we conclude with the final question:

DIALOGUE ABOUT WHAT?

Boys and Klenicki both raise questions about the use of typology in the Catechism. The former judges it to be "unimaginative, supersessionist, and a problem to relations between Catholics and Jews in our time," while the latter fears that the repeated emphasis on the preparatory nature of the Old Testament and the implied denial that Jews and Judaism still play a role in God's design will lead to the "teaching of contempt." I agree with Eugene Fisher that "the document in general is successful in avoiding 'supersessionist' language," and I find the overall tone of the Catechism so respectful toward Jews and Judaism and so different from anti-Judaic documents in the past, that the danger of conveying a spirit of contemptuousness strikes me as remote.

Yet, the issue at stake is crucial, not only in interfaith dialogue, but also in Christian ecumenical theology. Typological interpretation, an approach not unknown in Judaism, seeks to establish a correlation between historical realities, past, present, and future. What is the relationship between the "new thing" God is constantly doing and what has gone before or what is yet to come? Specifically, what is the relevance of the Old Testament for the church today?

Theologian Paul van Buren sees a danger in texts like Hebrews 8:13, because it "could support a theology of displacement," and hence, he states, "we dare not repeat the answer we thought we heard [there]."[1] Many biblical texts didn't say what we made them say. So, let us talk about interpretation.

Clark Williamson, who finds "bizarre" arguments in the letter to the Hebrews, goes much further than van Buren. To him, not only is misinterpretation dangerous, but the text itself represents a displacement theology which has "to have a long and tragic history."[2]

I personally see a danger in the eagerness with which some scholars raise the specter of the Holocaust, because it can too easily be used as a technique to silence the arguments of others. Harold Attridge has made what seems to me the correct observation that "it might be fair to characterize [Hebrews], not as the first *adversus Judaeos* tract but as the first exhortation to martyrdom" (*The Anchor Bible Dictionary*). In short, the author of Hebrews uses strong language in an urgent attempt to help believers endure and to "hold on" to their "confession of hope," not to engage in polemics against Judaism.

The issues of biblical interpretation and the continued significance of the Old Testament for the church are too fundamental and far-reaching to be dealt with in a put-off fashion. As Arnold van Ruler observed, "In the course of the centuries the Christian Church has treated the Old Testament just as uncertainly and unsuitably as it has treated the Jews."[3]

The Catechism might offer us a wonderful opportunity to deal with these issues in depth. The document draws heavily on the writings of the church fathers, many of whom had a tendency to slip from the typological method into a Philo-like allegorizing of the text, detaching the message from its historical roots as well as the mundane realities (politics, culture, economy, etc.). Martin Buber used to say that throughout the centuries the church has never really been faithful to the Old Testament vision concerning the sanctification of the earth—how could we, with a Christomonistic (against a Christocentric) view of the Bible? And how can we today, when so many preachers rarely deal meaningfully with the writings of Moses and the prophets from the pulpits?

In the midst of so much encouraging language in the Catechism, we find the following quote: "All sacred scripture is but one book, and that one book is Christ, because all divine scripture speaks of Christ, and all divine scripture is fulfilled in Christ." Is Christ, the center of the Christian *kerygma*, also to be made the end of all things? Or worse yet, as the Catechism quotes certain church fathers as saying: "The world was created for the sake of the Church. . . .The Church is the goal of all things." Was the world created for the sake of Christ, or did Christ come to save the world for the sake of the kingdom of God? Will the kingdom really mean the ecclesialization of all of life? Can the church engage in a meaningful "ministry of the Word" in the world today without a "Jewish reading" of the book of Israel, which later was also adopted as the canonical Word of God for the church?

The current Catechism shows that the Catholic Church has come a long way, as have many Protestant communions. However, the journey goes on. Dialogue must be an important part of that journey. But so must the moments when people of faith say: "Here we stand; we can do no else." Rather than being the end of dialogue, such moments of truth can become a point of renewal, the beginning of truly in-depth discussions.

The original, unedited form of this chapter was first published in the March, 1995, issue of Crisis–A Journal of Lay Catholic Opinion. Reprinted by permission.

[1] Paul van Buren, *Discerning the Way: A Theology of the Jewish-Christian Reality* (New York: Seabury Press, 1980).

[2] Clark M. Williamson, *A Guest in the House of Israel: Post-Holocaust Church Theology,* (Westminster: John Knox Press, 1993).

[3] Arnold A. van Ruler, *The Christian Church and the Old Testament* (Grand Rapids MI: Eerdmans, 1971).

DIALOGUE AND DOCTRINE

CHAPTER 6

Restoration Theology:
What Kind of Revolution
Will It Be?

"After being marred for nearly two millennia by Judaeophobia and anti-Semitism, Christianity is experiencing the beginnings of a revolution, as scholars, ministers, leaders, and laymen in virtually every denomination of the body of Christ are engaged in the quest to reclaim the church's Judaic heritage." Thus states an informational folder of the Restoration Foundation. But what will that "revolution" look like? What will be its implications for the foundations of historic Christianity? What changes in theology and practice are required by a faithful listening to the Scriptures and their witness to the restoration of Israel?

Those are some of the questions being raised by the contemporary quest to reclaim the church's Judaic heritage. Let us look at them in light of the work of one scholar who seeks "the dismantling of the anti-Jewish tradition of Christian theology and restatement of some of the central themes of the Christian faith." That quote is taken from the preface to a book by Clark M. Williamson, professor of theology at Christian Theological Seminary in Indianapolis, Indiana. This one-volume "systematic theology" is entitled *A Guest in the House of Israel: Post-Holocaust Church Theology*,[1] and is offered to the churches as a serious attempt to re-Judaize the Christian faith.

Dr. Williamson's work contains a wealth of historical and biblical analyses that are worthy of our careful and grateful attention. So much is to be learned about the history of Christian anti-Judaism, yet so little of what recent scholarship has brought to light is actually being taught in Bible schools and seminaries. But the book also raises fundamental questions for those of us who stand in a broadly evangelical tradition, and it thus poses a challenge to engage in an internal Christian debate about the nature of the "revolution" we seek.

Let us begin by taking a closer look at the title of the book: *A Guest in the House of Israel*. Right from the start we Christians are called to a little humility and, in light of a long history of Christian triumphalism and replacement theology, quite appropriately so. We Gentiles are latecomers in God's dealings with the world. As a matter of fact, we are the true proselytes–we are the wild olive branches that have been engrafted into the covenant tree of Israel, with its deep roots in the irrevocable promises of God (Romans 11:29). But, contrary to Paul's urgings, Gentile Christians became boastful, setting themselves above chosen Israel, and eventually claiming exclusive right to the covenant and kingdom of God for themselves.

So, Williamson believes it is about time that we recognize our true status and start behaving as guests in the house of Israel. I sympathize with the author's good intentions, but I cannot accept the underlying premise. We are not guests in the house of Israel; we are adopted children into the household of God (Ephesians 2). We have been made part of the family, which did not give us the right to take over the place, but neither can adopted children be referred to as guests. We are co-heirs of the kingdom! Our status in the covenant community is not established by the fact that our Jewish brothers and sisters are our hosts, but that the God of Israel is our Father through Christ the Son. The answer to the churches' false claims of supersessionism does not lie in toning down this central gospel truth.

Still, Williamson is right when he points out that, as Christians in dialogue with Jews, we should never forget the horrible history of anti-Semitism which culminated in the Holocaust. This leads us to the sub-title of the book: *Post-Holocaust Church Theology*. The author presents a double affirmation here: a) theology post-*Shoah*, as was already stressed above, must be done in a spirit of repentance because of past sins of the church, and b) theology should be done "in and on behalf of the Church" as well as "under the guidance of the Church."[2] These are both laudable goals, but how does it all work out in practice?

For me, a red flag went up very early in the text when the author, referring to the post-Holocaust nature of his theology, used phrases like "a revisionist understanding of a range of Christian teachings"[3] and the need to "reconstruct Christian theology in the light of the searching critique to which examination of its anti-Jewish past subjects it."[4] In post-Holocaust literature, this is often the language of those who call for radical revisions in basic Christian doctrines. As I shall show, that proves to be true in this case as well.

On the matter of presenting a "church theology," Williamson points out that "every chapter articulates a thesis already propounded in and by one of the post-Holocaust teaching documents issued by the churches."[5] In support of this position, he heads each chapter with a quote from one of the many church pronouncements on the relationship between Christians and Jews issued by denominations over the past decades.

Those "official" ecclesiastical documents do indeed represent a significant body of literature, meriting the careful attention of students in the field. But Mr. Williamson uses those materials so selectively and, in some cases, interprets them so tendentiously that his conclusions cannot be supported by a careful analysis of the full texts. In those instances, instead of ending up with a church theology that reflects the thinking of synods and councils, we are presented with the views of a small inner group of scholars who call for a radical reconstruction of the faith.

Let us look at some specifics:

WHAT CONSTITUTES ANTI-JUDAISM TODAY?

In answering that question, Williamson finds a prime example, not in the abundant literature still available that defames the Jewish people or denies God's faithfulness to his original covenant people Israel, but in a seminary advertisement that offers an M.A. degree in Missiology "with concentration in Judaic Studies and Jewish Evangelism." Mind you, the content of the course is not the issue at stake here, but rather the very fact that there are still Christians who believe that witness to the Jewish people is part of the gospel mandate.

Now, no one who has studied the history of Christian-Jewish relations, who knows the truth about forced conversions (under the threat of death!) and forced baptisms (often of little babies torn from their mothers' arms), will deny that this is a very sensitive and complex issue. That fact is clearly and rightly reflected in the language used by the formulators of church statements on the issue in recent decades.

Never should we forget the centuries of Gentile triumphalism which has struck terror in Jewish hearts. In the post-Holocaust era, Christian witness to Jews can only be done in a spirit of humility and repentance. In his novel, *The Gates of the Forest*, Elie Wiesel has one of his characters say, "Stop thinking about our salvation and perhaps the cemeteries won't be so full of Jews."[6] What a horrible indictment! Nevertheless, one we need to hear, because it is a judgment rooted in a long history of atrocities perpetrated against the Jewish people.

For some post-*Shoah* scholars, the solution to the dilemma lies in a cutting of the Gordian knot by declaring that a Christian proclamation (*kerygma*) to Jews is never justified. At best, we can maintain a Christian witness in terms of service (*diakonia*), usually interpreted as showing an active concern for Jewish interests. No major church body has articulated such an either-or position in their pronouncements.

They have evidenced a spirit of caution and ambiguity, sometimes by using intentionally vague language. As Williamson correctly points out, many of those documents have declared that Jews and Christians have a common responsibility to be "a light to the nations."[7] But surely there is no contradiction in gratefully acknowledging Jewish obedience to the eternal truths of Torah and at the same time believing that God's revelation through Jesus in the midst of Israel, as confessed by the church, is worth sharing with Jews and Gentiles alike.

Israel plays a unique role in God's dealings with the world. The very survival of this people is a witness to the faithfulness of God. Some church statements correctly emphasize that witness to the Jews, who have received Torah, is not the same as mission to the "heathen." Others warn against all attempts to make Jews conform to our Gentile ways, a position which, in Williamson's opinion, "contradicts any notion of a conversionary mission to the Israel of God."[8] Yes indeed, if conversion is made to mean adopting a de-Judaized faith. But no, if witness means confronting our Jewish brothers and sisters with one of their own, the Jewish Jesus, an encounter that has meant a radical transformation for multitudes of people, both Jews and Gentiles.

Professor Gabriel Fackre, commenting on a pronouncement of the United Church of Christ on the relationship between the church and the Jewish people stated the dilemma as follows: "Anti-supersessionism does not forbid sharing the gospel with Jewish people. Exclusion, in fact, is a subtle form of discrimination. . . . How this non-exclusionary mission mandate is carried out, while honoring the continuing covenant of God with Israel, is not clear."[9] Well, we ought to talk about that in the spirit of a true ecumenical dialogue. According to Vatican declarations, Roman Catholics are struggling with the same issues.

Finally, it should be pointed out that many Jewish leaders fully recognize the fact that the missionary imperative is a matter of conscience and not an optional choice for millions of Christians. In the words of the late Dr. Jakob Petuchowski, ". . .while I, as a Jew, have no right to demand from my Christian neighbor that he give up an essential part of his religious obligation in order to suit my Jewish convenience, I would plead with him to have some regard for both historical realities and the power of God."[10] That seems fair enough.

Robert Israel Lappin, a businessman who has held top positions in major Jewish organizations, said it about as well as anyone: "I would like my fellow Jews to know and to understand that the essential religious mandate of Evangelicals is to share the gospel of Jesus with all people–Jews and Gentile alike. Suggestions that this activity be curtailed, be they implied or expressed wishes, are inappropriate and insensitive. Just as true enlightened Christians are sensitive in their witnessing, so should my fellow Jews learn to distinguish between those who 'proselytize,' an illegitimate form of sharing, and those who 'witness;' that is those who leave to God the change of people's hearts. Jews should further recognize that enlightened Christians will witness with unconditional love; that is the kind that does not require of Jews to accept Christian theology in order to merit their support. . . ."[11]

SHOULD CHRISTIANS REFER TO JESUS AS THE MESSIAH?

As noted before, in order to buttress his argument that he is offering a church theology, Williamson heads every chapter with a quote from an ecclesiastical pronouncement. Chapter 7, dealing with Christology, opens with the following affirmation by the Synod of the Evangelical Church of the Rhineland: "We confess Jesus Christ the Jew, who as the Messiah from Israel is the Savior of the world and binds the people of the world to the people of God."[12]

Chapter 8, entitled "The God of Israel and Church," features a pronouncement by the Mennonite European Regional Conference: "In the end, we know God–specifically in the Messiah–as no one other than the God of Israel."[13] Good points!

But, our author would really prefer that Christians learned "to articulate the significance of Jesus Christ without using the title 'the Messiah.' "[14] First of all, as is generally acknowledged today, the Hebrew Scriptures, and later Jewish tradition, do not attribute a coherent and universally accepted meaning to the term *messiah*. And secondly, however Christians may interpret the inauguration of the new age, through salvation achieved in Jesus Christ, the Jewish expectation of a messianic age in which justice and peace reign upon the earth, did not materialize.[15]

However, reinterpretation of transmitted tradition in light of new historical experiences was not uncommon in the Judaism of that day. And that is precisely what the early Christians did in light of what they believed about Jesus, his life and ministry, his death and resurrection. God, they confessed, was in Christ reconciling the world to himself (2 Corinthians 5:19), and that was an event of supreme significance for all creation. Hence, the New Testament witness is clear: He is the One in whom the promises of the God of Israel and the hopes of Israel's prophets and seers have come true. *Ergo*: He is the Messiah! Millions of Christians continue to confess that, including the Catholic Church, which in its Catechism repeatedly refers to Jesus as "Messiah of Israel, Son of God and Savior of the world."

Reconciliation has come in Christ, and now God's people look forward with ever-greater intensity to the redemption of the whole creation. The New Testament constantly emphasizes that Christians, like the Jews, live their historical existence as a people of hope. We share a common sense of the unredeemedness of the world. The forces of sin (principalities and powers) are still very strong. In hope we have been saved (Romans 8:24), just as conversion to Christ means a rebirth of hope (1 Peter 1:3). The difference is that the central foundation for Christian hope is believed to be God's mighty act in Jesus Christ. Witnessing is one way of giving an accounting of the hope that is in us (1 Peter 3:15). Sin has been atoned, reconciliation is offered, forgiveness received, and the Holy Spirit opens people's lives to a new future.

IS THE DOCTRINE OF ATONEMENT WORKS-RIGHTEOUSNESS?

Throughout this book, Dr. Williamson puts strong emphasis on "God's thoroughly gracious covenant with Israel"[16] and on "the radical free grace and total claim of the God who redeems the ungodly, hence in ways that do not 'nullify the faithfulness of God' (Romans 3:3) to the Israel of God."[17]

As the renowned theologian Karl Barth used to say, Christians who claim that Jews do not deserve to be called a covenant people any longer because they have fallen short in their performance of the divine will, cut off the very branch on which they themselves are sitting. Is God faithful to us Christians because of our superior performance? Nothing could be a greater distortion of gospel truth!

In the parable of the laborers in the vineyard (Matthew 20), the master asks those who complain about his payments to the "less deserving" (from the point of view of a tit-for-tat mentality): "Do you begrudge my generosity?" This parable reflects the resentment Gentile Christians have often displayed toward their Jewish brothers and sisters, as they failed to apply their belief in the gracious faithfulness of God, whose promises are irrevocable, to the Father's first love–the people Israel. That, indeed, is works-righteousness at its worst.

Williamson is so right to emphasize that point. But, amazingly enough, he then proceeds to undermine the central Christian (and Jewish!) belief in atonement by claiming that it smacks of works-righteousness. Atonement, as historically taught, is interpreted as a "punitive doctrine" lacking in *agape* love. Writes he: "Seldom noticed is that the impact of an understanding of God as power devoid of sympathy on the doctrine of atonement is works-righteousness: someone has to perform the good work of setting things right between us and God."[18]

The whole meaning of Torah as embodying God's righteousness and holy will is at stake here; of course, the law of God must be done! The will of God must be established upon the earth. That's not legalism; it is the gospel of the kingdom. The gift-nature of the law was clearly and joyfully recognized in Israel, because the law is an essential element in God's saving dealings with the world. It is the law of the kingdom, the mold, as it were, in which the new creation will be cast when God's righteousness will dwell upon the earth. The divine demand that the law be fulfilled has nothing whatsoever to do with works-righteousness. Works-righteousness of the wrong kind has to do with our "handling" of the law as if God had not acted in the midst of Israel when, in an initiative of sovereign grace, Christ did what we could not do: fulfill the law in holy love.

Atonement through the cross of Christ as a once-for-all act of redemption, leading to reconciliation between God and the world, troubles some post-Holocaust theologians, because of what they see as exclusivist claims. They prefer a Christology which makes Jesus the way of salvation for Gentiles, while Torah remains the way for Jews. Such a view evangelical Christians cannot accept and, in this case, "evangelical" refers to a broad spectrum of believers to be found in virtually all denominations. The Vatican has stated emphatically that it does not accept that position either.

In the sacrificial cult, as practiced in Israel, the emphasis falls on the confession of sin on the part of the person who appears before the Holy One and a gracious assurance that the God of Israel "covers" our transgressions and thus takes care of a past that is beyond our grasp, except in the memory of guilt which can put us in the grip of despair. Through forgiveness comes a new freedom and a new openness to the future. "Blessed are those whose iniquities are forgiven and whose sins are covered; blessed is the person against whom the Lord will not reckon his sin" (Psalm 32:1-2). That is the gospel of grace and *agape* love, rooted in the faith of Israel and, for Christians, fulfilled in the cross of Christ.

My critical remarks should not obscure the fact that anyone who is engaged in the quest to reclaim the church's Judaic heritage can learn much from Williamson's book. But those of us who seek radical changes in the churches' relationships with the Jewish people and in the way we have done theology must be honest with each other. The word "radical" literally means going back to the roots–our roots in Israel–as well as our roots in the gospels and the apostolic writings, with their witness to Jesus the Christ.

Every believer must face fundamental choices. It is not enough to critique the views of others. We are challenged to set forth how we are conducting the quest and how we are dealing with the question as to what aspects of historic Christianity can and must be retained and what elements of our traditional views must be revised unless we hold on to the heresy of supersessionism and fall into sinful anti-Judaism.

May "the God of our Lord Jesus Christ, the Father of glory give [us] a spirit of wisdom and revelation . . ." (Ephesians 1:17).

[1] Clark M. Williamson, *A Guest in the House of Israel: Post-Holocaust Church Theology* (Westminster: John Knox Press, 1993).

[2] *Ibid.*, p. viii.

[3] *Ibid.*, p. 10.

[4] *Ibid.*, p. vii.

[5] *Ibid.*, p. viii.

[6] Elie Wiesel, *The Gates of the Forest* (New York: Holt, Rinehart, Winston, Inc., 1966), p. 38.

[7] Williamson, *A Guest in the House of Israel*, p. 3.

[8] *Ibid.*, p. 29.

[9] Gabriel Fackre, *New Conversations*, Summer 1990, p. 26.

[10] Jakob Petuchowski, *Face to Face*, Fall/Winter, 1977.

[11] Robert Israel Lappin, *Network News of the Christian Community of the North Shore of Boston*, February 1993.

[12] Williamson, *A Guest in the House of Israel*, p. 167.

[13] *Ibid.*, p. 202.

[14] *Ibid.*, p. 244.

[15] *Ibid.*, p. 42.

[16] *Ibid.*, p. 37.

[17] *Ibid.*, p. viii.

[18] *Ibid.*, p. 208.

CHAPTER 7

Dialogue and Doctrine

The following brief survey of three areas of doctrinal concern is meant to be illustrative of why the dialogue between Christians and Jews would be well served by a lively internal Christian debate. Marcus Braybrooke's book *Time to Meet* will be used as a sort of launching pad, mainly because it provides a handy framework for the kind of limited discussion that is offered here. The works of the leading scholars in the field cannot be dealt with in the context of this brief discussion.

The Doctrine of God

Historically, Christian Trinitarian dogma, as developed during the early centuries of the church, has been a major subject of dispute between Jews and Christians. This is still true today because, despite Christian disclaimers that belief in the Trinity does not involve a denial of biblical monotheism, Jews remain persuaded that the credal language of the church concerning Jesus crosses the boundaries of belief in the Oneness of God.

That ancient debate remains on the agenda, but in recent years another issue has become the focus of attention in the dialogue. It can be summed up in this question: "What belief in God is still possible after the Holocaust?" A concomitant question then is this: "To what extent must traditional teachings about God be changed?"

Braybrooke notes that "reflection on the Holocaust has not, at an official level, yet had much influence on Christian theology in, for example, the understanding of God's power and love."[1] But, besides the observation that Christians may perhaps still "have to come to terms with the impact of the Holocaust on all faith in God's goodness,"[2] he offers no further specifics.

However, on the non-official level of individual theologians, the tone tends to be much less hesitant. Quite the opposite, it frequently has a hype quality about it. The Holocaust is referred to as an event of "ultimate significance," an "Alpine event," unique in human history. Some speak about the Holocaust in revelatory terms, as a reorienting event which changes the way we think about God and human history. It has even been suggested that every year after 1942 should now be termed A.F.S.– "After the Final Solution," thus replacing the designation *Anno Domini.*

True, the horrors of the Holocaust are such that people understandably find it hard to handle the subject calmly and coolly. Sometimes silence would seem to be the better choice, but in the face of evil, silence should not have the last "word." Hence, the struggle with language as found, for instance, in the writings of Elie Wiesel. Poets can help us to hear the unspeakable, but trying to imitate their language in doctrinal discussions has its danger, especially the danger of ending up with a faddist theology. One person's *cri de coeur* becomes the next person's slogan.

"Holocaust theologians" have made a significant contribution in forcing the churches to face their past. They have documented the long history of Christian anti-Judaism, which, quite frequently, led to anti-Semitism, which, in turn, culminated in Hitler's "Final Solution." But there are also those who seem to assume that the degree of one's penitence can be measured in direct proportion to the radical rhetoric one uses.

What does it mean, for instance, when we are told that anyone who does theology today without beginning with Auschwitz continues to live in the "Kingdom of Night?" Most of us, even those of us who lived under Hitler's murderous reign and lost many relatives in the "Kingdom of Night," have no idea what a theology looks like that starts, not with Moses and the prophets, Jesus and the apostles, but with Auschwitz.

Michael Wyschogrod has stated the issue quite well in his critique of Rabbi Irving Greenberg's claim that traditional views of God the Redeemer must be abandoned "in the presence of the burning children," which would supposedly constitute a revelatory event. Writes Wyschogrod: "Inserted at the heart of Judaism as a revelational event comparable to Sinai, the holocaust [Wyschogrod does not capitalize the word] will necessarily destroy Judaism and give Hitler the posthumous victory we all wish to deny him."[3]

Just as Wyschogrod refuses to assign a place for the Holocaust at the inner sanctum of Judaism, so should Christians deny it a determinative influence on their confession of God. That does not, of course, preclude raising agonizing questions about the issue of evil, forced upon us with greater urgency than ever in the face of demonic acts of such a historic scale.

THE DOCTRINE OF CHRIST

Braybrooke's book contains a segment on "The Jewish Jesus," in which the author makes some valid points: Jesus must be interpreted in continuity with, and not exclusively in opposition to, the Judaism of his day; the Law should not be portrayed one-sidedly as a burden, ignoring the biblical message about delight in the Law; Jesus' arguments with the

Pharisees were no greater than the arguments among the Pharisees, etc. Through the dialogue, new insights have been gained on these and other issues.

However, in his eagerness not to exalt Jesus at the expense of Judaism, Braybrooke displays a tendency to go overboard on the other side, denying, for instance, that any tensions existed between Jesus and elements in the Jewish leadership. Reputable scholars, both Jewish and Christian, would contest such a conclusion.

But the pendulum really swings into extreme territory when the Christian confession of Jesus' lordship comes up. Such a confession, according to Braybrooke, "seems unavoidably to be a criticism of Judaism."[4] Here he seeks support in Rosemary Ruether's dictum that anti-Semitism is "the left hand of Christology." Confessing that Jesus is the Messiah, so the argument goes, amounts to an implicit claim that Christianity contains a "plus" over Judaism and is tantamount to declaring Judaism to be inferior.

Once again, an appeal to Auschwitz is supposed to supply the justification for a radical (and for most Christians, impossible) theological stance. "To affirm that Jesus was the Messiah vindicated by God not only seems to invalidate Jewish faith, it also appears to ignore the evil of the world, so horribly revealed at Auschwitz and for which the very Christian teaching of the triumph of the cross [i.e., the resurrection!] must take some blame."[5] By all means, let us call the church to account for the sinful triumphalism which has so often dominated its actions, but to say that this can be done only through a denial of any redemptive fulfillment in the cross and resurrection of Christ is a *non sequitur* of massive proportions.

In some Christian circles it has become commonplace to argue that New Testament fulfillment language is *ipso facto* triumphalistic, because it allegedly claims for the here and now what is promised only for the eschatological future. The text does not support such a position. Rather, the opposite is true: the New Testament is intensely eschatological in tone precisely because God's salvation in Christ has filled the air–even the creation itself (Romans 8) with expectation.

Since Braybrooke views all religions as being equally valid windows "on to ultimate reality," he sees no point in arguing about which window might give the clearest view. With such a theological position, the dialogue can be safely and comfortably confined to questions of general religiosity. But that would also limit the dialogue to a very narrow circle of participants who do not generally represent the professed views of the churches.

The christological formulations of ancient councils are not to be considered sacrosanct and off limits to critical inquiry.[6] Revision of past theological traditions must always be left open as a possibility. More than once churches have had to confess their past doctrinal incorrectness. But for a real dialogue to take place on such crucial issues, there needs to be room around the table for a broad spectrum of theological positions within the church.

THE DOCTRINE OF THE CHURCH

The New Testament recognized a variety of ministries: apostles, prophets, teachers, evangelists, agents of mercy, all people called to serve not only the church, but to serve Christ in the world–for the sake of the kingdom. Just as Israel was not called for its own sake, but in order that the Name of the God of Israel might be known upon the earth and the future of the Lord might be established, so the church is called to proclaim the gospel of the kingdom to the nations. If one can speak of a "philosophy of history" in the Scriptures, that, in a nutshell, is it. There is a *Missio Dei,* a divine rescue mission that reaches out to all creation. The people of God are those who have been "called out" to serve that mission.

From its earliest beginnings, the church has understood itself as a sent (apostolic) community. As we would say today, that was part of their self-definition. Thus, in a relatively short period of time the gospel traveled throughout the Greco-Roman world, then across Europe, to the continent of America, and, especially during the past two centuries, to the ends of the earth. This story is one of mixed motives and mixed blessings, to say the least. Even when done with the best of intentions, the missionary movement remained a very human and, hence, very fallible enterprise. The church's mission, like the history of Israel, although divinely ordained, is not beyond the power of sin.

The apostolate of the church takes on many forms, but the authority of all of them derives from the Word and the Spirit. The church, when faithful to its mission at all, has understood it as a mandate; not an elective, not one of many options, not an activity added to the life of the church, but belonging to its *being*, its *esse*. The church is Church-for-the-world, and proclamation is an essential aspect of serving the world.

Jews, as Braybrooke rightly observes, "find it hard to appreciate why it is so difficult for Christians to abandon the missionary appeal."[7] Indeed, to many Jews, this is a problem, but some leading Jewish spokespersons have come to appreciate very well how, for multitudes of Christians, this is a matter of conscience. They have openly written about that and have called for a dialogue on what *form* witness ought to take, particularly with respect to Jews who, after all, are no strangers to the prophetic Word.

However, some Jews as well as some Christians have recommended a "wordless witness," usually emphasizing a moral lifestyle, or social involvement, or support for the Jewish people and Israel. While not denying the need for all those forms of witness, Christian theology has never been able to totally detach itself from the belief that the Word of the Lord needs to be proclaimed. Revelation and its redemptive message are not to be found in the exemplary behavior of the Jewish people, but in the prophetic witness to Israel's God. In Christian history, any idea that the *Missio Dei* can be embodied in the good deeds of church members has usually been rejected as moralistic, which, of course, in no way implies a defense of "deedless witness."

Finally, and this will be the focus of what follows, the mission issue, as well as dialogue itself, are further complicated by the existence of a growing Messianic Jewish movement, which not only refuses to accept every aspect of a de-Judaized Gentile church as valid for them but also insists on arguing their case with the Jewish community in terms of the earliest period of the church, when Jewish-Christians remained within the fold of Judaism. This is one of the most emotional and controversial issues today. Mainline Christian dialoguers are caught in an uneasy alliance with some Jewish spokespersons who characterize the whole movement as fraudulent, while evangelicals are engaged in a precarious balancing act, trying to convince both Jews and Jewish Christians that they are "on their side."

When a Jew confesses what Christians believe, namely, a new and decisive redemptive act of God in Jesus Christ, he or she is likely to end up in a spiritual "no-man's land." Jewish leaders in the dialogue movement will repudiate them and, in subtle or not-so-subtle ways, demand that Christian partners in dialogue do the same. So, for all practical purposes, those people are "excommunicated" from the fellowship of faith and treated as adversaries, except if they promise to live as quiet Jews who are well-adjusted to the words and ways of a de-Judaized church and refrain from sharing their new-found faith with their brothers and sisters.

TRUTH-PASSION-PAIN

The late Rabbi Pinchas Peli, whose "Tora Today" columns in the *Jerusalem Post* provided education and inspiration to Jews and Gentiles alike, has reminded us that a dialogue in search of truth does not come without pain. "I am convinced," he wrote, "that the basis and aim of dialogue should not be less than that required by the prophet Zechariah [8:16,19] and which includes both 'truth' and 'peace.' The truth may be painful at times, but no real peace can be achieved without facing it."[8]

Braybrooke, too, declares that "at its deepest dialogue will raise questions of truth," but when it comes to affirmations of truth in open confrontation, his book–like so much dialogue literature–is filled with ambiguity and, at times, double-standard thinking. Since he considers all religions as equally valid windows onto ultimate reality, he is content to leave everybody alone with their own truth. In short, it simply does not make sense even to discuss such matters. After all, while dialogue may be called "a serious search for truth . . . it does suppose that no one religion has a monopoly on truth,"[9] a pious truism which does not help much in determining the dynamics of a valid dialogical debate.

According to page one of *Time to Meet,* the book is about "issues which now need to be tackled," i.e., it presents a dialogue agenda for Christians. However, after one finishes the book, Christians with more traditional views are left with plenty to defend, but there seems little left to debate between Christians and Jews. According to Braybrooke, Christianity must abandon major tenets of its faith, its missionary mandate, and–because of its guilty past–the right to affirm any truth that might give offense to Jewish dialogue partners. Christians have many sins to confess, but a guilt-ridden approach to dialogue will never produce a genuine relationship.

Braybrooke cites a document issued by the Lambeth Conference, which states that "genuine dialogue demands that each partner brings to it the fullness of themselves and the tradition in which they stand."[10] Christians should also be prepared for the fact that their Jewish partners will come to the dialogue with severe criticism of "Christian" history. Dialogue literature contains such critiques in abundance. It may be painful, but we must listen.

However, Braybrooke's constant concern about the "security" of the new relationship between Jews and Christians, which must be maintained at all cost, and the frequent warnings in dialogue literature that Christians refrain from mentioning confessional elements of their faith that speak of the fullness of redemption in Christ, because it allegedly implies that Judaism is "inferior," would seem to suggest a dialogical immaturity and delicateness that requires the avoidance of honest confrontation.

When Rabbi Henry Siegman, in the article mentioned before, says, "As a believing Jew I affirm that Judaism is the 'truest' religion," only wishy-washy Christians would object that such a statement is an insult to their faith, or would feel a restraint in making a similar affirmation about their own religion. The problem starts–and it started early in Christian history–when one person's confession of truth is used to malign another person's faith. The church father John Chrysostom gave an example of such vindictive logic when he wrote: "If the Jewish rites are holy and venerable, our way of life must be false. But if our way is true, as indeed it is, theirs is fraudulent."[11] The realization that quite a few of his listeners had attended service in the synagogue the day before, to a large degree, explains Chrysostom's resentful mood, but in no way excuses his strident language.

In his foreword to the book, *Overcoming Fears between Jews and Christians,* Irvin Borowsky observes that "dialogues that are merely polite and passionless are limiting at best."[12] He feels passionate about revising New Testament texts, and is willing to contribute considerable resources toward that goal. We may argue and disagree about specifics (Mr. Borowsky's first attempt when he published his "American Holy Bible," dedicated to Thomas Jefferson, was not an entirely unblemished effort), but it involves a legitimate concern, even though the process may be painful for some. On the other hand, there are many Christians who feel passionate about the church's missionary mandate. A mature dialogue, one would hope, can deal with a variety of passions in the same room at the same time.

Father Edward Flannery wrote the following sentences: "Because of its immaturity, theological conversation between Jews and Christians has thus far not proved to be overly fruitful. Until now dialogues of this sort have exhibited overcautiousness, excessive fear of offending, preoccupation with agreements and consonances, and also over-readiness to take offense."[13] There is a danger that the dialogue will deteriorate into a mutual-affirmation society between a circle of scholars who welcome each other's views, while the convictions of a large majority of Christians who, in some cases, represent the growing edge of the church, are avoided.

On the other hand, we all realize that, after many centuries of estrangement and hostility, the search for rapprochement is still relatively young. It is therefore to be hoped that, from the present mainstream of dialogue, a variety of tributary streams will be formed, enriching the landscape, and bringing new, refreshing resources to the movement. The Christian ecumenical movement has, by and large, gotten stuck in an establishmentarian statism. The same should not be allowed to happen to the interfaith dialogue movement.

[1] Marcus Braybrooke, *Time to Meet: Towards a Deeper Relationship between Jews and Christians* (Philadelphia: Trinity Press International, 1990), p. 15., p. 36f. See also I.C. Rottenberg, "'Comparative Theology' versus 'Reactive Theology': Jewish and Christian Approaches to the Presence of God," in *Pro Ecclesia,* Fall 1994, Vol. III, No. 4, pp. 411-418.

[2] *Ibid.,* p. 113.

[3] Cf. *Tradition,* Fall 1977, Vol. 16, No. 5, p. 75. Gershon Mamlak sees the specter of commercialization in all that talk about the role (or non-role) of God in the Holocaust. None of those theories, he states, "reach the bottomless profundity of Job and the comprehensiveness of the Talmudic statement: "We are helpless to grasp the success of the evildoers and the suffering of the just." (Cf. "The Holocaust: Commodity?", *Midstream,* April 1983, p. 13). Cf. also I.C. Rottenberg, "The Holocaust and Belief in a God of Holy Love" in *The Reformed Journal* (May, 1982) and "The Holocaust and the Development of Church Doctrine" in *Pro Ecclesia* (Spring, 1995, Vol. IV, No. 2).

[4] Braybrooke, *Time to Meet,* p. 59.

[5] *Ibid.,* p. 69.

[6] Cf., I.C. Rottenberg, "A Re-Judaized Jesus?" in *Perspectives* (December, 1992).

[7] Braybrooke., p. 97.

[8] Cf. *The Jerusalem Post*, International Edition, November 21, 1987, p. 22.

[9] Braybrooke, *Time to Meet*, p. 95.

[10] *Ibid.*, p. 30.

[11] John Chrysostom, quoted in *Interwoven Destinies: Jews and Christians through the Ages*, Eugene J. Fisher, ed., (New York: Paulist Press, A Stimulus Book, 1993), p. 78.

[12] James H. Charlesworth, *Overcoming Fear between Jews and Christians* (Philadelphia: New York: American Interfaith Institute; Crossroad, 1993) p. XII.

[13] Cf. *Face to Face*, Winter/Spring, 1976, p. 4.

CHAPTER 8

The Holocaust and Belief in a God of Holy Love

Feminist author Germaine Greer once described herself as a person who had thrown out the baby but kept the bath water; she still professed profound appreciation for the Roman Catholic Church, but without God. "If he did exist," she added, "I would have to fight him." The charge, I gathered from her remarks, was mismanagement. Novelist Elie Wiesel, in his play, *The Trial of God* and other writings, does not deny God, but he, too, indicts him. God must be called to account; he must at last justify his ways to a suffering humanity.

People have argued with God before. Job did, as had many before him and as have many since. In the face of evil, traditional religious "explanations" frequently begin to sound feeble and barely believable. In a world so filled with horror, how is one to confess faith in a God who is at once infinitely good and all powerful? How is one to continue to pray: "Infinite is Thy power, even so is Thy love?" In the final analysis, must not one or the other give?

The urge to give "answers" to the unanswerable has always been strong, particularly among theologians. Believers rush to defend God against questioning doubters and troublesome atheists. "Just are the ways of God and justifiable to men; unless there be who think not God at all." Thus wrote John Milton in his *Samson Agonistes*. To this the poet and pundit A. E. Housman was moved to write in response:

> And malt does more than Milton can
> To justify God's ways to man.
> Ale, man, ale's the stuff to drink
> For fellows whom it harts to think.

The 18th century has been called "the golden age of theodicies." Many shared Milton's confidence that, everything considered, evil and suffering could be made to fit into a rational scheme. Leibnitz published his famous book on "theodicy" in 1710, defending the thesis that ours is "the best of all possible worlds." He did not mean to deny the dark side of existence, but rather to affirm his faith that this world, created by an all-powerful and perfectly good deity, represents the best option out of an infinite number of possibilities.

But the anguish of the human soul and the voices of doubt are not to be silenced that easily. In times of crisis, the questions of those whose faith is challenged by the horrors of history burst forth with renewed power. People experience the shaking of the foundations of traditional beliefs, and the God of conventional wisdom is no longer acceptable. Religious leaders are forced to wrestle anew in order to find a saving word that can be spoken to the world with integrity. Two literary references may help to illustrate this point.

Father Paneloux, in Albert Camus' *The Plague*, called for a week of prayer as the devastating pestilence that had struck the community was claiming ever more victims. Looking upon the large congregation that had assembled in the cathedral, he began his sermon with these words: "Calamity has come upon you, my brethren, and my brethren, you deserved it." The priest then proceeded to explain how the calamity was not willed by God, but that, as a punishment for sin, God had turned his face away from his people.

Some time later, Father Paneloux delivered a second sermon. His opinions remained unchanged, but through suffering, he had become a different person. His preaching had become less pretentious, and significantly, the "you" had become "we." "The difficulty began," writes Camus, "when he looked into the nature of evil, and among things evil, he included human suffering."

A second illustration is found in Chaim Potok's book, *The Chosen*, where Reb Saunders represents the Orthodox position. "How the world drinks our blood," he sighs, "how the world makes us suffer." But, he concludes immediately, this is the will of God. "We must accept the will of God." Then, after a long silence, "he raised his eyes and said softly, 'Master of the Universe, how do you permit such a thing to happen?' "

Toward the end of the novel, Reb Saunders asks forgiveness of Reuven, a close friend of his son whose father's Zionism had angered him and had led to severe frictions. The answer to the six million Jews killed in the Nazi Holocaust could not lie in the establishment of a Jewish State before the coming of the Messiah. Says the devout Rabbi: "I–I found my own meaning for my–brother's death–for the death of the six million. I found it in God's will–which I do not presume to understand."

It is not always easy to affirm the traditional faith, at least not for those who have moved beyond abstract speculation or pompous preachments and have become participants in suffering. Solomon bar Simson, a chronicler of the First Crusade, struggling with the question of divine judgment on human sin, is one of a multitude who have confessed with burdened hearts because of their inability to comprehend. "God, the maker of peace, turned aside and averted His eyes from His people, and consigned them to the sword. No prophet, seer, or man of wise heart was able to comprehend how the sin of the people infinite in number was deemed so great as to cause the destruction of so many lives in the various Jewish communities. . . . Yet, it must be stated with certainty that God is a righteous judge, and we are to blame."

After the Nazi Holocaust, some Jewish thinkers find it, not just difficult, but impossible to utter such a confession. They call for a radical reconstruction of traditional teachings.

Only in recent years has the Holocaust become the subject of intense theological reflection in Jewish and Christian circles. As is usually the case after catastrophic events, some years had to pass before the haunting voices of the victims and the survivors could be heard. How is belief in God still possible after the Holocaust? In Wiesel's play, *The Trial of God*, an orthodox priest continues to speak of "heavenly love" in the midst of abominable horrors. Is that not blasphemy?

Among Jewish thinkers one finds, as might be expected, a variety of responses to the challenge to faith that is posed by the Holocaust. Some simply take for granted that traditional answers to the problem of evil must be discarded; others view proposed new answers as a threat to Judaism itself. Richard Rubenstein is still willing to believe in the "God of Holy Nothingness," but not in the God of history. Death is proclaimed the true Messiah and the land of the dead the place of God's true kingdom. Emil Fackenheim and others are not prepared to abandon faith in the presence of God, but to them, Auschwitz becomes "the commanding voice of God in exile," charging the Jewish people with the sacred responsibility to survive as Jews in order that Hitler not be handed a posthumous victory.[7]

Irving Greenberg and Michael Wyschogrod, both Orthodox Jews, have been engaged in a lively debate on the question whether the Holocaust should be considered a "revelational event" and what its implications are for traditional Judaism. "The cruelty and the killing," writes Greenberg, "raise the question whether even those who believe after such an event dare talk about God who loves and cares without making a mockery of those who suffered." Nor is there any longer room for ideas like "punishment for our sins" or for neat theological constructions presented in the name of faith. At most, we can speak of "moments of faith . . . moments when Redeemer and vision of redemption are present, interspersed with times when the flames and smoke of the burning children blot out faith though it flicker again."

Wyschogrod denies the centrality of the Holocaust to Jewish thought and faith. "The Holocaust was such an event of total evil that only insane lessons can be drawn from it." To these observations one might add the following statement by Jacob Neusner: "We are not well served by the appeal to the Holocaust either as the rationalization of our Judaism or as the source of our slogans for our Jewish activities and self-assertion. . . . What then are the implications of the Holocaust? In one sense I claim there is no implication–none for Judaic theology, none for Jewish community life–which was not present before 1933."

The Holocaust must be remembered as other catastrophic events are remembered, such as the destruction of the Temple in 70 A.D., the expulsion from Spain in 1492, and the apostasy of the pseudo-Messiah Sabbatai Zvi in 1667. Those turned out to be formative events in Jewish history. Yet, some would say, the Holocaust is not to be regarded an orienting event in the sense that it demands a redefinition of historic teachings.

In Christian circles, too, theological reflection on the Holocaust is of recent date. Robert Willis, after pointing out that an examination of major Protestant theological developments since 1950 leaves one with the impression that the Holocaust implies nothing of significance for the doing of Christian theology, goes on to state that "at the very least, one would have thought that the problem of theodicy . . . would have proved to be a minor stumbling-block for those theologies which continue to assert the ultimate meaning and fulfillment of history through God's action, but such, with few exceptions, is not the case."

John Hick's important study on *Evil and the God of Love* is a good case in point. The index does not contain the word "Holocaust," but it does occur once in the text (referring to World War I!). However, on page 397 of this 400-page work, there is a reference to "the Nazi programme for the extermination of the Jewish people" with its "horrors which will disfigure the universe to the end of time." Today, I dare say, such a study would struggle with the issues posed by the Holocaust in a much less afterthought fashion.

How shall we affirm tradition, especially belief in a God who is holy love, in the face of absurdity–in the face of the burning children? In Camus' *The Plague*, one of the characters says to the priest, "No, Father, I've a very different idea of love. And until my dying day I shall refuse to love a scheme of things in which children are put to torture." But in the Holocaust we are not dealing with "a scheme of things" that leaves room for pestilences to break out; we are confronted with a humanly devised scheme for the systematic murder of a whole people, including the children.

The following short passage from the Nuremberg trial record speaks of a depravity that is virtually without compare in the chronicles of human cruelty.

> WITNESS: . . . women carrying children were [always] sent with them to the crematorium. [Children were of no labor value so they were killed.] The mothers were sent along, too, because separation might lead to panic, hysteria–which might slow up the destruction process, and this could not be afforded. It was simpler to con-

demn the mothers too and keep things quiet and smooth. The children were then torn from their parents outside the crematorium and sent to gas chambers separately. [At that point, crowding more people into the gas chambers became the most urgent consideration. Separating meant that more children could be packed in separately, or they could be thrown in over the heads of adults once the chamber was packed.] When the extermination of the Jews in the gas clambers was at its height, orders were issued that children were to be thrown straight into the crematorium furnaces, or into a pit near the crematorium, without being gassed first.

SMIRINOV (Russian prosecutor): How am I to understand this? Did they throw them into the fire alive, or did they kill them first?

WITNESS: They threw them in alive. Their screams could be heard at the camp. It is difficult to say how many children were destroyed in this way.

SMIRINOV: Why did they do this?

WITNESS: It's very difficult to say. We don't know whether they wanted to economize on gas, or if it was because there was not enough room in the gas chambers.

How to affirm anything in the face of such unspeakable evil? Who would dare to give "answers" or "theological explanations" in response to the screams of the children? Irving Greenberg proposes that "no statement, theological or otherwise, should be made that would not be credible in the presence of the burning children." That seems like a somewhat dramatic way of calling for silence. In the presence of the burning children we cannot go about our usual business, including our theological business. God-talk, traditional or otherwise, must sometimes cease in order that God's message may be heard in silence. There is a silence of awe, when we stop demanding "answers" in the presence of the Holy One. There is also the stunned silence, when we stop giving "answers," because we find ourselves in the presence of unspeakable suffering. Living with questions is one of the essential elements of faith; it is a dimension of living in the presence of mystery.

Greenberg has come to the conclusion that "we are entering a period of silence in theology–a silence about God that corresponds to his silence. In this silence, God may be presence and hope, but no longer the simple *deus ex machina*." Fewer "explanations" and less cheap talk about God would indeed improve the theological climate. Yet, in my view, there remains room for witness–through the spoken and written word as well as through acts of love and compassion. But after the Holocaust, it ought to become a more humble and halting witness, particularly when Christians enter into dialogue with Jews about their understanding of God as holy love.

Why especially in dialogue with Jews? Because the cross, which through the centuries has for Christians been the central symbol of their faith in divine holy love, has to Jews become the great sign of cruelties perpetrated against them by people who presented themselves as Jesus' disciples. Here we touch on one of the most tragic aspects of Jewish-Christian relations over the past two thousand years.

The prophets and poets of Israel have taught us to speak of God in terms of "transcendence" and "presence." It is the mystery of Immanuel, God with us, even in the depth of our suffering. This is at heart what divine holy love is all about. "Thus says the high and lofty One who inhabits eternity, whose name is Holy: I dwell in the high and holy place, and also with him who is of a contrite and humble spirit" (Isaiah 57:15). "God is our refuge and strength, a very present help in trouble" (Psalm 46:1). Additionally, the book of Hosea has probably given the most profound expression to the unity of God's holiness and love.

In the Christian faith, this confession has come to focus in the message of Jesus' cross and resurrection. Theologians have expressed its meaning in many different ways. Paul Tillich, in his usual philosophical style, spoke of "a participation of the divine life in the negativity of creaturely life" and in this direction sought the ultimate answer to the question of theodicy. Others speak of God's willingness to take upon himself absolute self-sacrifice, his dramatic sharing of human suffering, and Christ's fulfilling the pattern of redemptive suffering.

"At the cross," write J. S. Whale, "the whole human problem of suffering and sin comes to a burning focus. So far as the enigma of man's pain is concerned, the light that comes from the cross is not an intellectual illumination but the startling discovery that God Himself bears our pain with us."

But, the symbol of the "agonizing God" became the symbol of hatred in his name. The cross, the New Testament tells us, is an inherent scandal: it speaks of suffering. At odds with our cults of success, it calls to confession and honest self-confrontation. To that scandal we have added a scandalous record of almost two millennia of "Christian anti-Semitism" and thus we have obscured the gospel.

Sholem Asch, who is best known for his books, *The Nazarene, The Apostle,* and *Mary,* wrote a booklet entitled, *One Destiny: An Epistle to Christians.* There he presents his spiritual credo that Judaism and Christianity are two parts of a single whole. Referring to the crufixion he states:

> The legend about the Jewish crucifixion of the Messiah has
> cost millions of Jewish lives. It carries a long streak of blood

after it, right down to our own time. It has become the microbe of hate in the spiritual body of Christianity. It has caused and still causes daily trouble for the Jews. It brings tears to mothers, anxieties and terrors to children. I myself suffered throughout my childhood from the accusation of blood guilt. Every Christian holiday was transformed by the legend into a day of fear and sorrow for the Jews.

"That cross makes me shudder," said a Jewish woman to Father Edward H. Flannery as they passed by a cross displayed in New York City at Christamas time. "It is like an evil presence," she added. Roy Eckardt, after referring to this incident, added this comment: "It was in and through the *Endlösung* that the symbol of the cross was taken captive by ultimate devilishness." He came to the conclusion that "the endlessly woeful consequence is that the cross is robbed of its redemptiveness. All that remains upon the hill of Golgotha is unmitigated evil. After Auschwitz, a question mark is nailed to the cross as the reputedly determinative symbol of redemptive suffering. From the point of view of the Holocaust of the Jews, God is not met on the cross–even in his 'Godforsakenness.' Once upon a time he may have been met there, but he is met there no longer."

I do not share this conclusion. Nevertheless, I am convinced that attempts to move beyond it will lead nowhere unless we have really listened to what the Jewish woman and the Christian theologian just mentioned are saying to us. In the shadow of the cross and in the shadow of the *via dolorosa* of the Jewish people, it has become extremely difficult for Christians and Jews to engage in dialogue. One of the main reasons is that the reality at the very heart of the church's gospel has been used as a rationalization for hatred and murder. Such a statement staggers the imagination, but as is becoming increasingly clear, it has historical evidence on its side.

In his book, *A Theology of Auschwitz*, Ulrich Simon has sought to probe these perplexities from a perspective of faith. Despite the valuable insights which his book contains, it left me with a deep sense of dissatisfaction. The essential facts are there in all their disturbing and horrifying truth; and yet one gets the feeling that Christians are not really helped to face the truth–while they face their Jewish brothers and sisters. In short, the dimension of confession, absolutely crucial in the biblical understanding of redemption, seems to be lacking. I am not talking about a "guilt trip," but rather the opposite: the potential of a liberating experience of grace because guilt is being dealt with in accordance with the gospel message.

Some Christians and Jews have begun to struggle together with these issues. For instance, the Roman Catholic scholar Hans Kung and Pinchas Lapide, professor at the Bar Ilan University in Israel, engaged in an exchange of views on Jesus over a German radio network. In that conversation, they ventured into the shadows of the *viae dolorosae* of Jesus and the Jewish people. Kung, pointing to the great Jewish painter, Marc Chagall, who constantly represented the sufferings of his people in the image of the Crucified, wondered "whether the history of this people can be understood differently and more deeply precisely from this standpoint: in the light of the Crucified who might almost stand as a personal symbol of Jewish history."

Lapide responded by stating that the Jews of his generation have fundamentally come to a "a paschal self-understanding," with Auschwitz as a Golgotha on a national scale and the founding of the State of Israel as a resurrection event. "For this Jewish people," he goes on to say, "what better embodiment could you find than this poor rabbi of Nazareth? . . . Is not this rabbi, bleeding on the cross, the authentic incarnation of his suffering people: all too often murdered on the cross of this hatred of Jews which we had to feel ourselves when we were young?"

We find here a probing for interconnections and for new approaches to Christian-Jewish dialogue which at the same time seeks to avoid an over-simplified identification of the fate of Jesus and the fate of the Jewish people. Obviously, because of the format of a radio program, but also because of our lack of experience in dealing with these issues, we are offered little more than first soundings. Where will such searchings lead us? How will they finally affect our "speaking of God?"

It seems to me that we ought not to settle for quick conclusions on such questions. There is always a danger that new insights become prematurely solidified in the deep freeze of a rigid theological system. Reconstructed theologies, even radical ones, have a way of becoming the new vogue, at least for an inner circle. It would be more than ironic if this were to happen to what has come to be known as "Holocaust theology."

All theological affirmations begin to sound hollow when they lose their confessional nature, when they are taken out of the context of a living encounter with God. So often the blasphemous nature of theological statements derives less from their content than from the spirit in which they are uttered. For instance, the theory of divine punishment for sin as a general explanation of things and the confession of guilt by people who have wrestled with themselves and with God are two entirely different worlds.

"How shall we live with God after Auschwitz?" asks Emil Fackenheim. "How without him? Contend with God we must, as did Abraham, Jacob, Job. And we cannot let him go." There are moments in the divine-human encounter when the cries of anguish become mixed with angry accusations against God. But even defiance can be an expression of faith, a claim on the promise of covenant, a prayer for some sign of presence in the midst of death. At the thresholds of the ovens of Auschwitz and other concentration camps, in moments of Godforsakenness, last words have been whispered to the Holy One, whose mercy is from everlasting to everlasting.

Dare we make the witness of the martyrs our own? As a mere rehashing of words, no. As a theory to explain the way things are, no. That kind of cheap God-talk indeed makes a mockery of other people's agony. We can only join their witness as people who know the meaning of remembrance and compassion, who know what it means to enter at least in some measure into the dark nights of human experience. There we stand on holy ground and perhaps, by the miracle of grace, we shall be able to affirm the great "Nevertheless" and speak the Name aright.

The original, unedited form of this chapter was first published in the May, 1982, issue of The Reformed Journal. Reprinted by permission.

CHAPTER 9

The Holocaust and the Development of Church Doctrine

The dialogue has become quite "established" since the humble beginnings of the workshop in 1973, when a group of mostly Catholic and Jewish scholars met in Dayton, Ohio. Few would dispute the advances that have been made in Christian-Jewish relations over the past decades. But some of the faithful *do* question the direction in which the dialogue has been moving. One of the principal "founders" of the National Workshop suggested to me that the dialogue had become "too much of a left-wing free-for-all," leaving less and less room for traditional church positions. Radical views are to be expected in a movement that seeks to redirect the thinking in the Christian world with regard to Jews and Judaism. The issue is no longer whether certain positions that have a long tradition in Christianity need to be changed. Most major church communions have answered that question in the affirmative and have taken steps to do so. But the questions today may be whether the dialogue is in danger of taking on certain radical chic aspects. A concomitant question is whether a sustained conversation is being maintained between individual theologians who tend to function in a more "free-for-all" environment, and the "official" positions of churches and ecclesiastical councils as expressed in their public pronouncements.

A National Workshop with about 800 participants may not be the best forum to debate various theological issues, but a few counter voices to radical claims of the predominant trend of thinking would, no doubt, enliven the proceedings and bring new excitement to a somewhat tired dialogue. As things stand today, all sorts of radical claims are being made, particularly in the name of post-Holocaust theology which, through constant repetition, tend to take on the appearance of a dialogical consensus while, in fact, those positions are not reflected in the growing body of ecclesiastical and ecumenical declarations.

My purpose is not in any way to minimize the monstrosities of the Holocaust or the historical role of the churches in helping to create the cultural climate in which such horrors could take place. Dozens of my relatives died in Nazi camps, including my father. My own experiences with Storm Troops were mild compared to theirs, but still brutal enough to have left a permanent imprint upon my soul. Holocaust experiences and/or studies might well make a difference in the way we conduct theology and correct wrong conclusions from the past. But, they should not determine how churches define doctrine.

For some, the *Shoah* is a revelatory event which requires a radical reconstruction of basic Christian tenets of faith. Auschwitz thus becomes an interpretative theological principle of the first order. Church theology must now pass through the crucible of Hitler's ovens to come out purged of all "exclusivist claims."

At the same time, the New Testament text is viewed as heavily, if not hopelessly, tainted by anti-Judaism. The question no longer is how to deal with certain passages in which harsh language is indeed used with respect to Jews. Rather, the poison of anti-Judaism is said to have seeped into the very root sources of the Christian *kerygma*, requiring that their most basic claims about God, Christ, and the Holy Spirit be questioned and reconstructed. In practice, this often means that they are to be relativized because, in their present form, they allegedly stand in the way of positive relationships to Judaism, as well as other non-Christian religions.

Hence, the impression is created that a hypercritical attitude toward the Scriptures is one of the prerequisites for an authentic post-Holocaust theology. In such a context, it is not surprising to find the God of classical Jewish and Christian theism described as "the ancient God," who is declared to be beyond belief for those who have come to terms with the *tremendum* of the Holocaust. In short, the traditional notion of a beneficent and providential God must be abandoned.

In some cases, disbelief in divine intervention is combined with passionate calls for human initiatives to save the world. It never ceases to amaze me how some post-*Shoah* scholars, who have lost faith in God, the sovereign Lord of history, still find it within themselves to put their hope for the survival of the planet in improved human behavior. To me, holding on to belief in divine grace and providence, even in the face of monstrous evil in the world, although perhaps in the form of an anguished cry of protest *de profundis*, seems more plausible than putting one's trust in human conduct.

As was to be expected, traditional Christology comes in for the heaviest critique. To use another bit of Rosemary Ruether's rhetoric, "Is it possible to say 'Jesus is Messiah' without, implicitly or explicitly, saying, at the same time, 'and the Jews be damned?' "[1] By such criteria, the Catechism of the Catholic Church would find itself immediately placed on the post-Holocaust "index" of condemned books.

The doctrine of atonement, especially with its New Testament emphasis on the once-for-all nature of God's redemptive act in Christ, poses another serious post-*Shoah* stumbling block. If the cross of Christ is that decisive in the divine drama that runs from the creation to the recreation of all things, what then remains of the role of God's covenant with Israel? Once again, there is the concern that the *kerygma* about a unique act of God in Christ implies a replacement theology–i.e., the ancient heresy that a more deserving church has taken the place of a disobedient and rejected people Israel.

Post-Holocaust theological literature tends to be absorbed with a fear of fulfillment language, which is so liberally used in the New Testament writings. Fulfillment is then one-sidedly interpreted to mean that all that has gone before is now declared to be inferior and that salvation has come into the world with a finality that leaves no room for future development in the story of redemption. The word *prolepsis* (ultimate outcome) has gained great favor as a replacement for the New Testament emphasis on *pleroma* (fullness). It involves a consistent effort to minimize the reality dimension of redemption in the here and now. The gospel is declared to be all about hope, but a hope that finds its basic motivating force in the incompleteness of the redemption in Christ. *Prolepsis* implies what is called an "unfulfilled messianism," a notion that is considered necessary in order to safeguard Jews against an anti-Semitism that is rooted in Christian triumphalism. Any idea that, in certain ways and forms, the future kingdom of God is present in history is viewed as an illegitimate claim upon the future, or a "historicizing of the eschatological."

But isn't that precisely what historical revelation is all about: the presence of the future kingdom in the power of the Holy Spirit? Does not the God of Israel and the Father of our Lord Jesus Christ enter this world in the "power of futurity"? Isn't it precisely through the presence of the promised future that the signs and first fruits of the new creation are established upon the earth? And does not the foretaste of the age to come fill existence with expectation and eschatological hope?

Post-Holocaust theologians like to claim that they, and they alone, take history seriously. But their positivist attitude toward historical reality gives them endless hangups about the interrelationship between history and eschatology, constantly playing out the one against the other. In truth, however, the eschaton and history are correlative realities.

Historical existence is drawn by the dream and the power of the future of the Lord. The *eschaton* is not a *nova creatio*, plunging from the heavens into a sort of black hole of history, an empty interim between the resurrection/ascension and the redemption of the world. The interim is the dispensation of the Holy Spirit, the time for sanctification, the apostolate of God's co-workers and responsible stewardship of the creation. In light of God's act in Christ, these are also experienced and proclaimed as "the last days."

Rosemary Ruether scathingly talks about "tricks of realized eschatology" played upon history and assures us that "unredeemed reality" will turn out to be stronger than such fantasies.[2] Hence, she calls for "historical realism" which she believes will serve as an antidote to triumphalism. I, on the other hand, maintain that prophetic realism and not a positivist type of historical realism, is the true heritage of Israel's faith. Belief in the covenant and divine presence, trust in the coming future of the Lord, and the victory of divine righteousness, these are the ingredients of prophetic realism.

Post-Holocaust theologians tend to excise the triumphant notes from Christian theology and church life in an attempt to exorcise the demon triumphalism. Some find a peculiar attraction in the tragic view of life that comes to expression in the writings of the Kabbalists. So we are left with Christian hope minus the hallelujahs. A triumphant faith, they say over and over again, is a sure sign that the evil in the world is not taken seriously.

Well, the voices of tragedy, doubt, even despair and protest against God, need to be heard as well, as they are heard repeatedly throughout the Bible. But exile, with its sense of divine absence and silence, while real enough, never has the last word in Israel's faith and worldview. "The world of prophetic faith," wrote Martin Buber, "is in fact historic reality, seen in the bold and penetrating glance of the man who dares to believe."[3] Such prophetic faith does not involve an escape from history, although it often does have a "nevertheless" quality about it. "Though he slay me, yet I will trust in him" (Job 13:15). Or, in the words of the prophet Habakkuk: "Though the fig tree does not blossom, and no fruit is on the vines; and though the produce of the olive fails and the fields yield no food; though the flock is cut off from the fold and there is no herd in the stalls, yet I will rejoice in the Lord. I will exult in the God of my salvation" (Habakkuk 3:17-18).

Such a "nevertheless of faith" was also heard in Hitler's camps when the *Shema* was recited within sight of the gas chambers. In the midst of historic reality, even in the midst of the kingdom of death, prophetic faith dares to believe in the God of the covenant.

Prophetic faith is also a faith that dares to proclaim. Few who know the horrors of Christian history *vis-à-vis* the Jewish people, and who believe in the continued covenant with Israel, will deny that Christian witness to Jews confronts us with dilemmas that are not always easily resolved. Many post-*Shoah* theologians do, however, offer an easy answer. As we have noted, when it comes to the Jewish people, they have suggested that the church does not have a *kerygma* to proclaim; at best it has a mission in the form of *diakonia*, meaning, in essence, support for Jewish concerns and causes. But, one must ask, does an ecclesiology with such a limited apostolate still reflect the church of

Jesus Christ as portrayed in the New Testament? I think not.

Christian triumphalism is a perennial temptation, and so is missionary imperialism. Sinful boasting on the part of Gentile Christians against which Paul sounded such grave warnings (Romans 9-11) has led to supersessionist theologies, which in turn have been the source of much Jewish suffering. Those are issues any post-Holocaust theologian has to deal with, but not, I believe, by depriving the church of its triumphant message concerning God's victory revealed in the death and resurrection of Jesus Christ.

The "principalities and the powers," which are frequently controlled by evil forces, remain very strong. We confess the lordship of a Christ who rules among his enemies. Our hope is not founded on a "hear-no-evil-see-no-evil" kind of faith. Jews and Christians are partners in hope, because they share a common belief in the *magnalia Dei* as manifested in the midst of Israel. The issue on which we differ is the decisive nature of God's dealings with the world in Jesus of Nazareth. In him, the church confesses, the God of Abraham, Isaac, and Jacob has done a new and wonderful thing, both for the salvation of Israel and the redemption of the world. That difference can never be dialogued away.

But what, then, about triumphalism? It is, as it has always been, as real as sin. Anti-Semitism, at least in some of its manifestations, is a revolt of the pagan heart against the God of Israel and the very idea of historical revelation. The question we now face in the post-Holocaust era is this: "Can we proclaim a triumphant gospel without, in the process, producing a triumphalistic church?" My answer is "yes," but it will require constant and radical conversion. Conversely, we also face this question: "Can we maintain an authentically Christian message and mission if we abandon the triumphant notes in the gospel?" I do not think so. To paraphrase the apostle Paul, if Jesus was not raised from the dead and if he is not the Lord who has overcome the world, then our Christian faith is in vain, and so is our theologizing.

The original, unedited form of this chapter was first published in the **Spring, 1995, issue of Pro Ecclesia. Reprinted by permission.**

[1] Cf. Rosemary Ruether, *Faith and Fratricide: The Theological Roots of Anti-Semitism* (New York: Seabury Press, 1974), p. 246.

[2] *Ibid.*, p. 243.

[3] Cf. Martin Buber, *The Prophetic Faith* (New York: Harper & Row, 1960), p. 135.

CHAPTER 10

Fulfillment Theology and the Future of Christian-Jewish Relations

Judaism and Christianity both point to the signs of God's active presence in history as the foundation of their hope.

The book *Auschwitz: Beginning of a New Era?*[1] contains an exchange between two theologians–Roman Catholic John T. Pawlikowski and Russian Orthodox Thomas Hopko–on the question of "fulfillment theology" and its significance for future Christian-Jewish relations. Pawlikowski, following other Catholic scholars such as Rosemary Ruether and Gregory Baum, challenges the traditional "fulfillment" concept as basically inaccurate and calls for new approaches in Christology which he believes will "profoundly alter Christianity's self-definition and make possible a more realistic relationship to Judaism and to all other non-Christian religions." The basic implication of his proposal is that Christians ought to abandon the claim that in Jesus the messianic age has been inaugurated.

Hopko responds to the challenge by expressing the hope that Pawlikowski's proposal will not be realized because, he says, "the 'fulfillment' understanding of Christianity [cannot] be abandoned without the destruction of the Christian faith." He fears that the suggested changes in Christology will portend "the end of all meaningful religious and spiritual dialogue" and will result in a "sterile relativism, a monistic spiritual syncretism devoid of creative, truly pluralistic conflict and fruitful, truly creative tension."

To this growing debate on "fulfillment theology" I would add a contribution from a Reformed theological perspective: the thesis that New Testament messianic claims can be abandoned only at the cost of sacrificing crucial aspects of the church's witness to the gospel of the kingdom, but that Christians do need to abandon a good deal of "fulfillment theology" that finds its source in ecclesiastical triumphalism.

The New Testament everywhere contains fulfillment language. In christological context, fulfillment terminology is used to assert that, in

Jesus of Nazareth, God acted in an ultimately decisive way in history.

According to the most ancient Christian confession, Jesus appeared when the time was fulfilled, and his coming meant nothing less than the breakthrough of the new age of the kingdom of God (Mark 1:15). In this faith Christians came to see themselves as people who had "tasted the goodness of the word of God and the powers of the age to come" (Hebrews 6:5). In short, an encounter with Jesus as the living Lord was experienced as a foretaste of the future of the Lord proclaimed by prophets and seers. The emphasis in New Testament fulfillment theology is on foretaste, not on the full realization of divine redemption in present history.

Nevertheless, the christological claims of the New Testament can hardly be overstated. We are told not only that time has been fulfilled, but also that in Jesus Christ the law and the prophets have been fulfilled. In Jesus, claim the early Christians, "all the promises of God find their Yes" (2 Corinthians 1:20). Jesus' death was interpreted as an act of atonement and as a victory over the forces of sin and death that hold humanity captive. Thus, he was confessed as "Lord of all" (Romans 10:12), who has overcome the world (John 16:33).

Traditional Judaism has countered these Christian claims with some very fundamental questions. How can one speak of a breakthrough of the messianic era in light of the fact that the world is so obviously unredeemed? Does not the entire "Christian era" provide one great testimony that the fulfillment of the prophetic promises is still a vision of the future? Some Jewish scholars maintain that empirical evidence shows a deterioration of the human condition since the death of Christ, rather than an improvement.

Redemption, as Martin Buber never tired of pointing out, will mean *Die Vollendung der Schöpfung*, a fulfillment of the creation, which will amount to the re-creation of the whole world. That particular redemption surely has not taken place.

How then do Christians validate their "fulfillment theology"? A common Jewish view is that Christians seek to escape from this dilemma by spiritualizing redemption. "The thesis of historical Christianity has been 'otherworldliness,' " writes Steven S. Schwarzchild. The messianic idea, according to Gershom Scholem, is totally different in Judaism and in Christianity; Judaism in all its forms and manifestations has always maintained a concept of redemption as an event which takes place publicly, on the stage of history, and within the community. In contrast, Christianity conceives of redemption as an event in the spiritual and unseen realm; an event which is reflected in the soul, in the private world of each individual, and which affects an inner transformation which need not correspond to anything outside.[2]

Once redemption becomes spiritualized and thus effectively removed from the realm of daily life, the danger of Christianity's becoming a *status quo* religion is real. Why try to change a world that is so obviously of inferior spiritual significance compared with the salvation of eternal souls for heaven?

Scholem's and similar views do not show the whole picture of Christianity through the centuries; nevertheless, the first response of a Christian to his kind of challenge should be one of *peccavi* ("I have sinned").We finally ought to face up to the false claims made in some of our "fulfillment theologies" which have contributed immensely to the prevalent misconceptions about Christian views of redemption. In no way am I suggesting that we compromise our faith, but rather that we confess our sins.

For example, patristic literature is full of polemics that seek to prove the superiority of Christianity to Judaism. "Remember," said Paul, "it is not you that support the root, but the root supports you" (Romans 11:18). Faith in Christ's victory, however, was frequently turned into something quite different: ecclesiastical triumphalism.

As a result of this trend, "fulfillment" became interpreted as God's rejection of his covenant relationship with the people of Israel. When the church declared itself to be the "New Israel," it usually did so, not in order to acknowledge in gratitude God's new initiatives in Jesus Christ, but rather to reinforce false imperialistic notions about the church's calling. Ecclesiastical claims that run counter to the biblical witness (for example, Paul's affirmation in Romans 11:29 that "the gifts and the call of God are irrevocable") became accepted as New Testament doctrine. The Jewish scholar Uriel Tal was mistaken when he wrote that the idea of God's continued covenant with the Jews "is of course contrary to the theology of the New Testament." That idea is only contrary to the church's false claims of being the "New Israel," replacing and superseding God's covenant relationship with the Jews.

Krister Stendahl has pointed out that the only New Testament passage claimed for calling the church by the name "Israel" rests on a mistranslation of Galatians 6:16, a text that really speaks of the original Israel as "the Israel of God." A careful reading of the Greek text, says Stendahl, "must lead to the translation: 'And as many as walk according to this standard [the new creation in Christ], peace be upon them–and mercy also upon the Israel of God.' The Revised Standard Version has suppressed the striking and strong *kai* (also) before 'the Israel of God.' "

Equally unscriptural claims were made about the New Testament declaration that, in Jesus' coming, the law and the prophets were fulfilled. A text particularly significant is Matthew 5:17, the opening words of the Sermon on the Mount. The church has struggled for centuries to gain a clear understanding of the meaning of these words. But the text makes unequivocally clear what Jesus did not mean to say. An interpretation that this verse seeks to avoid is that the law of God–the law of the kingdom as embodied in the Old Testament–has been abolished, set aside, or in any way declared defunct because of Christ's fulfillment. In fact, Jesus came to affirm and give a new foundation to the righteousness of God as embodied in the law. Another interpretation the text wants to make impossible is that the fulfillment of the prophetic promises means that Christians no longer live by promise, whereas the exact opposite is true: fulfillment implies that we live by promise more than ever.

The combination of law and fulfillment, as well as the combination of law and love, is mentioned repeatedly in the New Testament, particularly in the letters to the Romans and the Galatians. The New Testament leaves no doubt of its witness that something radical has happened in Christ's act of sacrificial love. Somehow, Torah, which certainly is more than a set of legal rules and which refers to a dynamic reality–namely, God's righteousness as it comes to us in our historical existence–has been given embodiment. That embodiment is what Christ came to accomplish, and he continues to do so through the power of the Spirit. In this sense, the law is called "spiritual" (Romans 7:14), while at the same time we are told that only "doers of the law will be justified" (Romans 2:13) and that through faith we do not overthrow the law but uphold it (Romans 3:31).

Criticism of the law is not an exclusively New Testament phenomenon; it is found in the prophetic writings as well. In neither case does it reflect a disrespectful view of divine law (which both the Old and the New Testament see as grounded in divine grace), but, rather, it refers to what is bound to happen to the law when we start "handling" it and using it to establish our own righteousness rather than letting the rule and righteousness of God dwell and become embodied in our midst. Any suggestion that such misdeeds occurred among the people of Israel but are not happening among Christians would bespeak a self-righteousness that suffocates the very truth of the gospel message.

All Christian claims that Judaism confesses a God of law in the formal/legal sense in contrast to a "Christian God" of grace are based on false views of fulfillment; such views not only damage Christian-Jewish relations, but are devastating for the life of the church itself. First we lose the law, then we lose the gospel of the kingdom, and finally we end up with a spiritualism and/or moralists with scarcely a meaningful word to say to the modern world. Gerald Sloyan makes an important point when he states that "the teaching church cannot allow the confusion to continue with its grandiose–and often quite wrong-contrast between the law and the gospel."[3]

Another false interpretation of "fulfillment" is the claim that the people of the Old Testament era lived by promise, while Christians possess the reality itself. I shudder when I read Lawrence E. Toombs's advice to preachers that they should see "the Old Testament related to the New as hope to fulfillment, as question to answer, as suggestion to reality."[4] It is sheer heresy to suggest that those who believe in fulfillment are no longer saved by hope (Romans 8:24).

Faith in Christ means that people have become "partakers of the promise with the people of Israel" (Ephesians 3:6), and one of its main fruits is a rebirth of hope (1 Peter 1:3). How can we describe the Old Testament as "question" and "suggestion" and the New Testament as "answer" and "reality"? Does not the Bible, from beginning to end, witness to the reality of God's presence in the world, and does not an encounter with him always make people dreamers of the kingdom of God?

Abraham Heschel expressed a basic insight found throughout the entire Bible when he wrote, "What lends meaning to history? The promise of the future. If there is no promise, there is no meaningful history. Significance is contingent on vision and anticipation, on living the future in the present tense."[5] The Christian believes that, in Jesus Christ, God's future has broken into our midst and that the promised future is already present in the power of the Spirit. But, it is precisely through this presence of the Spirit, which is called "the Holy Spirit of promise" (Ephesians 1:13), that the whole creation is made pregnant with longing for the final coming of the future of the Lord (Romans 8). The Holy Spirit is also called "the guarantee of our inheritance until we acquire possession of it" (Ephesians 1:14). To receive the fullness of the Spirit means to be filled with expectation.

Jakob Jocz wrote some years ago that "a bridge theology" between Judaism and Christianity "can be accomplished only at the point of a diminution of traditional Christology." The process is being attempted today by a number of theologians, but more promise may be found in a reexamination of the New Testament pneumatology.

Rosemary Ruether repeatedly makes the point that the church preaches a fulfilled messianism whenever it forgets the *parousia*, the second coming, losing its vision of the future. Historically, many false claims of fulfillment have indeed found their basic source in a loss of the eschatological perspective. On the other hand, the New Testament witness to fulfillment is rooted precisely in the eschatological vision, and in the belief that the future of the Lord, albeit in a hidden and fragmentary way, is present in our midst in the form of signs, first fruits, foretaste and so on. These are all pneumatological categories. The key concept of *pleroma* in the New Testament illustrates that fulfillment is essentially an eschatologically charged reality.

"God was in Christ reconciling the world to himself" (2 Corinthians 5:19). In the incarnation and the act of atonement, according to Christian confession, reconciliation has taken place and the possibility of forgiveness is offered to humankind. But the act of reconciliation does not mean that redemption of the world is now a reality. For Christians it means a renewal and broadening of the covenant (Gentile branches are grafted onto the tree of Israel–Romans 11:17) and a new foundation for hope in the ultimate coming of the future kingdom. Through the presence of the Spirit, signs of that kingdom are established in the world. In faith, first fruits of the eventual harvest of God's new age are experienced; we receive a foretaste of the fullness of history that is yet to come (Ephesians 1:10).

These occurrences take place through the presence of the Holy Spirit; they are spiritual realities. But it is a tragic misunderstanding of the Christian message to interpret that truth as meaning that redemption becomes "spiritualized." One must excise major portions from the New Testament in order to claim that redemption and the life of faith have nothing to do with the poor, justice, the state, and other earthly realities.

Gregory Baum states that "the redemption brought by Jesus to mankind in the present is prophetic or anticipatory of the future glory; it is a token, a pledge, a first installment of the complete redemption promised in the Scriptures." This assertion is correct, but the christological and pneumatological aspects of such a statement, while intimately related, should not be confused with each other.

Rosemary Ruether rightly rejects an "illegitimate historicizing of the eschatological." The church is not the kingdom of God; sanctification is not yet glorification; in the first fruits we taste the promise of the harvest but do not possess the harvest itself, and the fulfillment of time is not the same as the consummation of history. Yet, the presence of God in history, through the Spirit, is real. There must not be an illegitimate dehistoricizing of the *inhabitatio Spiritus sancti*, either.

Martin Buber used to speak of Judaism and Christianity in terms of "two types of faith." David Flusser, who had a profound knowledge of early Christian literature, advocated the view that Judaism and Christianity are "one faith." Said he: "When both Judaism and Christianity acknowledge that it is fundamentally one religion, one faith, and do not deny it–as still happens so much, either out of ignorance or out of dogmatic prejudices–then they can really debate with each other."[6] Flusser's statement seems closer to the truth than Buber's arguments in his book *Two Types of Faith*.

Flusser does not wish to ignore the real differences between Judaism and Christianity. Nor do I. But Jews and Christians share a vision concerning the new heaven and the new earth. They also share some basic perspectives on the nature of God's redemptive presence in the world today, even though the Christian view of history "between the times" is influenced in a decisive way by its christological confession.

At a time when Christians of various traditions are wrestling with questions of political theology, it does not seem to make sense for Jews to insist that Christianity holds an essentially ahistorical view of salvation. That would be tantamount to saying that the Satmar Rebbe and his followers, who deny any form of historical realization of eschatological expectations, represent Judaism as a whole. We must move beyond caricatures of each other's faith. When Seymour Siegel notes that "the State of Israel is salvation but not redemption," he seems to come very close to what many Christians mean when they speak about "signs of the kingdom" in historical existence. Such signs are an embodiment of the promise–fragmentary and constantly threatened by the sinful impulses of humanity, but nevertheless the beginning of the dawn of our redemption. Of course, there are also the birth pangs of the Messiah. Both Jewish and Christian literatures have much to say about positive as well as negative signs of the approaching end.

Emil Fackenheim has pointed out that "all attempts to link the precarious present with the absolute future are themselves precarious. . . . Yet, unless the Messianic future is to become ever-elusive and thus irrelevant, its linking with a possible present, however precarious, is indispensable . . ." The Jewish scholar here touches on a basic issue with which both Jews and Christians struggle as they seek to read the signs of the times and to approach their historical responsibility with a sense of honesty as well as hope.

Judaism and Christianity both point to the signs of God's active presence in history as the foundation of their hope. The role of Jesus in God's historical-eschatological dealings with the world remains a point of radical difference between the two faiths. Distorted Christian interpretations of "fulfillment" have had destructive consequences for meaningful dialogue. The debate on "fulfillment theology" is therefore of crucial importance, both for Christian-Jewish relations and for the life and mission of the Christian church itself.

The original, unedited form of this chapter was first published in the Christian Century. Copyright 1989 Christian Century. Reprinted by permission from the April 12, 1989, issue of the Christian Century.

[1] Eva Fleischner, (ed.), *Auschwitz: Beginning of a New Era?: Reflections on the Holocaust:* Papers Given at the International Symposium on the Holocaust, Held at the Cathedral of St. John the Divine (New York: Ktav Publishing House, 1977).

[2] Fleischner, *Auschwitz*, p. 218.

[3] Gerald Sloyan, *Is Christ the End of the Law?* (Philadelphia: Westminster Press, 1978), p. 101.

[4] Lawrence E. Toombs, *The Old Testament in Christian Preaching* (Philadelphia: Westminister Press, 1961), p. 27.

[5] Abraham Heschel, *Israel: An Echo of Eternity* (New York: Farrar, Straus & Giroux, 1967), p.127.

[6] David Flusser, *Jews and Christians Between Past and Future*, p. 30.

CHAPTER 11

Jewish and Christian Views of Messianic Redemption

DISPUTATION AND DIALOGUE

Judaism and Christianity have their disputes. It has always been thus. The gospels portray Jesus engaged in arguments with certain religious leaders of his day. The apostolic letters tell us about disputes between the emerging church and the synagogue. We live with our profound differences to this day.

Where there are real differences between faith communities, disputes are bound to be part of their interaction. Christianity came to be so called because it is a Christ-centered faith involving messianic claims about Jesus that run counter to the overwhelming view among Jews that a breakthrough of the messianic age still lies in the future. Hence, Christology is a major subject of dispute between Jews and Christians, even though Jesus is viewed much more positively in broad Jewish circles today than was the case only decades ago.

A HISTORY OF CONFLICT

What forms has that dispute taken? This question leads us straight to the sad history of Christian-Jewish relations. Dispute led to separation, separation led to estrangement, and estrangement led to enmity. Differences were turned into dichotomies and eventually acts of violence. Both parties have, in various ways, contributed to these disastrous developments, but the churches bear by far the greatest burden of responsibility for what has happened as a result. Once Gentiles constituted the majority of congregational membership, church leaders turned to Hellenistic rather than Hebraic modes of thought. Furthermore, attitudes toward Jews and Judaism became increasingly hostile, and after the church gained the upper hand as an imperial power, it resorted to coercive force. Soon polemics was matched with persecution.

The second century church father Justin Martyr entitled one of his famous treatises *A Dialogue with Trypho*. In fact, it read more like a diatribe than a dialogue. By accusing his Jewish opponent of "obstinacy of heart and feebleness of mind," this Christian defender of the faith set the stage for the later stereotype of the obstinate Jew who, against all reason, refuses to renounce his/her faith and accept baptism. The historian Adolf von Harnack rightly observed that this tract was in reality a "victor's monologue."

The disputations forced upon the Jewish community in the Middle Ages, designed to prove Jesus' messiahship to Torah-faithful Jews, also did not have even the semblance of a dialogue. Their true intent was not mutual understanding, but the humiliation of Jews and the deprecation of their faith. These staged events were, in effect, opportunities for Christians to propagandize under police protection. Woe to any Jew who would dare to protest. For many Jews it became a matter of being baptized or banished, or much worse. All this was done in the name of Jesus, whom the church confesses as the Messiah of Israel and Savior of the world.

I shall not rehash this history of horrors, which has been so abundantly documented over the past decades by both Jewish and Christian scholars. Instead, I shall focus on some voices in the post-Holocaust era on the issue of disputation and dialogue, with special reference to the churches' messianic claims.

THE NEW DIALOGUE

Dialogue is widely being praised by many Christians and Jews as the great new positive reality in Christian-Jewish relations. In my view, there are good reasons for that. Some Jewish scholars, however, have their doubts, especially about theological dialogues as distinguished from exchanges about socio-cultural and political matters. There are those who feel that dialogues on questions of faith are basically meaningless, if not dangerous. Meaningless because the two faiths have, theologically speaking, little if anything in common–are, in fact, incompatible–and dangerous because such encounters tend to perpetuate the alleged "myth" of a Judeo-Christian tradition.

I offer a few brief samples for illustrative purposes. Rabbi Jacob Neusner, a highly esteemed scholar and prolific writer, is not impressed with the dialogue thus far. In his book, *Telling Tales*, he accuses dialogue devotees of engaging in "a form of shadow-boxing," of dealing mostly with "surface matters" while avoiding issues that go to the heart of each other's beliefs. In his often provocative style, he even uses the phrase "a conspiracy of hypocrites."

Neusner offers some proposals on how the dialogue might be moved to a next stage, but, unfortunately, he sees as the precondition of an honest dialogue the mutual acceptance of the fact that "Judaism and Christianity are entirely different and essentially unrelated religions." Levi Olan made the same point when he wrote that "Jesus and the New Testament are wholly outside the Jewish realm," and that "Jews have no more and no less interest in discussing these than they do the founders and scriptures of other faiths." In short, the relationship of Judaism to Christianity is no different than its relationship to Hinduism or Buddhism.

Rabbi Henry Siegman presented that dichotomous perspective in a 1975 *Worldview* article. He used such phrases as "the ultimate incommensurability of Judaism and Christianity" and the "incompatibility of Sinai and Golgotha" (i.e., observance of Torah versus redemption *sola fide* through the cross of Christ). He believed that acknowledgment of these "facts" would be a good starting point for dialogue.

Others have used even stronger language. As we have noted, Eliezer Berkovits, in a famous 1966 essay in the journal *Judaism* stated quite bluntly that "Judaism is Judaism because it rejects Christianity, and Christianity is Christianity because it rejects Judaism." Thus, the sin of the youthful church is visited upon us. Christians so disastrously defined themselves in opposition to Judaism, causing the enmity which now makes it seem desirable to some that we accept that judgment as the norm.

During the 1980s, Gershon Mamlak emerged as a passionate advocate of the dichotomous position. Assigning Christianity to the "syncretistic orbit of Hellas," we have noted earlier that he saw the uniqueness of Judaism to lie precisely in where it differed from Christianity. For us, he argues, the law embodies a covenant partnership with the God of Israel for the sake of the mending of creation, while they have abandoned the law and have chosen the way of an unworldly Gnostic-type spirituality. His wrath was directed in particular at the "Jesus-a-true-Jew" school.

David Flusser was one of the prime representatives of that "school." Despite the fundamental differences between Christianity and Judaism, he was not reluctant to describe them as "really one faith" nor to enter into dialogues about Jewish and Christian understandings of messianic redemption. A number of scholars in the United States have pursued a similar path.

Rabbi Irving Greenberg wrote an essay entitled, "The Relationship of Judaism and Christianity: Toward a New Organic Model," a clear attempt, not to move to consensus on core beliefs, but, to a more balanced view of each other's position. Greenberg posed the following question: "Is it possible for Judaism to have a more affirmative model of Christianity, one that appreciates Christian spiritual life in all its manifest power?"[1] In other words, as an Orthodox Jew, he sought to enter into dialogue about some of the central faith claims of Christianity.

This courageous and creative attempt to move beyond dichotomy to a deeper dialogical relationship unfortunately did not receive the response it so richly deserved. Rabbi Greenberg tells me that some of his

Orthodox compatriots reacted with bitter attacks while there were few serious discussions about his proposal among Christian dialogue partners.

As to the messianic question, Greenberg reflected on how Jews might better understand the reaction of the early Jewish followers of Jesus to his ministry and then his disastrous death. How did they come to confess him as Messiah? For the author's arguments, I must refer the reader to Greenberg's article in the *Quarterly Review* (mentioned above). Let me just mention his discussion about a "failed messiah" who, as distinguished from a "false messiah," can still advance the cause of redemption. "In the Messiah ben Joseph," he writes, "you have a messiah who comes and fails, indeed is put to death, but this messiah paves the way for the final redemption." The same may be said of Jesus.

Michael Kogan, also writing from a conservative Jewish perspective, has made similar proposals in two noteworthy articles.[2] Can't we move, asks Kogan, from mutual respect to mutual influence, and eventually even to mutual enlightenment? He sees Christianity as basically a "Jewish outreach into the world," one which has spread the message about the God of Israel to the nations. As to key Christian doctrines (*viz.* incarnation, vicarious sacrifice, and the resurrection) Kogan renders a more positive Jewish evaluation of such core Christian beliefs than has usually been the case.

Jesus, while not accepted as Messiah, is–in line with Martin Buber's thought–portrayed as one of the greatest among the sons of Israel. But if Christian dialogers were to either drop the designation "Messiah" for Jesus or follow Kogan's idea to define it "in an internal and spiritualized way unknown to Judaism," that, in effect, would constitute an admission that Mamlak and others have been right all along in describing Christianity as a Gnostic-type spirituality.

THE "REALIZED ESCHATOLOGY" ISSUE

Gnosticism was a severe threat to Christian orthodoxy. It took a fierce intellectual struggle to resist its seductive powers to replace the notion of an historical revelation with a spiritualistic immanentism. In the end, biblical faith in creation, the incarnation, and the resurrection of the body won out, even though the church has succumbed time and time again to an unworldly spiritualization of the faith.

"Jesus is Lord" became the central confession in the faith of the post-resurrection church and that belief had not only internal-personalistic implications, but political ones as well, as the early martyrs who refused to worship the emperor all too soon found out. The church proclaimed a triumphant message of redemption. Jesus was proclaimed as the Christ, the One promised in the message of Israel's prophets. In his birth, his ministry, his cross and resurrection, the God of Israel had acted decisively on behalf of a world gone astray. The gospel of salvation in Christ was seen as being of world-historical, even cosmic significance. The apostles, with Holy Scripture in hand (which for them meant "Moses and the prophets") went out into the Greco-Roman world claiming nations and cultures for Christ the Lord.

Our Jewish brothers and sisters have two basic responses to this message. First, the Christ of the church is not the Messiah of Jewish expectation, and the best evidence of that is that the world has so obviously not been redeemed, the Jewish people did not gain political sovereignty, and an era of world peace was not inaugurated. So, how can Christians claim that there is a presence of the kingdom of God in the here and now?

Secondly, the triumphant gospel of the church was turned into an ecclesiastical triumphalism and supersessionism that has brought untold suffering to the Jewish people. How can they be expected to receive the church's message as a redemptive faith? Instead, the Jewish people have come to see Christian messianic claims as a threat to their very survival.

These Jewish responses and concerns need to be taken very seriously by Christian believers. Sinful Christian triumphalism has frequently obscured rather than promoted the triumphant message of the gospel. Ecclesiastical hegemony has all too often been used as a power tool to oppress others. The church has at times made claims that conveyed the idea that it represented the kingdom of God on earth in all its glory, thus losing the eschatological perspective of the Bible, and with it, the life lived in faith, hope, and love. As already noted, the Jewish people became the prime, although certainly not the only, victims of these distorted versions of biblical faith.

Profound shock has filled the souls of many Christians who have studied this history of horrors. Scholars have struggled to find ways to revise the manner in which we witness to the Jewish people, or even to reconstruct basic doctrines of the church. Again, proposed solutions can be presented here only in very summary fashion. The following examples are mostly for illustrative purposes.

Some Christian scholars (e.g,. the late Paul van Buren and Clark Williamson) have recommended that Christians do indeed avoid the designation *Messiah* when referring to Jesus. It just seems inappropriate to take such a central concept in Judaism and endow it with an entirely new meaning. For others, the very confession "Jesus is Lord" contains anti-Judaic implications of a replacement theology and therefore should be abandoned. The late Roy Eckardt, in a provocative fashion equal to Rosemary Ruether, posed this question: "How can the resurrection of Jesus be proclaimed as a special act of God without the Christian triumphalism that paved the way to Belzec and Sobibor?"[3] For him, Jesus was indeed a failed messiah who came very close to being a false messiah.

The basic problem for these theologians–and for those who share their views–is the claim of the presence of redemption in the here and now. In order to minimize the emphasis on such a presence of salvation, the term *prolepsis* has gained popularity in certain circles. Jesus is the Christ/Messiah "in an anticipatory way" (Gregory Baum). Jesus was a Jew who died hoping for the coming of the kingdom, not the Messiah who inaugurated the promised new age. Hence, we are dealing with an "unfulfilled messianism" (Ruether). Thus, these scholars believe, the futuristic dimension of biblical faith is preserved, while the unredeemed nature of the present is fully recognized, and Christian triumphalism is avoided. To say it differently, any notion of a "realized eschatology" must be rejected.

FULFILLMENT AND CONSUMMATION

There is no denying the fact that the New Testament message has a *fait accompli* dimension to it. What needed to happen has happened. The divine law was fulfilled in holy love and righteousness. Atonement has been accomplished. Indeed, "God was in Christ reconciling the world to himself" (2 Corinthians 5:19). The gospel now is good news about "fulfillment," a concept that runs through the New Testament in a variety of contexts. It is used in connection with the law, time, the church, etc. The idea of fulfillment is so problematic to a number of theologians that they simply want to get rid of it. According to Ruether, the use of this category is in effect a "historicizing of the eschatological," i.e., making illegitimate claims about the here and now as if the divinely promised future is already fully present. This has led some scholars, like Father John Pawlikowski, to declare that we ought to abandon once and for all the idea that fulfilled history exists anywhere. As I have argued in various writings over the years, the problem here lies in the fact that the New Testament notion of the fulfillment of history is being confused with the consummation of history in the kingdom of God. There is a dynamic relationship between the two, but they are not the same, certainly not in the New Testament.

In fact, I would claim that there is an element of "realized eschatology" in the New Testament message, but that rather than representing a historicizing of the eschatological, this aspect of the gospel has a strongly futuristic content about it. In other words, in Jesus Christ the future of God's kingdom has broken into our history and through the Holy Spirit the power of the reign of God is operative in the here and now, not only in human hearts, but in the history of the world. That is what the New Testament concept of fulfillment is all about. It is about a *fait accompli* that is not a *finit*. Fulfillment is an historical-eschatological dynamic. That divine promises are fulfilled before the end of time as we know it never means the end of it, not in the Old Testament nor in the New Testament. It is all part of covenant history where the divine establishment of a "new covenant," rather than meaning the abolition of the existing covenant, is, in fact, a confirmation of God's faithfulness as the divine plan of redemption unfolds. Fulfilled promises open up history to new futures and new expectations.

When the New Testament proclaims that in faith people receive a taste of the powers of the age to come (Hebrews 6:5), I would say that is a form of "realized eschatology." We are not talking about something ethereal that can be spiritualized out of concrete historical reality. Quite the contrary: these powers become embodied in a renewal of life, in healings, in good deeds, in just laws, etc. Furthermore, through the presence of the powers of the kingdom to come, expectation and hope are intensified. Fulfillment does not mean that we have taken hold of the new heaven and the new earth, but rather that we have become "partakers of the promise with the people of Israel" (Ephesians 3:6). Thus, we become partners in hope, and coworkers with the Lord of the universe. To be saved and become a born-again Christian in the New Testament sense means to undergo a rebirth to hope (1 Peter 1:3; Romans 8:24). It also means that one "strains forward to what lies ahead" (Philippians 3:13) in active service to the kingdom of God.

Key concepts in the New Testament understanding of the presence of redemption in the here and now are foretaste, first fruits, signs, and a first installment of an inheritance to come. These terms suggest a certain eschatological reservation. The gifts of God are glorious, but they pale in comparison with the glory of the full redemption of the earth when "God will be all in all" (1 Corinthians 15:28). That, indeed, will be the consummation of history.

I realize that the New Testament use of the word *pleroma* and its various derivatives can be confusing. I can understand how a wise and diligent student of both Jewish and Christian sources such as Michael Wyschogrod can conclude that Christians hold the view of a "completed history." In that case, the life of faith would no longer mean a straining forward to what lies ahead.

I agree with Clemens Thoma that "[in] the last analysis neither in Judaism nor in Christianity is it a question of the messiah but of the Kingdom of God."[4] Yes, the life and ministry, the death and resurrection of Jesus are central and decisive in the Christian understanding of the divine plan of redemption. Therefore, the differences between Judaism and Christianity run very deep. Unfortunately, the commonalities that remain have all too often been obscured by the atrocities committed by Christians against the Jewish people.

Thus, as Martin Buber wrote, we came to face each other across "a gulf which no human power can bridge." Yet, we still have some important things in common: namely, "a book and an expectation." So, the gulf "does not prevent the common watch for a unity to come to us from God."[5] Christian expectation finds its confirmation not only in the great acts of God recorded in the Old Testament, but above all in the "Christ-event," the "Pentecost event," and the presence of the power of the kingdom in the present age.

In the meantime, the watchword is waiting. Not, as was already pointed out, a waiting in passive resignation; but waiting while "hastening the coming of the day of God" (2 Peter 3:12). It is to be hoped that through continued dialogue we will discover new and common ways of serving the cause of divine *Shalom* in the world. It will require more than colloquia in comfortable surroundings. It really demands what Greenberg has called a new "worldliness in holiness" or what might be called "biblical this-worldliness" on the part of both Christians and Jews, a wonderful way of describing our common need for divine and sanctifying grace.

[1] Irving Greenberg, "The Relationship of Judaism and Christianity: Toward a New Organic Model," *Quarterly Review,* Winter 1984.

[2] Michael Kogan, "Toward Total Dialogue," *The National Dialogue Newsletter,* Winter 1990-1991; and "Toward a Jewish Theology of Christianity," *Journal of Ecumenical Studies,* Winter, 1995. (For more extensive discussions by Kogan and myself on the issues involved, see the *Journal of Ecumenical Studies,* Fall, 1989; Winter, 1992; Spring, 1993; Winter, 1995 and Spring, 1996).

[3] Roy Eckardt, "Reclaiming the Jesus of History," *Christology Today,* 1992, p. 211.

[4] Clemens Thoma, *A Christian Theology of Judaism,* Helga Croner, tr. and ed., (New York: Paulist Press, 1980), p. 135.

[5] Martin Buber, *Disputation and Dialogue: Readings in the Jewish Christian Encounter,* F. E. Talmage, ed., (New York: Ktav Publishing House, 1975), p. 282.

CHAPTER 12

Comparative Theology vs. Reactive Theology

JEWISH AND CHRISTIAN APPROACHES TO THE PRESENCE OF GOD

For centuries, Judaism and Christianity have existed in a basically adversarial relationship to each other. As a result, adherents of the two communities have often defined themselves, at least as far as some central tenets of their faith are concerned, in terms of contrasts *vis-á-vis* the other party.

The desire to accentuate differences rather than common perspectives has frequently led polemicists to bear false witness, either by caricaturing the other person's beliefs, sometimes to the point of defamation, or by presenting one's own tradition in the most favorable light, while emphasizing what are perceived to be vulnerabilities in the other's positions. For example, antinomian tendencies within Christianity were often motivated by a desire to attack Judaism's alleged inherent legalism. Jewish scholars, on the other hand, have tended to treat the church's christological and trinitarian tradition in terms of absolute antitheses.

In recent decades, some participants in the dialogue movement have sought to move away from polarization and such a reactive type of theology toward what is sometimes referred to as "comparative theology," which is more inclined to explore common grounds. To some degree their efforts have been successful. Concepts like Torah, covenant, and peoplehood have become more nuanced for many Christians. The question now being raised in what follows is this: Can we have more nuanced exchanges on christological and trinitarian themes as well, not for the sake of a false harmonization, but in an effort to achieve greater mutual understanding?

In Chapter 3, I referred to three Orthodox Jewish scholars in connection with a discussion of incarnational/christological questions. Professor Michael Wyschogrod gave us an example of his own move away from a reactive theological position when, in his book *The Body of Faith*, he described how, having freed himself from the need to be as different from Christians as possible, he was able to recognize incarnational motifs in Judaism. In other words, he came to an acknowledgment that Judaism's reaction to the church's Christology had led to an extreme position on the incorporeality of God, one that represented a distortion of Jewish tradition.

Reference was also made to Hebrew University professor David Flusser's thesis that the church's Christology has been influenced significantly by a Jewish theology of the hypostasis of God, and that this line of inquiry has not been sufficiently explored. Also, this position would seem to offer interesting prospects for a comparative theological analysis. More specifically, if the views of Wyschogrod and Flusser are taken together, might they open the door for a discussion on trinitarian modes of thought that is not conducted entirely in terms of polarization?

The following is intended as a tentative attempt to explore that question and to suggest a few affirmative answers, while realizing that this is a somewhat risky enterprise. Anyone who is not a Hebraic scholar (as this author certainly is not), well-versed in all aspects of Rabbinic Judaism, must necessarily feel like an amateur in dealing with Jewish sources. When dialogue enters into the profoundly theological issues between Christianity and Judaism, participants soon discover how difficult it is to gain even a measure of familiarity with, not to speak of expertise in, the authoritative sources of each other's faith.

By the same token, if dialogue is going to involve more than scholars treating each other to their latest academic treatises at conferences, exploratory questions from non-experts in certain technical fields should not just be tolerated, but welcomed. After all, if dialogue is about trust, it should also mean that people can take chances.

At first, Christian-Jewish differences focused on issues pertaining to Torah, but as the church's doctrinal positions developed, the Trinity became a matter of fierce disputes. Christian apologists were ever eager to find evidence of a full-fledged dogma of the Trinity in the Hebrew Scriptures. In fact, of course, this doctrine was formulated in the course of a long process of theological reflection and many internal ecclesiastical debates and conflicts about Gnostic heresies and dualistic (or even tritheistic) tendencies. The rabbis responded to all this by seeking to show that the very idea of a Trinity was diametrically opposed to biblical monotheism, with its fundamental confession of the oneness of God.

The arguments started with the very first words in Scripture: "In the beginning God created. . ." (*bereshith bara Elohim*–a singular verb with a plural noun) and the statement in Genesis 1:26: "Then God said, 'Let us make humans in our image. . .' " Christians were inclined to interpret the use of the plural *Elohim* instead of the singular *El* (or *Eloah*), not in the sense of a plurality of gods, but as an indication of multiform divine manifestations that reflect a pluriformity within the divine Mystery. Jewish interpreters, on the other hand, read the text either as a *pluralis majestatis* (the convention in which a monarch speaks of himself/herself in the plural) or as God addressing the heavenly council. In the latter case, Christians in turn wondered: must we presume that created beings functioned as co-creators whose image humans carry in conjunction with the divine image? It should also perhaps be mentioned that the use of the plural in the Hebrew text when referring to God is not always reflected in English translations (e.g., in both Joshua 24:1 and Jeremiah 10:10, the plural Hebrew *Elohim* is translated "God," not Gods).

Other texts favored by Christians have been those that contain the notion of "sonship." As an example, we might cite Psalm 2:7 ("You are my son; today I have begotten you"). This word "begotten" (generated) instead of "created" recurs, of course, in the later creeds of the church when referring to Christ the Son. When the Psalmist goes on to declare that this "son" will inherit the nations and possess the ends of the earth, Christians found that to be further confirmation that he was referring to a very unique "person," namely the coming Messiah. Daniel 7:13-14, with its reference to "one like a son of man" to whom was given everlasting dominion, and glory, and kingship and who would be served by all peoples and nations, also became a prominent passage in Christian trinitarian apologetics.

Threefold repetitions found in the Hebrew Scriptures also fascinated the defenders of trinitarian foreshadowings in Moses and the prophets. Most familiar has been the *trisagion*, "Holy, holy, holy" (Isaiah 6:3), but one could also mention texts like Psalm 29: ". . . the voice of the Lord . . . the voice of the Lord . . . the voice of the Lord" or Psalm 96: ". . . sing to the Lord . . . sing to the Lord . . . sing to the Lord." The threefold Aaronic blessing (Numbers 6:24-26) would be another illustration.

References to the Spirit of God, as in Psalm 51:11 ("do not take your holy spirit from me"), Psalm 139:7 ("Where can I go from your spirit?"), or Ezekiel 37:14 ("I will put my spirit within you, and you shall live"), have often been quoted in support of Christian pneumatology. The *Ruach Elohim* or *Ruach haKodesh* (the Holy Spirit) is interpreted in both Judaism and Christianity as the presence of divine power or the presence of God himself in power. The concept of the Spirit as "advocate" (Hebrew, *senegor*) can also be found in both traditions.

When Flusser referred to Judaism's theology of hypostasis, one assumes that he also had in mind such concepts as *Metatron*, *Memra*, and *Shekhinah*. Judaism is an historical religion *par excellence*. Its theology could be called a "theology of the presence of God." YHWH, the God of Israel, dwells with his people. The word *shekhinah* literally means "in-dwelling." The God of the covenant is confessed as the Creator of heaven and earth and the Lord of history, the "God who acts." Covenant came before Torah, but through Torah we know that the Holy One of Israel, who dwells in heavenly glory, is very near to those who call upon his name.

In John's Gospel, too, "the Word became flesh and dwelt among us. We have seen his glory, glory as of the only Son from the Father" (John 1:14). In the Hebrew Scriptures, "glory" represents the presence of God. Christian theology of the presence of God became Christ-centered, and Hebrew categories used to convey this message were often reinterpreted, at times radically so. But that does not necessarily preclude a common vision. For instance, in the book of Revelation the final eschatological vision is of God dwelling among his creatures, when death will be no more and the former things have passed away (Revelation 21:1ff.). In other words, the new creation, or the consummation of the kingdom of God, can be described as the presence of God in final and full redemptive power.

The question being raised here is not whether certain concepts in Judaism lead one directly to the Nicene Creed. They do not. Nor do we need to argue whether Christian apologetic literature has often contained overstatements and exaggerated claims about trinitarian "proofs." It has. The question raised is whether the early Jewish Christians and the later predominantly Gentile church, in order to express their incarnational/christological faith, drew on concepts and categories current in Judaism, while both faiths at the same time were influenced by Hellenistic sources.

The use of some categories in Christian doctrinal formation ought to be critically reexamined and perhaps questioned. But that is not our purpose here. The main purpose of this exercise in "comparative theology" is to inquire whether the oneness of God, as confessed in Judaism, in addition to precluding any form of polytheism, also excludes pluriform revelations of God indicating, in the words of Clemens Thoma, "a rich life within the Deity, various manners of God's efficacy outside of himself, and unfathomable dialectical and dialogical movements between the infinity of God and his efficacy in the world."[1] Furthermore, do not Jewish ideas of hypostasis and the Christian doctrine of the Trinity, each in their own way but still drawing on common sources of Hebrew spirituality, basically seek to deal with the same question: "How does the covenant God of Israel act redemptively among his people and in the history of the world?" And in doing so, have they not had to deal with quite similar problems?

The *Shema*, "Hear, O Israel, the Lord our God, the Lord is One," continues to resonate throughout the New Testament (Matthew 19:17; 23:9, Mark 12:29, John 17:3, Romans 3:30, James 2:19). It could hardly be expected that Jewish followers of Jesus would so soon abandon this most fundamental tenet of the tradition in which they had grown up.

They struggled, however, with the question of how the divine unity can be maintained while God's full revelation (presence) in Jesus and through the Holy Spirit is affirmed. No language is adequate to deal with the Mystery of mysteries. But both Judaism and Christianity profess to believe in divine creation and historical revelation, and, hence, issues pertaining to the relationship between God and the realms of creation and history are unavoidable. Terms like covenant, *Shekhinah*, incarnation, and kingdom of God are all a way of witnessing to the presence (immanence) of the One who is holy (transcendent). But, then, the question arises whether the revelation of God in pluriform manifestations reflects the divine "nature" or "being."

The angel of the Lord (*Malak* YHWH) is commonly portrayed as the "representative" of God. But, the text frequently seems to obscure the distinction between YHWH and *Malak* YHWH. In Genesis 31:13 the angel of God says to Jacob "I am the God of Bethel." Later, in Genesis 48, Jacob (Israel), while blessing Joseph, speaks about the God of his ancestors, the shepherd of his life, and in the same breath talks about "the angel who has redeemed me from all harm" (Genesis 48:15 ff.).

In his commentary on Genesis 18:14, referring to the "three men" who appear to Abraham, the great sage Abraham Ibn Ezra (12th century) wrote: "According to some these three men are YHWH himself. He is one and he is three, and these may not be separated."[2] This does not make him a believer in the dogma of the Trinity, but it seems to show a freedom of language in Jewish speculative thinking about God when the need is not felt to polemicize against Christian views.

Particularly interesting and frequently discussed passages are Exodus 3:2 ff., where the angel of the Lord appeared to Moses and, calling to him "out of the bush," declares "I am the God of your father, the God of Abraham, the God of Isaac, and the God of Jacob," and Exodus 23:21 where the people of Israel are told concerning the angel: "Be attentive to him and listen to his voice; do not rebel against him, for he will not pardon your transgression; for my name is in him."

Does not "the name" signify God's *being*? In the *Targum Onqelos* to Exodus, an Aramaic translation of the Bible, the sense of the Hebrew is reversed, because the author was afraid that the angel would be too closely identified with God. The text there reads: "Beware of him and listen to his *Memra* (word), do not refuse to listen to him, for he will not forgive your sins, because his *Memra* is in My Name."[3]

Rabbi Moses ben Nachman (13th century), in his commentary on Exodus 3:2 wrote: "Indeed, the angel mentioned here is the same as the redeeming angel of whom it is written: 'My Name is in his inner being,' and who said to Jacob, 'I am the God of Bethel.' It is he of whom we read here (Exodus 3:2): God called to him. He is called angel with respect to his rule of the world."[4]

In Rabbinic literature *Metatron* is apparently the most common term used for God's presence in the form of an angel. The *Metatron*, or "the Prince of the Countenance" (namely, the one who is very near to YHWH), is, as Gershom Scholem points out, not a "second deity" nor a "lesser YHWH," as some kabbalists would have it. The disputations around this concept, however, point to the fact that, in Judaism, too, speculation about the manner of God's presence could rather easily drift into dualistic modes of thinking.[5]

Can the *Metatron* be given a supernatural status and still be distinguished from YHWH's own being? The same question arose with respect to Christ's relationship to God the Father. There are echoes of the *Metatron* concept in New Testament texts that portray Jesus as seated or standing at the right hand of God and interceding for us (e.g. Matthew 26:64; Acts 7:55; Romans 8:34).

The concept of *Memra* (Aramaic for "word") was mentioned in passing in the quote above from the *Targum Onqelos*. Even a cursory reading of the *Targumim* will show that almost all divine appearances in the Hebrew Scriptures and virtually every act of God are attributed to the *Memra* and the Holy Spirit. This does not make a Christian theology of Word and Spirit. But neither does it take an excessive dose of Christian speculation to reinterpret the idea of God the Father, acting in unison with the *Memra* and the Holy Spirit, in terms of christological and trinitarian theology. It would at least seem that we are not dealing with antithetical thought worlds as both faiths seek to witness to God's historical revelation.

The creative Word of the Lord (*Dabar* YHWH) is alive and active; God's Word is deed. He speaks, and it is there. In the *Targum Pseudo-Jonathan* Genesis 1:1 is rendered: "From the beginning with wisdom the *Memra* of the Lord created and perfected the heavens and the earth . . ." The transcendent God makes himself known in the world through the *Memra*. When, as for instance in 1 Samuel 15:11, 35, God is portrayed as showing regret (or as repenting), the *Targum* text attributes this divine disposition to the *Memra*. At Sinai, Moses called on the name of the *Memra*. Sometimes, deliverance and atonement are described as the work of the *Memra*. For instance, in the *Isaiah Targum*, chapter 12:2 is rendered as follows: "Behold, in the *Memra* of the God of my salvation I trust, and will not be shaken . . . he has spoken by his *Memra*, and he has become for me a savior."[6]

The virtual hypostatization of wisdom, as we find it, for instance, in Proverbs 8:22-31, and especially in writings like the *Book of Wisdom*, must be considered in this same context. Again, it does not take too giant a leap to move from this thought world into the Johannine *Logos* passages or Philo's *logos* speculations, even though the inner meaning given to those concepts may be radically different. The unity, incorporeality, and simplicity of God are supreme concerns for Philo. But in his case, too, Hellenism has not totally conquered Hebraic thinking and hence, he cannot escape the idea of the "multiform name of God."[7] "In scripture," he tells us, "the term one, when applied to God, means only numerical unity. It is merely a denial of external plurality: in this case denial of polytheism."[8]

The mainstream of Christian theology during the early centuries of the church was also eager to avoid any suggestion of dualism or polytheism. True, Justin Martyr's idea of the *Logos* as "the second God" came dangerously close to falling into the same kind of dualism Scholem found in some of the kabbalists. But these were basically aberrations that were rejected when the church formulated its authoritative creeds.

The *Zohar*, a central work in kabbalistic literature, also struggles to find language with which to speak about God the Ineffable One, the *mysterium tremendem* whose being "lies beyond any speculation or even ecstatic comprehension,"[9] but who is also God the Creator, Maker of heaven and earth. The notion of *Ein-Sof* (the Infinite) represents a hypostatization of the hidden God (*deus absconditus* in later Christian theology), while the *Sefirot* represent the power of emanations which relate God to the creation; i.e., God as he *reveals himself* as present. According to Scholem, "most of the early kabbalists were . . . inclined to accept the view that the Sefirot were actually identical with God's substance or essence"[10] and that there was an "interchangeable identity of God with His Names or His Powers: 'He is they, and They are He.' "[11] In sum, "the emanation of the Sefirot is a process within God Himself."[12] For the uninitiated, this is a thought world which it is very difficult to enter into. But even an amateur in the field might find a certain fascination in such kabbalistic speculations about unity and pluriformity within the divine Being, the One (*Echad*) with three "Names." To say the least, it may seem suggestive to Christians who are struggling with trinitarian thought forms or who seek to engage in a comparative dialogical theology.

The church's theological journey from the Jerusalem Council (Acts 15) to the Council of Chalcedon (A.D. 451) was a tortuous, tumultuous, and often tragic one. It was marked by conflicts and divisions, imperial politics and persecutions. After the sad and bitter estrangement between church and synagogue, an increasingly gentilized Christianity with a de-Judaized theology faced persistent challenges from its pagan environment, often leading to accommodation for the sake of acceptance. In the end, especially with the conversion of Constantine, the church conquered the Empire, but only after the spirit of imperial power had invaded the church to a dangerous degree.

When faced with the assaults from Neoplatonism, Gnostic dualism, and Marcion's anti-Judaism, Christian apologists marshalled their arguments to defend the faith, but, unfortunately, they themselves had often lost touch with the foundational truths of the Hebrew Scriptures that had nourished the sacred Christian texts. Hence, the battle against heretical views, although fought valiantly and often brilliantly, was hampered by a failure to utilize the most effective weapon against the pagan mindset, namely, the Hebraic thought forms found in the law and the prophets.

The debates about Torah and Trinity have never fully come to rest, not between Christians and Jews and not among Christians themselves. Both issues fundamentally affect the way the church understands God's historical revelation, the destiny of Israel and the nations, and the mission of the church in the world.

A Christian comparative theology which, through dialogue, seeks to (re)discover common roots with Judaism, must do so, not for the sake of compromise–and certainly not for the sake of camaraderie–but in order to come to a deeper understanding of the gospel of the kingdom of God as it has been revealed in the Jewish Jesus. Our search should lead to new insights about the Johannine statement that salvation is from the Jews (John 4:22).

The original, unedited form of this chapter was first published in the Fall, 1994, issue of Pro Ecclesia. Reprinted by permission.

[1] Clemens Thoma, *A Christian Theology of Judaism*, p.13.

[2] J. Rottenberg, *De Triniteit in Israel's Godsbegrip* (Wageningen: Veenman, 1939), p. 64.

[3] Cf. *The Aramaic Bible*, by Bernard Grossfeld, Vol. 7 (Wilmington: Michael Glazier, Inc., 1988), p. 69.

[4] Rottenberg, p. 70f.

[5] Cf. Gershom G. Scholem, *Kabbalah* (New York: The New York Times Book Co., 1974), p. 377ff.

[6] Bruce D. Chilton, *The Aramaic Bible*, Vol. 2 (Wilmington: Michael Glazier, Inc., 1987), p. 29.

[7] Cf. Harry Austryn Wolfson, *Philo*, Vol. II (Cambridge: Harvard University Press, 1947), p. 127.

[8] *Ibid.*, p. 98.

[9] Scholem, p. 88.

[10] *Ibid.*, p. 107.

[11] *Ibid.*, p. 103f.

[12] *Ibid.*, p. 98.

CHAPTER 13

Law and Sin in Judaism and Christianity

Years ago, John Shelby Spong, now a retired Episcopal bishop, and Jack Daniel Spiro, a Jewish rabbi, published a book containing the text of actual exchanges between them and the congregations they were serving in Richmond, Virginia. When they came to talk about their understanding of sin and the function of law in the religious life, Spong made the interesting suggestion that it would perhaps be on this point, even more than on Christology, that Jews and Christians today would find their greatest diversity of views. "The way each of us defines sin," he stated, "grows out of our particular understanding of humanity." Earlier he had observed that "this becomes such a vital question because the way we understand sin determines the way we will both understand savior."[1]

Of course, Christian–and particularly Pauline–interpretations of Jesus (not to mention the development of trinitarian theology in subsequent centuries) remain an area of crucial differences. H. J. Schoeps maintained that Paul's Christology was "the radically un-Jewish element" in his thought. More recently, David Flusser, while holding that "Christian teaching about the Father and the Son departs from its Jewish premises," has also stated that "the most important motifs in the church's conception of Christ already existed independently in pre-Christian Judaism." In short, he denies that the New Testament Christology was a pagan invention of Hellenistic Christian communities. The Christian confession of Jesus as Lord perhaps remains the most fundamental issue that divides Judaism and Christianity, but increasingly sophisticated research into ancient sources is providing us with a better basis for discussion.

However that may be, Spong's focus on anthropology offers fruitful possibilities for Christian-Jewish dialogue. I propose to approach that issue from the perspective of law and sin. It is the better part of wisdom to proceed with caution through this veritable minefield of misconceptions and misrepresentations, but the issues here are so central to our mutual faiths that we must take our chances. Needless to say, the limited scope of a chapter requires that this extremely complex topic be treated in a somewhat summary fashion.

"The law of the Lord is perfect, reviving the soul; the testimony of the Lord is sure, making wise the simple; the precepts of the Lord are right, rejoicing the heart . . ." (Psalm 19:7-8).

During public worship, Christians regularly recite the Psalms, which emphasize delight in the law of the Lord and the desire to be taught the divine statutes and commandments. However, most Christians find it extremely difficult to understand that such sentiments are still part of a living Jewish tradition. The reason is that Christians have come to equate Judaism with dry and dreary legalism, not rejoicing in laws and precepts.

TORAH IN THE HEBREW SCRIPTURES

In the Hebrew Scriptures–referred to among Christians as the Old Testament–Torah is the "way of life" in the profoundest sense of the word. When Moses conveys the words of the law to Israel, the people are urged to take them to heart, because "it is no trifle for you, but it is your life . . ." (Deuteronomy 32:47). In Leviticus, the admonition is put this way: "You shall . . . keep my statutes and my ordinances, by doing which a man shall live: I am the Lord" (18:5).

According to Leo Baeck, "Torah is an untranslatable word. It is untranslatable because no other people, no other cultural or language group has achieved an idea of its own like the one which found expression in the word 'Torah.' "[2] But translated it was. The Septuagint, the Greek translation of the Hebrew Bible, used *nomos,* "law," for "Torah," a rendering which has created numerous misunderstandings, aggravated when the biblical message entered Roman culture with its ideas of legal order.

Torah actually means "teaching," "instruction," and "guidance," but none of these words alone, nor all of them together, exhaust its meaning, because in the last analysis, "Torah" refers to God's own gracious and righteous presence. Laws, statutes, and precepts are part of Torah, but they are not its essence. Torah must be primarily understood in dynamic terms, not as a set of legal rules.

Israel received Torah from YHWH who reveals his righteousness and who seeks to establish his justice on the earth. He is the God of the covenant, the one who says, "I shall be your God and you shall be my people" (Jeremiah 7:23; 31:33). The law of the Lord is the book of the covenant (Exodus 24:7) and the Ten Commandments are called "the words of the covenant" (Exodus 34:28). In short, God's law is to be received as a gift of grace.

Torah offers a liturgy of life; it calls to obedience. Yet, as the Hebrew Scriptures show so well, one can stick to the letter of the law without obeying God. The danger is always great that we will focus on the laws and forget the Lawgiver. The prophetic cry "Their hearts are far from me" (Isaiah 29:13) expresses the pathos of such a situation; hence the prophets' critique of religious observances and the call for a "circumcision of the heart": "And the Lord your God will circumcise your heart and the heart of your offspring, so that you will love the Lord your God with all your heart and with all your soul, that you may live" (Deuteronomy 30:6). In the final analysis, the law is fulfilled in love.

Torah provides an ordering of life and thus it contributes to its livability. It is a dynamic reality, and through rabbinical interpretation it has found a continuing development in the Talmud and post-Talmudic tradition. For Judaism, the priority lies in *halachah*–the precepts that produce a "way of life" which leads to sanctification–not in dogma. Does such an approach not pose the threat of legalism? That temptation is never absent, not even from the most noble of human spiritual aspirations. We need divine guidance. As it says in the words of the daily morning prayer: "Blessed is our God, who has created us for his glory and has separated us from them that go astray, and has given us the Torah and thus planted everlasting life in our midst. May we open our hearts unto his Torah."

Torah in the Apostolic Scriptures

One could cite a whole series of texts to show that many of these themes reappear in the New Testament. "The law," Paul proclaims, is the law of God, and as such, it "is holy, and the commandment is holy and just and good" (Romans 7:12). The true intention of the commandment is to offer life (vs. 10). "I delight in the law of God, in my inmost self," he declares (vs. 22). Confession without commitment, and faith without obedience, are sham. It is not enough to say "Lord, Lord . . ."; the will of the Father must be done (Matthew 7:21). Those who profess to know God but deny him by their deeds are called "detestable, disobedient, unfit for any good deed" (Titus 1:16).

According to Romans 2:13, "it is not the hearers of the law who are righteous before God, but the doers of the law who will be justified." In the last judgment the Lord "will render to every man according to his works," and it is emphasized that this applies to both Jews and Gentiles (Romans 2:6ff.); however, when it comes to doing the law, "circumcision of the heart" is essential (vv. 25ff.).

Still, when all the parallels have been pointed out, it remains clear that the New Testament confronts us with a radically new dimension, which has far-reaching implications for the question of law and sin. We refer, of course, to Jesus, whom the church confesses to be the Christ who has fulfilled the law and thus revealed the divine triumph over the power of sin. Most scholars, both Jewish and Christian, agree that Jesus was a faithful observer of the law of Moses. As Flusser points out, there were tensions between him and the local "orthodoxy" in Galilean villages, but that kind of tension is found in all religious communities. Jesus had his arguments with certain Pharisees, but in that, he was very much a child of his time and a participant in the internal polemics of contemporary Jewish society. Flusser states that all the motifs of Jesus' famous invective against the Pharisees in Matthew 23 can be found in rabbinical literature.

PAUL'S VIEWS ON TORAH AND SIN

The real debate usually focuses on Paul and his interpretations of law and sin. The arguments have raged for centuries, not only between Christians and Jews, but also among Christians themselves. Two elements seem crucial in Paul's position: (1) his confession of God's saving act in Christ, who had fulfilled the law, and (2) his belief that he was called to be an apostle to the Gentiles and the impact of a growing Gentile participation in the life of the earliest Jewish-Christian community. The latter factor led to a variety of tensions, not only between Judaism and Christianity, but also between Jewish Christians and Gentile Christians. Those tensions have greatly affected later developments, both in theology and in Christian-Jewish relations. The Dutch scholar Willem Zuidema concludes: "The tragedy of Paul is that a Gentile Christian church, which came into being because he wanted to make room for non-Jewish participation in the messianic community, has severed itself from its Jewish background and has subsequently appropriated Paul (i.e., his letters) for the purpose of its own theology."[3]

Does that absolve Paul too easily? I think not. Paul's belief in God's historical act of fulfillment in Jesus led him to raise radical questions about the "fulfillability" of the law. Those questions sometimes took the form of a critique of how the law functioned in the lives of those who professed to be its adherents. Similar themes can be found in prophetic criticism. While Paul's "new eon" perspective caused him often to draw very sharp contrasts, he never ceased to affirm the divine claims of the law. As a matter of fact, even his most radical negations are charged with this basic affirmation.

Paul believed that, in Jesus the Christ, the true, faithful, and obedient covenant-partner had appeared. In him, God had resolved the requirement that the whole law must be fulfilled in order for the righteousness of God to be revealed on the earth (Galatians 5:3). In light of God's act of fulfillment in Jesus, Paul condemned not the doing of the law, but human reliance on "works of the law," and boasting in one's own righteousness (Galatians 3:10; Romans 2:17). In light of Christ's fulfillment of the law and the "new eon" situation it had created, Paul saw all talk about human "fulfillability" as a form of self-righteousness which refused to acknowledge the revelation of God's righteousness in Jesus' obedience.

However, this does not mean that the righteousness/justice of God need no longer be manifested on the earth through human service. Quite the opposite. The Holy Spirit has been given precisely in order for that to happen. Romans 8 is most revealing in this respect. God has done what we, because of our sinful nature, could not do. He acted in Christ, "in order that the just requirement of the law might be fulfilled in us, who walk not according to the flesh but according to the Spirit" (8:4; cf. Ephesians 2:8-10).

Paul's understanding of the law must be seen in terms of his views on redemptive history rather than in terns of his alleged guilt complexes. Krister Stendahl has offered a severe criticism of the psychologizing tendencies of Christian theologians, especially when it comes to interpreting Paul. He has referred to "the introspective conscience of the West" as a "plague" and offers New Testament evidence for what he considers to be Paul's "robust conscience."[4]

Too often Paul has been interpreted from the perspective of Luther's personal struggle and theology. The function of the law is frequently seen exclusively as convincing humanity of sin (*lex semper accusat*). Classical dogmatics, with its "threefold use of the law," offers a broader perspective. The law was defined as (1) pedagogical (to make us know our misery), (2) didactic (as a rule of gratitude and life), and (3) political or civil (as a basis for the ordering of society). Such an approach, which became predominant in Reformed theology, is hardly an invitation to antinomianism!

The law in the biblical sense is not a formal set of rules. It is the law of the kingdom of God and embodies his righteousness. He seeks to establish his order of divine justice on the earth, the order of Torah, which is something quite different from the *lex Romana*. The doctrine of the fulfillment of the law in Christ in no way reduces the believer's calling to serve the kingdom nor the role of God's law in the sanctification of life on the earth.

There is a profound paradoxical element in all this. The confession of the continued validity of God's law should not be interpreted as meaning that nothing has changed. The dynamic character of the law finds its ultimate source in God's redemptive presence; he does something with his law. For instance, according to the Christian faith, he fulfilled it in Christ's sacrifice of love.

When the Lord of history is redemptively present in our midst, things do not stay the same. However, the eschatological reality that remains is that his righteousness and justice shall be established on the earth. According to Christian confession, the cultic, moral, and juridical dimensions of the law have found embodiment in the life and death of Christ.

On the one hand, the law is given into human hands in order that

God's will may be done on the earth: the God of the Bible enters into covenant with his people. On the other hand, the law proves more than we can handle. As a matter of fact, precisely when we start "handling" the law as if it were ours, we refuse to let God's righteousness rule in our midst, and the law of God is turned into a law of sin. Thus, the cultus, our moral aspirations, and our attempts to establish an order of justice in the world frequently become the very occasion for disobedience. However, the New Testament claims God himself has acted in order that his righteousness and justice may find final embodiment in the kingdom of God.

H. J. Schoeps concluded a discussion on Paul's teaching about the law with the following statement: "Because Paul had lost all understanding of the character of the Hebraic *berith* as a partnership involving mutual obligations, he failed to grasp the inner meaning of the Mosaic law, namely, that it is an instrument by which the covenant is realized,"[5] According to Schoeps, the Jews have never despaired about the "fulfillability" of the law. My thesis is that Paul understood the mutuality of the covenant full well, but that his perception of Jesus' role in the realization (fulfillment) of the covenant caused him to question severely the ability of any human being to fulfill the whole law. While he retained the notion that we are called to be "God's co-workers" (1 Corinthians 3:9), the concept became incorporated into a radical theology of grace.

JUDAISM AND TORAH

Leo Baeck has referred to Judaism as "the religion of ethical optimism" and the Dutch scholar K. H. Miskotte has spoken of "an untamable optimism" in the predominant Jewish view of the human task to bring the creation to its fruition. In the continued dialogue on these issues, it is of the utmost importance that we avoid facile and false antitheses, for instance, by setting one-sided descriptions of "Jewish optimism" over against "Christian pessimism," or by contrasting the alleged legalism of Judaism with the grace-orientation of Christianity.

As Charlotte Klein has shown so clearly in her excellent study, *Anti-Judaism in Christian Theology,*[6] Christian scholars have for years been busily engaged in footnoting their books with the biased opinions contained in a number of "standard works" that were mostly based on secondary sources. In most Christian seminaries, students are taught a caricature of what so-called "late Judaism" in the time of Christ was all about and receive virtually no instruction whatever in contemporary Judaism. In many Christian studies, Judaism, and particularly the Talmudic tradition, are portrayed as representing casuistry, sophistry, and legalistic piety. Genuine Jewish spirituality is rarely mentioned. Such misrepresentations have permeated the whole Christian educational system and have made fruitful conversations on the issues that divide us very difficult.

The relationship between covenant law and grace is regularly expressed in the liturgy of the synagogue: "With everlasting love hast Thou loved the house of Israel; Thou hast revealed to us a law and commandments, statutes and judgment. . . . They are our life and the measure of our days."

At the same time, Judaism is deeply aware of the *yetzer ha-ra,* the evil urge which operates within the human heart and makes our lives the scene of a continual moral struggle. Yet, I must confess that when I read descriptions of the human being as God's partner, the agent called upon to share in the completion of divine creation, whose task it is to make the world worthy of redemption through his or her *mitzvot* (deeds in accordance with God's will), I am both fascinated and puzzled by what seems to me an incredible confidence in human nature. Here, differences in accent reach a point where we must indeed speak of substantial differences in basic perspective.

Judaism recognizes that human beings fail and commit sins, while the Christian faith has a sense of what the New Testament calls "the power of sin," which corrupts even the best of human aspirations and endeavors–especially the best ones, such as the search to attain righteousness before God. According to Christian teaching, this power is more than a personal impulse to do evil; it represents the demonic potentials that are operative in history and often become embodied in supra-individual realities such as the structures of society.

In Judaism, the concept of covenant relationship and divine-human partnership often implies a mutuality which, to the Christian, almost seems to amount to mutual dependence. Or, to say it differently, Judaism appears to accept a concept of human freedom which seems to most Christians contrary to both the Old and the New Testament. An illustration can be found in the following statement by Abraham Heschel: "There is a partnership of God and man. God needs our help. I would define man as a divine need. God is in need of man. In history, He cannot do the job alone. . . . And the whole hope of messianic redemption depends on God and on man. We must help him. And by each deed we carry out, we either retard or accelerate the coming of redemption. Our role in history is tremendous. I mean, our human role."[7]

On the other hand, Arthur A. Cohen sees the need for a profound correction of the anthropology of Christianity, which, according to him, may have been appropriate to the period immediately succeeding the death of Jesus, but "is hopeless for a humanity that has none of the chiliastic opportunities of the monk, solitary, or ascetic in which to withdraw, but must–like the Jew–maintain the whole of the religious life while earning bread, raising a family, building a home, and waiting for the Messiah."[8] In short, he raises the question whether Christian anthropology is relevant for a responsible existence in modern society.

I hesitate to use the expression, but Jewish faith contains a "heroic" element which Christians find hard to reconcile with their perception of historical realities. On the other hand, it seems to me that an understanding of the Jewish historical experience, and the whole of *halachic* tradition in it, could immensely enrich and broaden Christians' perception of their calling to live in the world as God's covenant partners. There is a paradox here, but also a promise, in genuine Christian-Jewish encounter. Because the truth is that, while the church was eagerly pointing its finger at "Jewish legalism," its own life was often paralyzed by a dismal legalism on the one hand and "cheap grace" on the other. In short, Christians, while witnessing to the fulfillment of the law in Jesus Christ, must confess that they have often used attacks on Jews and Judaism as a convenient way of avoiding the painful process of facing themselves and their failure to manifest the love which they confess to have received from Christ.

The Johannine admonition seems an appropriate conclusion: "This is the love of God, that we keep his commandments. . . . let us not love in word or speech but in deed and in truth" (1 John 5:3; 3:18).

The original, unedited form of this chapter was first published in the November, 1979, issue of the Reformed Journal. Reprinted by permission.

[1] John Shelby Spong and Jack Daniel Spiro, *Dialogue: In Search of Jewish-Christian Understanding* (New York: Seabury, 1975), pp. 75, 63.

[2] Leo Baeck, *This People Israel, the Meaning of Jewish Existence* (New York: Holt, Rinehart and Winston, 1965), p. 194.

[3] Willem Zuidema, *God's Partner, an Encounter with Judaism* (London: SCM Press, 1987), p. 55

[4] Krister Stendahl, *Paul Among Jews and Gentiles, and Other Essays* (Augsburg: Fortress Press, 1977), pp. 78f.

[5] H.J Schoeps, *Paul: The Theology of the Apostle* (Philadelphia: The Westminster Press, 1961), p. 218.

[6] Charlotte Klein, *Anti-Judaism in Christian Theology* (Philadelphia: Fortress Press, 1978).

[7] Abraham Heschel, cited in Frederick Holmgren, in *The God Who Cares: A Christian Looks at Judaism* (Atlanta: John Knox Press, 1979), p. 117.

[8] Arthur A. Cohen, *The Myth of the Judeo-Christian Tradition* (New York: Harper & Row, 1969), p. 51.

CHAPTER 14

Apocalypse Now and Then Again

I do not wish to exaggerate the ecumenical quality of life among Christian supporters of Israel nor the number of people who find bonds of Christian unity through a common interest in demonstrating solidarity with the Jewish people and the State of Israel. Still, I have seen trust relationships develop among persons who would not likely have come to know one another had it not been for a common interest in "Jewish issues," some of which they recognized as rooted in Christian unfaithfulness to the basic tenets, not only of faith, but of common decency as well. In facing such issues together, Christians have sometimes been moved to reevaluate the importance of differences between them, as well as the elements of faith they hold in common.

The sharpest differences among Christian supporters of Israel are to be found in the area of eschatology. People have come to very diverse interpretations of the biblical vision of the future, particularly the more apocalyptic passages in the Bible. But, as was often the case as well when Protestants and Catholics did not talk with each other, theological ideas are usually not the only or primary cause of separation. Cultural and educational factors tend to play an important role as well, as for example, different forms of spirituality or even a different ethos about such things as a glass of sherry before dinner.

I owe a debt of gratitude to evangelicals who, over the past years, have broadened and deepened my sense of the catholicity of the Christian faith, even though they themselves might avoid that term. The Genesis story suggests that it is precisely through the otherness of the other that mutual enrichment is found (male and female the Lord created them!). But, in daily life, the fear of diversity can be very real, even among members of the various brands of Christianity. In the New Testament, on the other hand, variety is frequently mentioned as a major characteristic of the working of the Holy Spirit.

Before I sound overly romantic about my experiences, I should emphasize that I have never thought very highly of an ecumenicity of the backslapping kind. Honest disagreements and critiques should not be silenced for the sake of ecumenical alliances in support of Israel or

any other cause. As I have become better acquainted with premillenialist/
dispensationalist circles, there are elements in their life and faith that I
have learned to appreciate. In some cases, however, I have also experienced a growing concern about possible excesses, especially among adherents of a highly apocalyptic theology.

A major source of criticism and controversy, with respect to the
premillenialist/dispensationalist movement, has to do with its so-called
"Armageddon Theology." Many Jews distrust the apocalyptic scenarios
of Christian dispensationalists because of the descriptions they contain
of future destruction that will be visited upon Israel, even though divine
intervention is expected to provide a last-minute victory of miraculous
proportions. Furthermore, the fact that the final deliverance implies
the conversion of a major "remnant" of the Jewish people to Jesus as
Messiah makes the scheme even less attractive for most Jews.

Others are concerned that an apocalypticism, which proclaims that
the "true believers" will be "raptured" out of this world before disaster
strikes, is not conducive to developing a sense of social responsibility.
This is a frequent charge against premillenialists, that they tend to encourage escapist attitudes. In some cases, that is no doubt true. On the
other hand, history shows that an intense futurism can also become the
strong motivating drive to "redeem the time" that is still available and,
thus, lead to activism.

For me, personally, the problem is not with millenialist views *per
se*, nor with apocalyptic visions. These seem to be valid aspects of the
biblical message, which deserve our consideration. Furthermore, apocalyptic imagery has been an "in thing," not only among the Religious
Right but among the radical Christian Left as well. A glance through
issues of the radical evangelical magazine *Sojourners* yields plenty of examples of apocalyptic language, as will literature issued by certain
anti-nuclear and environmental groups. Apocalypticism seems to fit
well with the mood of our day and the Left as well as the Right,
each in their own way, uses the fear in the "politics of doom" as an
important motivating force.

Premillenialists, it is sometimes claimed, lack a proper dose of fear
because of their views on ultimate divine intervention. Ironically enough,
on some topics, certain liberal writers would like to see more effective
hellfire preaching. "While it is right to ground peacemaking efforts on
faith and Scripture," wrote Paul Johnson, "it seems highly inappropriate to minimize the fear that people do and should have over what nuclear
weapons can do."[1] In other words, faith is fine, but let's keep the fires of
fear burning as well.

By their very nature, apocalyptic writings tend to have an "out
there" quality to them. They are written, if not out of a sense of panic,
certainly from a sense of extremity and semi-finality, a feeling that the

world, inflicted with a terminal illness, has fallen into a measure of decay that virtually puts it beyond human redemption. Direct and dramatic divine intervention is our only hope. Cataclysmic events lie ahead, and those who feel called upon to announce that kind of future are inclined to speak in high-pitched voices. Hence, the language of apocalypticism is usually not only very vivid and symbolic but often sensationalist as well.

It is easy to get carried away when one is enraptured by that sort of spirit. Some obviously do. I see a danger when Christians become too preoccupied with the apocalyptic segments of the Bible. How pervasive should that perspective be in Christian preaching and teaching? Some ignore it altogether; others seem to make it the sum total of the biblical message. I prefer to see the apocalyptical perspective balanced by other eschatological categories in the Bible, like the emphasis on the kingdom of God found in all sections of the Hebrew and Christian Scriptures. The hope of such a kingdom perspective seems less in a hurry and tends to nurture greater openness to ongoing historical developments.

Karl Barth said that one should do theology with the Bible in one hand and the daily newspaper in the other. Premillenialists often seem to live like that. The headlines in the daily paper become incorporated into the message from the pulpit. But one can get carried away by current events. Enthusiasm sometimes leads to unfortunate carelessness.

Similar questions are being raised by people within premillenialist circles as well. For instance, Douglas Shearer published a document entitled "The Messianic Scenario." He himself believes that "in all likelihood its consummation will occur during our lifetime."[2] He objects, however, to an "emotional appeal that verges on an uncontrolled sensationalism," which is sometimes attached to basic premillenialist doctrine. He complains about the "paperback dilettantes" or "army of self-proclaimed decoders and Christian cryptologists" who hold their audiences in an atmosphere of endless hype and "frivolous debates, which seem to be forever centered upon the meaning of '666,' the legitimacy of Israeli invasions, the reestablishment of blood sacrifices, the personality of Ariel Sharon, etc."[3]

These observations express sentiments that are shared by many persons observing the movement from the outside. One wonders what to make of the excessive speculations, the forced and seemingly farfetched interpretations of biblical texts and the predictions about imminent end-time events which are revised or simply ignored and then soon replaced by new predictions as history refuses to follow the prescribed scenario. To some, it appears like an endless script about *Apocalypse Now*, but no, not yet, but then again and again and again. True, some prophecy teachers carefully avoid the trap of date-setting. However, much of the literature in the field relates historical events and figures to biblical texts in ways that seem to feed on and then, in turn, further nurture a ferocious appetite for sensationalism and new prophecy thrills.

No text is quoted more frequently in pro-Israel fundamentalist circles than Genesis 12:3: "I will bless them that bless thee, and curse him that curseth thee. . . ." I personally do not find it farfetched when people hold the view that those words have found repeated confirmation in Israel's history. But the way some people apply the text in the context of contemporary events can surely tax one's credulity.

Now, one does not need to be a dispensationalist to believe that the Holy Spirit is very much alive and operative in history today. I too believe in divine presence and guidance. Far be it from me to deny *ipso facto* the validity of mystical urgings or the fact that the power of God moves people to respond in faithful obedience. What makes me suspicious, however, is all that cheerful chuminess in the walk of mortals with the Sovereign Lord of history, the familiarity that seems to lack a sense of mystery, the manipulative potentials when people too easily claim to have received instructions from the Lord.

Again, when someone tells me "God has led me to do so and so," I am quite willing to listen. There is a simplicity and lack of self-consciousness in some people's walk with God that strikes me as genuine, sometimes even enchanting. I have little desire to show hyper-sophistication and skepticism in the presence of those who seek with intensity to be instruments of the Spirit. But my attitude changes when people write letters assuring me and many others that they have received a mandate from the Lord that they are prepared to obey if only the person receiving the mailing will pay. As the Roman saying goes, "Corruption of the best is the worst." Is it not one of the worst corruptions of the best impulses of human spirituality when pious language is used for purposes that have at least the appearance of exploitation about them?

Finally, the God-told-me-so game can be played by both sides in a dispute. And that is precisely what is happening in fundamentalist circles today. One leading charismatic figure is a foe of all evangelical talk about the eternal covenant with Israel, and he preaches supersessionism with a vengeance. Describing TV evangelists who urge their audiences to "bless Israel" as deceivers of Christ's flock, he views their corrupting influence in the church as a major cause for the delay of Christ's return. How does he know? The Lord Jesus told his sister![4] According to this view, Christians have no business blessing Israel, "a nation that has rejected Christ"; our only task is to preach salvation to the Jews.

On the other extreme of the apocalyptic spectrum is theological reconstructionism. There are theological reconstructionists in liberal church circles; however, it is not generally recognized that a Reconstructionist Movement is going on within fundamentalist circles as well. But the goal here is to restore supersessionism, not to overcome it. We hear about "new wave theologies." One aspect of the movement is so-called "dominion theology," which is not only supersessionist *vis-à-vis* Jews and Judaism, but also triumphalistic in the social-political realm. These people reject premillenialism as escapist and as lacking a social agenda. In its stead, they advocate a postmillenialist position; i.e., the view that Christ will return after the millenium, brought about by the progressive triumph of Christ's people in the areas of politics, law, education, and culture in general.

Both the Jewish and Christian communities are extremely complex, filled with internal dynamics that must be understood by those who wish to engage in interfaith activities. Generalizations are not very helpful in dealing with the issues. Alliances based on naive stereotypes that are devoid of a sense of nuances usually end in disillusion. On the other hand, a refusal to cooperate on issues that involve common interests because of disagreements on other matters, while appearing noble, can involve a naiveté of its own.

It is, of course, true that Israel is only one item on the agenda of interfaith relationships. Most alliances that involve interfaith issues are of a somewhat limited scope, and both the potentials and the problems that such ventures entail will vary from group to group. I have attended meetings between Orthodox rabbis and fundamentalist Christians. They found common interests in such areas as homosexuality, government subsidies to private schools and, of course, Israel. I have also attended meetings between evangelical Christians and Reform rabbis. They talked about the clear distinction that is made in dispensationalist theology between the church and Israel, about the eternally valid covenant between God and Jewish people and, of course, Israel. I have been part of National and World Council of Churches dialogues with Jewish leaders, and in that case, the dynamic was different again: considerable agreement on social and church-state issues, and considerably more discomfort when questions pertaining to Israel come up.

In the midst of all the soap operas and side shows going on in the religious communities, it may be easy to shrug one's shoulders and forget about it all, including the fact that Israel's future security may well, in large measure, depend on the broadest possible support among various constituency groups in the United States. Certainly, in that context, the various Christian groups are not a minor factor.

So, my own feeling is that a healthy dose of skepticism in all such interfaith efforts will do no harm. That is, unless it leads to a kind of isolationism which, I believe, none of us can afford. Least of all, Israel, whose enemies have always put great hope in the idea that in a world full of gruesome tyrannies, they might yet succeed in singling out Israel as the one country that should be declared an outcast among what is euphemistically called the "family of nations." To friends of Israel, that ought to be a concern of perhaps not apocalyptic, but, nevertheless, frightening proportions.

The road of interfaith alliances will never be easy. It requires a good deal of patience, understanding, honest confrontation and, hopefully, a touch of humor. Rubem Alves' statement, "humor keeps hope alive," applies even, I would say, in an apocalyptic age and in a world where we religious people do some strange things.

[1] Paul Johnson, *Christian Century*, December 21, 1983.
[2] Douglas Shearer, "The Messianic Scenario," 1982.
[3] *Ibid.*
[4] Earl Paulk, *To Whom is God Betrothed: Examining the Biblical Basis for the Support of National Israel*, (Decatur GA: K Dimension Publishers, 1985), p. 2.

DIALOGUE AND MISSION

CHAPTER 15

Witness in Christian-Jewish Relations

The question of witness in relationship to the Christian-Jewish dialogue has long been a difficult and often contentious issue. As the dialogue has emerged, however, even this important issue has been opened for discussion between Christians and Jews. In the unfolding dialogue, some important facts have emerged.

I. There is a growing biblical/theological interest among mainline Christian circles in the question of the church and the Jewish people.

This represents a significant change in outlook. For many years, the question of the people of Israel in the light of biblical revelation has occupied a central place mainly in the more speculative aspects of the sectarian theologies. For instance, it has always been a favored subject among millennial theorists. Helga Croner's book, *Stepping Stones to Further Jewish-Christian Relations*, contains a collection of both Catholic and Protestant documents dealing with the issue, which give clear evidence that the topic has become of great interest in broader circles.[1]

Three themes receive particular prominence in these recent developments:

1. God's promises to the people of Israel are irrevocable (Romans 11:29). The apostle Paul, therefore, strongly affirmed the continued validity of God's covenant with his chosen people. Hence, in our encounter with the Jewish people, we come face-to-face with the sovereignty of divine love, often an offensive notion for moralistic Christian hearts and minds. One of the great ironies of Christian history is that those who claim grace as the sole basis for their salvation have found it so difficult to accept "the permanent vocation of the Jewish people."

2. The church has not replaced Israel. Rather, it consists of those people among the Gentiles who have become incorporated into the covenant community of Israel. The idea that the church has superseded the people of Israel, who no longer play a role in God's dealings with the world, must, therefore, be rejected as the worst kind of Christian triumphalism. As Krister Stendahl and others have clearly shown, the whole theory of the church being the "New Israel" is based on a wrong reading of Galatians 6:16, the text most frequently used as the basis for

such an interpretation.

Christian-Jewish polemics has often posed dichotomies where it should have stressed affinities. For instance, those who portray Judaism as a religion of law in contrast with Christianity as a religion of grace, forget that the Jewish Scriptures are filled with the message of divine love and mercy. Also, those who set the New Testament emphasis on fulfillment over against the Old Testament promises forget that Christians, too, continue to live by the promises of God. A Christian church that boastfully claims it has replaced Israel robs itself of contact with the very roots of its tradition. As triumphalism turned into anti-Judaism, the overheated language of some of the intra-Jewish disputes found in parts of the New Testament was frequently used for the demonic purpose of threatening the very existence of the Jewish people. Thus, the foundation was laid for the tragedy of pogroms and Holocaust.

3. The relationship between the church and the Jewish people must be approached from an ecumenical rather than a missionary perspective. In other words, the estrangement between the older and the younger brother in the one-covenant household is the first and most fundamental schism with which the church must come to terms.

Jürgen Moltmann put it this way: "Just as God is one, so His people are also one. Ultimately, the ecumenical movement and ecumenical thinking always come back to the first schism, the one from which non-Jewish Christianity developed, i.e., the separation of the Church and Israel. This is where schismatic thinking began, and this is where it must finally end. In Jesus Christ, the Jew, it is not only the true God and the true man who looks at us non-Jewish Christians, but also Israel. Through him, we perceive Israel and are linked with Israel, because, through him, the promises of the God of Abraham, Isaac and Jacob come down to us; the ecumenical movement will not find its completion without Israel."[2]

II. The confessional Christian stance, which views the Jewish people in terms of the continuing covenant, is still very much a minority position.

In other words, while a book like *Stepping Stones* gives one cause for rejoicing, because it shows that progress is being made, it also makes one aware of the fact that the churches have a long way to go before those views are even seriously considered among large numbers of their members. As a matter of fact, it has at times proven to be very difficult to get an ecumenical body to discuss documents on Christian-Jewish relations that were issued in its own name. As a result, in broad Christian circles, myths and misconceptions about Judaism continue to abound.

There are many reasons why the "new theology" (which, in fact, is quite old) has had a difficult time taking hold.

1. There is a problem inherent in the concept of historical revelation that is part of every biblical theology of Israel. It all has to do with

contextualization, namely, the biblical claim that revelation has taken place in the context of Israel's life and history. That means that, in order to learn to "spell the Name," we must enter into that story and history. This is a very difficult idea to accept for the "natural mind," particularly one that has been molded by the Hellenistic tradition. It is a problem peculiar to the knowledge of "the God of Abraham, Isaac, and Jacob," one that can usually be avoided when dealing with "the God of the philosophers."

The idea of historical revelation has its built-in "offense," what some decades ago used to be referred to as the "scandal of particularity." We much prefer to encounter God in "pure reason" or in "deep feelings." Revelation in historical context is hard to accept; even more so the claim that the context is a Hebrew one.

2. Then there are the problems relative to a certain christological perspective. Some theologies interpret the New Testament witness concerning the finality of Christ and the fulfillment that has come through him in a way that precludes the notion of a continued theological relevance of the Jewish people. Israel is seen as having played its role in the preparatory stage: since Christ has come, that function is no longer needed. Someone has used the imagery of the spaceship that, after it has been successfully launched, drops its first-stage rockets.

On the other side are the advocates of an "unfulfilled messianism," who argue that any theology of fulfillment constitutes an illegitimate historicizing of the eschatological. The kingdom of God is a future reality, and no claims of fulfillment in Christ should be made. I suggest that the biblical concept of "fulfillment" might be one of the most fruitful topics for exploration in a Jewish-Christian dialogue.

3. Finally, there are the problems relative to the politicized situation. Repeatedly, churches and church councils meet with resistance against considering the theological issues dealing with the relationship between the church and the Jewish people because of fear that it might give an unfair advantage to one party in the Middle East conflict.

As early as 1954, when the WCC met in Evanston, Illinois, and the question was raised as to whether or not something should be said about Israel, especially since the theme of the meeting was on Christian hope, a telegram from the Lebanese statesman Charles Malik, urging that no such statement be made, played an important role in the decision to remain silent on the subject. Suspicions cannot be avoided entirely, but at least we should strive to overcome any party-line mentality that might have crept into our theologizing.

III. The new confessional stance raises questions about the form Christian witness should take** vis-à-vis **the Jewish people.

In millennial circles, where the question of Israel has been a key concern for many years, the particular interpretation of the Bible prevalent there has given strong impetus to aggressive missionary endeavors.

The gospel must be preached, and it must be addressed first and foremost to the Jews. Since conversion of Jews is seen as a foreshadowing of the "fullness of Israel" that is to take place in the *eschaton*, missionary activity is perceived as a way of hastening the coming of the day of the Lord.

In mainline Christian circles (both Catholic and Protestant), on the other hand, the new biblical/theological understandings have led to a questioning of the whole concept of "mission to the Jews." In recent years, the emphasis has switched from "mission" to "dialogue." However, as soon as dialogue is viewed as more than an exchange of information, the old questions once again emerge. Christians, even those who accept the new confessional stance, remain deeply divided on the question of witness to the Jews. This came out clearly in a statement issued by the WCC's Consultation on the Church and the Jewish people. The participants admitted that, while they were engaged in a common search for "authentic and proper forms of Christian witness" in relationships with Jews, they held divergent views on the question of whether the bearing of a witness to Jews should include a call to faith in Jesus Christ as Lord and Savior.

There are three recurring viewpoints in the literature on the subject.

1. There is a widespread rejection of proselytism. Professor Tommaso Federici, in an address to the International Catholic-Jewish Liaison Committee in Venice, Italy, defined proselytism as follows: "By 'proselytism' is here understood attitudes and activities engaged in outside Christian witness. Essentially, it means anything which infringes or violates the right of every human person or community not to be subjected to external or internal constraints in religious matters, and also includes ways of preaching the Gospel which are not in harmony with the ways of God, who invites man to respond freely to his call and to serve him in spirit and in truth." But, while people may agree on a definition of proselytism and the wrongness of any coercive practices, they will often still hold different views as to what constitutes "pressure" when a person is engaged in witnessing to his or her faith. Some statements on the subject have stressed that both "overt" and "subtle" forms of proselytism are to be rejected. In that case, the demarcation line seems to become rather blurred.

2. A smaller group, but one that seems to be finding growing support, holds that separate missionary organizations and campaigns for the purpose of converting Jews are to be avoided. The WCC affirmed that position during its first meeting in 1948, advocating that "churches must consider the responsibility for missions to the Jews as a normal part of parish work, especially in those countries where Jews are members of the general community." The door was left open for a "special

missionary ministry" under certain conditions. Essentially the same position was taken by the Lutheran World Federation in a document published in 1964. While holding that "the witness to the Jewish people is inherent in the context of the Gospel and in the commission received from Christ, the head of the Church," it wants such witness to be pursued "in the normal activity of the Christian congregation, which reflects itself in the Christian witness of the individual members."

Professor Federici, in the paper referred to earlier, rejects any "attempts to set up organizations of any sort, particularly educational or welfare organizations for the 'conversion' of Jews." Instead, he writes, "encouragement is to be given to all efforts to get to know the history of Israel, starting with the Bible and exploring in depth the spirit, the existence, the history and the mission of Israel, her survival in history, her election and call, and her privileges which are recognized by the New Testament."

3. A smaller circle yet rejects any idea of Christian witness to the Jews that entertains even the slightest notion of "appeal" or "invitation" or even the hope that they might come to share the Christian confession about Jesus. Some among this circle hold that Judaism is a religion that is complete in itself, and therefore, any such witness is both unnecessary and offensive. Furthermore, the advocates of an "unfulfilled messianism" seem to say, the affirmations of the early Christians about Jesus were mistaken to start with. Or, if they were not mistaken, they have been misunderstood throughout Christian history. Finally, some would add, our burden of guilt as Christian churches calls for silence, particularly in this post-Holocaust era.

My own inclination is to look toward a dialogue that involves risks for both sides and that is open to the possibility of mutual transformation. I can argue that best from the Christian perspective. It seems to me that a really serious encounter with Judaism could have radical consequences for the life and theology of the church, and I believe that in the main that would be a good thing.

But what about changes in the beliefs and lives of individual members of the two communities? That question leads us to the very sensitive issue of "conversion." My final observation deals with that touchy topic.

IV. Even if we were to succeed in avoiding the concept of conversion, we will have to face up to its reality.

People do convert. Every year a number of Christians become adherents to Judaism. According to some estimates, 7000-8000 Christians per year have converted to Judaism during the past decade. Some Jews would not encourage this. They feel that it is unnecessary, since redemption is available to all who lead a righteous life. Others, like Rabbi Gilbert Kiddin, call for "a worldwide programme for conversions."

It should be pointed out that, in most cases, Christians do not turn to Judaism as a result of organized missionary efforts. Rather, instruction in the faith of Judaism is offered in response to inquiries by interested parties.

Jews also become converts to Christianity. This is a highly charged and emotional issue within Judaism. And for good reasons! The legacy of forced conversions and the history of some of the worst kinds of proselytism have left a profound mark on the Jewish psyche. For centuries, Jews were introduced to conversion in the context of persecution and the violation of their rights and beliefs. It is therefore not surprising that the reaction to converts was often one of a deep sense of betrayal.

Jewish views of Jesus and the New Testament were often highly colored by this climate of hostility and suspicion. In recent decades that has changed substantially. A thorough re-evaluation of Jesus has been going on within Judaism. And there are indications that the same may be happening in the case of Paul. Richard L. Rubenstein, in his book, *My Brother Paul*, refers to the apostle as "a loyal Jew" and "one of the greatest theologians the Jewish world has ever produced."[3] Is it possible for a person to be a follower of Jesus and yet remain a loyal Jew?

A phenomenon like the Messianic Jewish Movement, or what has been called Jewish Christianity, seems to pose questions different from those raised by Gentile Christian missionary movements. Buber referred to Jesus as his brother–a messianic figure, but not the Messiah. Under what conditions can a person who goes a step further and becomes a follower of Jesus still be accepted as a loyal member of the Jewish religious community? And is it possible that some day the witness of Jews who confess Jesus as Messiah will take place within the context of the Jewish community of faith? The Jewish community has been able to accommodate a wide diversity of views and allegiances. Am I stretching the limits beyond the breaking point?

Perhaps the question could be posed differently. Rabbi Henry Siegman once suggested that "the ultimate incommensurability" of Judaism and Christianity become the starting point for a dialogue between them. Are Sinai and Calvary inherently contradictory foundations of faith, or has Christian theological interpretation made it seem that way?

The original, unedited form of this chapter was first published in the June, 1978, issue of the Reformed World. Reprinted by permission.

[1] Helga Croner, *Stepping Stones to Further Jewish-Christian Relations: An Unabridged Collection of Christian Documents,* (London ; New York : Stimulus Books, 1977).

[2] Jürgen Moltmann, addressing the Faith and Order Conference at Lausanne, Switzerland, Pentecost Sunday, 1977.

[3] Richard L. Rubenstein, *My Brother Paul*, (New York: Harper & Row, 1972).

CHAPTER 16

Should There Be a Christian Mission to the Jews?

In interfaith dialogue we are not just exchanging information; we are also testifying to truths that have taken hold of us and shaped our commitments.

Christian evangelism among Jews remains one of the most sensitive and controversial issues in Jewish-Christian relations. When the Vatican issued its "Guidelines and Suggestions" for contacts between the church and the Jewish people, the document was greeted by Jewish leaders with a mixture of delight and distress: delight at the change of outlook it reflected, and distress that it still contained references to the church's "divine mission" and "witness."

Should there be a Christian witness to the Jews? Many of my Jewish friends, as well as a growing number of my Christian friends, would answer that question with a resounding "no." But many other Christians would respond with a firm "yes." Many years ago, the faculty of Fuller Theological Seminary's school of world mission called on "Christians in all traditions to reinstate the work of Jewish evangelism in their missionary obedience." According to these scholars, "Jewish-oriented programs should be developed. Appropriate agencies for Jewish evangelism should be formed."[1] Others would express themselves a bit more cautiously.

Missiologist Gerald H. Anderson, for example, has stated that "Christians have no special mission to the Jews, but neither is there any special exemption of the Jews from the universal Christian mission."[2]

Instead of a resounding "no" or a firm "yes," my own answer to the question usually comes out more like "Yes, but . . ." I must hasten to add, however, that for me the qualifying word "but" looms larger all the time. I increasingly feel drawn toward conclusions that I have resisted for decades.

Some years ago, I would probably have welcomed the suggestion made by a joint committee of the Christian Reformed Church and the Reformed Church in America, that these two denominations enter upon a united program of "Jewish evangelism." After all, the Apostle Paul tells us that, not only would that be the proper thing to do, but, in fact, it ought to be a priority–to the Jew first (Romans 1:16). My argument is not with Paul's position but with the motives and methods with which it is often applied today.

The early church argued the question of whether the Judaic tradition should be preserved in every detail: for instance, must Gentiles submit to circumcision when entering the church? Today we face an entirely different situation. One of the key issues now is that, through a long process of de-Judaization, the Christian church has lost contact with its basic roots in the Hebraic tradition. For the sake of its own wholeness, the church needs the encounter with Judaism. Christian-Jewish relations should be an ecumenical priority of the first order. However, between the debate in the early church and the contemporary debate lies a long and tragic history of estrangement and, in numerous instances, of the church's participation in persecution of Jews. The unwillingness of many Christians to come to terms with that history constitutes a major obstacle to presenting a genuinely Christian witness to the Jewish people.

A "Mission" or a "Witness"?

I purposely use the word *witness*. It has rich biblical connotations rooted in Israel's covenant history: "You are my witnesses . . ." (Isaiah 43:10); "I shall give you as a light to the nations!" (Isaiah 49:6). The life and ministry of God's covenant people always involve witness. I agree with Krister Stendahl's suggestion that this word may yet be exonerated and come to be of key value in relations among believers across all barriers.

In Greek antiquity, the word *witness* had already moved beyond its technical courtroom usage and had come to mean the proclamation and exchange of views felt with conviction. In the New Testament, however, witness is not just a matter of words; it involves the sharing of life. To me, the word lacks the connotation of an aggressive campaign of mission "drives" and evangelistic "crusades." That's why I like it.

The term *mission to the Jews* should definitely be abandoned. It will lead only to confusion and to the multiplication of existing misunderstandings in Jewish-Christian relations. Surely, the church has a worldwide mission. But because of the common bond in God's covenant promises, its relationship to the Jewish people is *sui generis*. That fact should be clearly expressed in the language we use. People who don't recognize this special relationship and who, contrary to Romans 11:29, insist that God has revoked his covenant with Israel are bound to become boastful and imperialistic in their approach to the Jews.

Believers who share the covenant faith that has come to it through Moses and the prophets don't missionize each other. Yet, there ought to be room for witness, the sharing of faith perspectives and the exchange of deeply held convictions.

"Faithful Dialogue"

Why not just use the word *dialogue*? Edwin Newman, in a TV commentary, called it "one of the most boring words to come along in years . . . a word that is bunk." According to Newman, dialogue means only that people are talking with each other. In Christian ecumenical circles, where the term is frequently invoked, it is often stressed that "dialogue" carries a broader meaning. Sometimes, in order to make the point that we are talking about "talk plus," the term *faithful dialogue* is used. The partners in dialogue are to be free to affirm their beliefs.

Nevertheless, when all is said and done, a basic rule of the game seems to be that one must not expect anyone to change. Any such anticipation, it is feared, will inevitably lead to manipulation. It is all right to share convictions so long as one does not try to be convincing; persuasiveness is seen as tantamount to proselytizing.

It is often said that the only legitimate motive for dialogue is to gain better mutual understanding. To be sure, that would be no minor achievement! An "I-thou" relationship–that basic prerequisite for all true dialogue–cannot be established until some of the prevalent misunderstandings and caricatures have been erased. I have the impression, however, that interfaith dialogue is frequently practiced at the level of intellectualizing; it thus tends to become a polite and somewhat elitist enterprise. In daily life situations, where faith perspectives meet and historical movements encounter each other, things are not so neatly managed.

It seems to me that all witness should have a dialogical quality; i.e., there should be a willingness to listen to and learn from the other. In other words, witness ought not to be triumphalistic–or, to use a biblical term, it should never be boastful. Whenever we feel called to witness, we ought to be aware of our true motives. They are rarely as pure and loving as we like to make ourselves believe.

Likewise, all dialogue should include a dimension of witness. All too often, interfaith dialogue is designed for safety. That unwillingness to risk leads to sterility. A little passion, even a bit of polemics will not damage a dialogue that has reached the stage of basic mutual respect and trust.

I am not pleading for a return to the old-time polemics, with its adversary mentality and its barely concealed insults. But in interfaith dialogue, we are not just exchanging information; we are also testifying to truths that have taken hold of us and shaped our commitments. There are profound issues at stake, such as the ones raised in Martin Buber's polemical book *Two Types of Faith*.[3] We ought to be able to reason–and occasionally to argue–with each other about those things.

According to a study published by the *Evangelischen Kirche* in Germany, "the point of Christian-Jewish encounter is to make their different confessions of the one God fruitful for mutual witness." In this way of stating it, I sense a dynamic which seeks to move beyond improved mutual understanding: it seeks to affect the life and witness of both communities.

THE MESSAGE OF CONVERSION

So we are talking about change after all–not about "convert the Jews" campaigns, which are supposed to take the place of conversation–but rather about mutual change. It seems to me that any Christian encounter with the Jewish people lacks integrity if it does not grow out of a profound recognition that the church itself needs to come to a radical transformation as a result of the experience.

By the same token, it should be pointed out that conversion is an essentially Hebrew concept. The question of conversion arises when we meet the God of Israel–the God of Abraham, Isaac and Jacob, the Holy One, who addresses us and calls us to respond. The faith of Israel is fundamentally different from the kind of religiosity that people have in their blood, that simply flows from their being, their gut feelings. Such religiosity does not demand ultimate decisions. Paganism comes naturally; therefore, the question of conversion does not arise.

At best, the message of conversion is good news about the transforming potential of faith. Jews and Christians both pray for the day when all humanity will turn to the Lord and give glory to his Name. Why, then, has it become such bad news to Jews when Christians start talking about making them converts? In order to begin to understand Jewish feelings on this matter, Christians will have to enter into the Jewish experience throughout Christian history in a way few of them have been willing to do.

Most Christian clergy have studied church history without ever being introduced to this shameful aspect of the church's story. The Jews, however, do know about it. They know about the anti-Jewish polemics of certain church fathers; about the forced baptisms, especially of children; about the church council decree that sanctioned the removal of such children from their parents; about a papal edict encouraging raids of Jewish synagogues by the faithful; about the expulsion of all Jews from Spain; about Luther's flaming language directed against Jews when they did not convert according to his timetable; about the prohibition against Jews living in Calvin's Geneva; and about all the cruelties Christians have felt justified in perpetrating against the people they called "Christ-killers." Is it surprising then that, to so many Jews, conversion came to mean "joining the enemy"?

We are not talking only about things that happened in some distant dark age; we are talking about the memories of our neighbors. Listen to Jewish novelist Elie Wiesel, as he spoke in the Cathedral of St.

John the Divine in New York:

"I do not feel at ease in a church. I hope you will forgive my frankness. I believe in the usefulness of dialogue, but it must be preceded by an honest exchange. As a child, I was afraid of the church to the point of changing sidewalks. In my town, the fear was justified. Not only because of what I inherited–our collective memory–but also because of the simple fact that, twice a year, at Easter and Christmas, Jewish children would be beaten up by their Christian neighbors."[4]

There is more. At an early stage in the church's history, a process of de-Judaization was set in motion that, through the centuries, has deprived the church of some of the richest elements of its Hebrew heritage. The U.S. Catholic bishops spoke frankly about these things in a pastoral message. But the vast majority of Christians have yet to recognize that fundamental fact, let alone come to terms with its implications for the life of the church and its relationships to the Jewish people.

To confront the Jewish people with the meaning and significance of the life and ministry of Jesus, as we understand and confess them, is one thing. To ask Jews to become well-adjusted denominational Christians in a Hellenized church is quite another. The best among those Jews who decide to take that step are likely to end up as lonely and misunderstood missionaries, calling an unrepentant church to renewal through a recovery of its roots in the Hebrew Scriptures.

A Recovery of Roots

Let me be clear. I have received perspectives of faith through the witness of the Christian church which I consider to be of ultimate significance to my life. As far as my faith is concerned, Jesus–his message and the reality of his Spirit as a transforming power–are normative. I believe that there are accents in the New Testament message of grace that will continue to have a powerful appeal to certain Jews.

On the other hand, I can testify from personal experience that, to be reared in the Christian church as we know it, makes loss of basic elements of one's Judaic background virtually inevitable, including elements that the church desperately needs for its own renewal. My father, son of a Polish rabbi, while completing his own rabbinical studies in Switzerland was introduced to the New Testament, not by an eager Gentile missionary, but by his overhearing (quite by accident) a discussion about Jesus in some university hall. After becoming a Christian, he stayed in close contact with his Jewish heritage. He shared his faith with his people, and during the Holocaust he shared their fate in the Nazi ovens.

For me and my family, however, things are quite different (even though my wife, too, grew up in a Hebrew-Christian home). In a number of ways, we live in alienation from very rich aspects of the Jewish tradition. And when I look at my children, I realize that, in many respects, they are tragically ignorant of their Jewish background.

The faculty members of the school of world mission at Fuller Theological Seminary said that it ought not to be so. They called on Jewish converts to maintain their cultural ties for the enrichment of the whole church. That, however, is not so easy to do when, for centuries, the church has followed policies (not unwittingly, as the Fuller professors state, but systematically and by unholy design) that sought to de-Judaize the Jews and submerge them in various brands of Christendom. Why, one wonders, such passionate desire to remove the otherness of the Jews? Could it possibly be related to our problems with the otherness of the God of Israel?

Such questions cannot he avoided. How can we talk about converting the Jews when we are not passionately concerned about the conversion of the church? The church needs change, in its theology and in its life and ministry.

THE CONCEPT OF "FULFILLMENT"

Some dramatic proposals for changes in Christian theology have been made by Rosemary Ruether, who holds that anti-Judaism has developed within the church as "the left hand of Christology"–that it is really the reverse side of the Christian confession that Jesus is the Christ–Ruether defends the position of "unfulfilled messianism." In his foreword to Ruether's book, *Faith and Fratricide*, Gregory Baum, a Jewish convert to Christianity, quotes her as stating: "We might say that Jesus is our paradigm for holy, aspiring man, venturing his life in expectation of the Kingdom."[5] Ruether has also argued that, "what Christianity has in Jesus is not the Messiah, but a Jew who hoped for the coming of the Kingdom of God and who died in that hope."[6]

Resolving the issues between Judaism and Christianity through this kind of "unfulfilled messianism" sounds to me somewhat like resolving the debate between capitalism and communism by eliminating the idea of private property. Such a proposal tends to create a brief sensation, only to be set aside as another radical fad that has come and gone. Yet I believe that there could be great mutual benefit to the concept of "fulfillment" as the focus of a serious Jewish-Christian dialogue.

The manner in which "fulfillment theology" has been developed by the Christian church has frequently led to ecclesiastical triumphalism and, in many cases, to anti-Judaism. Often, Christians have made claims for themselves and against the Jews that have no basis in the biblical message. The issue emerges as soon as we deal with some basic theological questions: How do we see the relationship between the Old and New Testament, between the church and Israel, the church and the kingdom of God, the presence of the Kingdom in the here-and-now and the church's eschatological hope?

Let us be more specific. Has the Old Testament become superfluous, or at least of secondary value? Has God's covenant with Israel been annulled? Can the church be equated with the kingdom? In what sense can it be said that redemption has come to the world? When called upon to answer such questions, Christians have frequently been led astray by unbiblical doctrines of "fulfillment."

THE "ALREADY" AND THE "NOT YET"

God was in Christ reconciling the world to himself. That is a basic Christian confession. Now we await with eager longing the redemption of all things. That, too, is a basic Christian confession, one that the church and the Jewish people share. It is when we seek to give an account of the foundations of the hope that moves us that the differences become pronounced. The church, in its witness to Jesus as the Christ, tends to emphasize the "already" of the redemption that has entered history. Sometimes, the distinction between the reconciliation which, according to Christian teaching, has already occurred and the redemption of all things yet to take place, becomes obscured in Christian witness. Then Judaism confronts us with its profound sense of the "not yet," born out of its burning vision of a new world of righteousness and peace.

In the New Testament, "fulfillment" (*pleroma*) is a key concept, a complex one applied in diverse ways. It has christological as well as pneumatological elements. Many things receive *pleroma* in Christ and through the presence and power of the Holy Spirit: time, prophecy, the law, people, the church, and even the cosmos.

In essence, the New Testament teaching about "fulfillment" deals with the question of the presence of redemption in history. I once traced that theme through various theological traditions in my book, *Redemption and Historical Reality*.[7] It is unfortunate that some Jewish scholars still pose an antithesis between Christian and Jewish positions on this issue, claiming that Christian theology conceives of redemption exclusively as an event in the spiritual and private realm of a person's inner life, but unrelated to history. True, Christian theology has frequently suffered from overspiritualization. But there is a vast body of Christian theological literature that struggles with the question of redemption in profoundly historical terms.

The New Testament speaks about signs of the kingdom and first fruits of the Spirit. The fulfillment of all things and the consummation of all things correspond to the presence of God's kingdom in the midst of historical ambiguities and redemption as it will be experienced in the end time. The Reformers, for instance, carefully distinguished between the *regnum Christi* and the *regnum Dei*. Fulfillment does not make hope unnecessary; it nourishes and intensifies it.

These themes are certainly not foreign to the history of Jewish thought, although they are, of course, developed differently there. I see the concept of "fulfillment" as a much more fruitful basis for Christian-Jewish encounter than all the talk about "unfulfilled messianism."

LIVING AS A PEOPLE OF HOPE

Such an encounter would force the Christian church to take a candid look at the duality of its own witness. Do we indeed live and work in the world as a people of hope? Perhaps the most persuasive witness of the church to the Jewish people would be for Christians to live as a pilgrim people engaged in the practice of the imperatives of the gospel. In that case, much of our witness would consist of answering the inquiries of those who want to know what moves us (1 Peter 3:15).

Isn't that what the Apostle Paul had in mind when he saw "evoking to jealousy" as the true strategy for the church's witness to the Jews (Romans 11:11)? It seems to me that the more we fail to be faithful to such a witness, the more we begin to act like what Paul called "peddlers of the Word" (2 Corinthians 2:17), holy hucksters who are prepared to apply the strategies of salesmanship, but who do not appear sincerely interested in the well-being of those whom we encounter. Behind our salesmanship, there is often insecurity and an intense desire to control others.

My intention is not to condemn all that has been done in the name of "Jewish mission." I have seen too many of those people witness not only in word but in deed, and during the Nazi persecution I saw quite a few of them demonstrate their love by risking their lives for their Jewish neighbors. However, I consider all honest encounters between the church and the Jewish people as a priority concern. This, it seems to me, can take place only if the churches become more willing to face their past and to acknowledge their need for radical transformation. Hence, for me, the great priority lies not in strategies, programs, and campaigns to convert Jews, but in a major Christian educational effort to help church members recover the roots of their faith in Judaism.

The original, unedited form of this chapter was first published in the Christian Century. Copyright 1977 Christian Century. Reprinted by permission from the April 13, 1977, issue of the Christian Century.

[1]*Missiology*, October 1976.

[2]*Missiology*, July 1974.

[3]Martin Buber, *Two Types of Faith*, Norman P. M. A. Goldhawk, tr. (London: Routledge & Paul, 1951).

[4]Elie Wiesel, as quoted in *Auschwitz: The Beginning of a New Era?*, Eva Fleischner (ed.) (New York: Ktav Publishing House, 1976), p. 406.

[5]Gregory Baum, in his foreword to *Faith and Fratricide* (New York: Seabury Press, 1974), p. 20.

[6]Ruether, cited in *Anatomy of Contempt*, John M. Oesterreicher (Seton Hall University Press, 1975), p. 32.

[7]Isaac Rottenberg, *Redemption and Historical Reality* (Philadelphia: Westminster Press, 1964).

CHAPTER 17

The Mission Dilemma

The mission issue impinges on Christian-Jewish relations in a variety of ways. First, there is the fact that a number of denominations have had mission programs in the Arab world for many decades. Several references have already been made to ways in which church policies have been affected by that reality. It is a complex situation, often influenced by a mixture of motivations and perceived missionary interests.

One force at work in the dynamic is love, affection, and often admiration for Arab peoples and their culture. The Arab world, too, has its mystique and its own kind of seductiveness. Arab culture, with its ancient traditions and customs, can get hold of people who open their minds and hearts to what it has to offer. Arab hospitality is a lovely thing to behold.

I shall never forget traveling in a four-wheel-drive Jeep with my son through the desert in Oman. When we approached a small oasis, he suggested that we pay a visit to the owner of the fruit orchard there. After the two of them had exchanged the customary Arab greetings, this man became our host in a way that cannot help but touch one's heart. I think about that Omani every time I might be tempted to conclude that terrorism is deeply embedded in every Arab soul.

Most Middle East missionaries I have known have developed a love affair with the region. In some missionary families those sentiments have been transmitted from one generation to the next, making them, in effect, like "leading families" in the land, in some cases with close ties to the ruling elite. Of course, less of that is happening in the more nationalistic climate of today.

But love is not the exclusive force at work here. There are other powerful factors, among them fear, guilt, and frustration. Christian denominations are constantly reminded that their missionaries operate in basically closed societies. Visas for their personnel are issued, refused, or revoked at the pleasure of the local ruler. When a missionary presence is permitted, it is done as a favor or because the church workers perform a function in education, medicine, agriculture, etc., that is seen as serving the national interests of the country. Expulsions of personnel and expropriations of facilities have occurred. Hence, there is a good deal of self-censorship in what churches say publicly about conditions in Arab countries. A more open society, like Israel, where one can criticize the government in the full assurance that one can return later for a repeat performance, tends to be somewhat at a disadvantage in the propaganda war, which is never absent from Middle East politics, including church politics.

The guilt and frustration factors can be traced to a variety of sources. It seems to me that they are engendered partly by the belief that U.S. foreign policy has been unfair to Arab interests, or at least, tilted in an unbalanced fashion toward Israel. U.S. missionaries in the Middle East feel a constant need to be apologetic about their own country. The situation is aggravated by the fact that missionaries to the Moslem world can rarely report dramatic conversions as a result of their work. Samuel Zwemer, the great pioneer in mission to the Arab world, is reported to have said that, after a lifetime of work, he could count the converts on the fingers of one hand. And he did not face the restrictions that are placed on Christian outreach in the Arab world today.

When these missionaries return home on furlough and pay visits to their supporting churches for fundraising purposes, they do not have the right stories to tell. Their audiences wish to be inspired, which means, above all, that they want to hear about the "souls" that have been saved. At the very least, that is true in the churches that contribute most of the money for missions.

In their talks or "Dear Friends" letters sent from the field, many Middle East missionaries make attempts to present foreign policy issues or even mild defenses of terrorist activities. But in most cases, their efforts to convert the folk at home prove to be as frustrating as their evangelizing activities abroad. Nevertheless, some have come to see advocacy of Palestinian rights as the *raison d'être* of their missionary calling.

A few years ago, Basheer K. Nijim, edited a book entitled *American Church Politics and the Middle East*. It was basically designed as a handbook to help those who seek to promote goodwill toward the Arab cause among church constituencies. In it, Peter Johnson makes some interesting observations. He believes that "for at least some time in the future, the WASP churches of the establishment grouped in the National Council of Churches will continue to play the most important organized religious role in influencing the formulation of foreign policy."[1] He says that missionaries were "increasingly to become 'more Arab than thou' as the Palestine question became a central issue in Arab national politics." He then continues: "The missionaries were intent upon protecting their own position as Americans in the Arab world . . . What we have here is what might even be called the religious face of the State Department, which is noted for its pro-Arab cast."[2]

As Peter Grose pointed out in his book, *Israel in the Mind of America,* long before the founding of the State of Israel, the missionary establishment had voiced its opposition to the idea of Jewish restoration, seeing it as a clear threat to the Christian presence, not only in the Holy Land, but in the Arab world at large as well. He quotes an elderly Presbyterian veteran of the faculty at the American University of Beirut as writing (shortly before Israel's independence was achieved): "Everyone zealous for Christian missions must feel a veritable heartbreak for the way in which the hasty and ill-advised endorsement of the Zionist program by Congress has nullified the sacrificial labors of generations of missionaries and educators."[3]

When, during the Fall of 1985, Shiite militants decided to release one of the hostages they were holding at that time, Presbyterian missionary Benjamin Weir became their candidate. He performed according to what I believe were their expectations. He returned home pleading for understanding of the reasons why terrorists engage in desperate murderous acts. When, after the seajacking of the Achille Lauro and the brutal murder of Leon Klinghoffer, the U.S. intercepted an Egyptian plane that was carrying the killers plus Abu Abbas, the architect of this despicable affair, the Rev. Weir did what many Middle East missionaries would do as an almost automatic reaction: he expressed outrage at U.S. aggression. The Presbyterian Church later elected him to serve a term as its Moderator, thus, for a season at least, making him the major denominational spokesperson.

But, as we have seen in conservative churches as well, like the Southern Baptist Convention, the mission establishment also plays a central role in molding the denomination's position toward Middle East issues. It should not be forgotten that, at least in many Protestant churches, mission boards are where a good deal of the churches' income is to be found.

But there is another side to the mission question that is relevant to our story, and that is what this chapter is really about. I am referring to that very controversial issue, mission to the Jews.

I have entitled this chapter "The Mission Dilemma," because, as defined by Webster's Unabridged Dictionary, "dilemma" involves, among other things, "a perplexing and awkward situation." To multitudes of Christians, the question of mission when dealing with our Jewish neighbors has a special dimension of perplexity and awkwardness about it that does not apply to what might be called "mission in general."

Some of my friends would disagree with the word choice. For them, the issue does not involve a dilemma at all. They pronounce an unequivocal "no" to the very notion of Christian mission to the Jewish people, or, putting it a bit more mildly, a Christian "witness" to Jews. The late Paul van Buren stated frequently and bluntly in speeches that were often widely quoted,[4] that Christians who try to convert Jews are "working against the will of God and the expressed command of Jesus." He argued that, if Jews had said "yes" to the church's message, the Jewish people, as a people with a Jewish identity and as a people set apart for a divinely appointed mission in the world, would have ceased to exist. But God wills that there be a Jewish people. And, more than ever since the Holocaust, we, too, should see the survival of that people with their own corporate identity as a moral mandate.

According to van Buren and other scholars, Christians must accept the Jewish "no" to the church and appreciate that "no" as a positive. "If there were no more Jewish people," van Buren never tired of emphasizing, "we would have lost the single most concrete and enduring sign in the world of God's faithfulness." In Romans 11:25-26, Paul admonishes Gentiles not to "be wise in your own conceits," but, rather, to understand the mystery of Israel, which will remain a mystery until the divine destiny for both Jews and Gentiles will be fulfilled.

In some instances, local or state councils of churches have taken up this theme in their assemblies. For instance, the Texas Council of Churches, by unanimous vote, passed a resolution condemning efforts to bring a witness about Jesus to Jews because "the Jewish people today possess their own unique call and mission before God." The council specifically singled out for criticism the establishment of organizations that target the Jewish people as a special "object" for mission. My own hunch is that such unanimity on very controversial issues usually says more about group dynamics during church meetings than about the quality of theological debate that took place there. But even if the resolution may not speak for the majority of Texan Christians, it does reflect the strong conviction of at least a minority of them.

There seems to be a growing number of Christians who are prepared to accept some kind of dual-covenant theology, positing that there are two parallel roads to approach the God of the Bible, the road of Christ and the road of Torah. All this is reminiscent of Franz Rosenzweig's view that both faiths are to be seen as manifestations of the same Truth. In other words, they represent equally true and valid views of reality and each must honor the other as a servant of God. Sometimes, I think Jewish listeners have a tendency to hear the sounds of a two-covenant theology when a non-supersessionist position is presented that may actually be very far removed from the Rosenzweig view.

At any rate, some Christian theologians who are strong advocates of dialogue with Jews and who are also profoundly aware of the church's history of anti-Judaism seem to feel that historic Christianity is in fact not a valid view of reality as understood in faith. They therefore propose a process of radical reconstruction.

Convinced that anti-Judaism goes to the very heart of New Testament teachings and is inherent in historic Christian doctrines, scholars like Rosemary Ruether and Roy Eckardt have called for changes in the church's teaching about the centrality of Christ and his resurrection that, to many other Christians sound like extreme positions or even apostasy.

"I am the way, the truth, and the life"; "There is no other name under heaven given among men by which we must be saved," These and other New Testament statements signify to some Christians the element of uniqueness expressed in the gospel of Christ's saving work. However, to other Christians they represent a claim to absolutism and exclusiveness that simply has to go because it inevitably leads to intolerance and missionary triumphalism.

To most Jewish scholars, the radical theological reconstructionists in the Christian community represent a true sign of hope. They make no secret of the fact that they wished that all Christians would think like that. But they are sophisticated enough to know that the voice of a few individual scholars, influential as they may be in certain intellectual circles, is quite a different matter from the voice of the church as it expresses itself through synods and councils.

In the minds of Jewish leaders, the mission issue is intimately tied up with the question of survival. To some, it may seem that such an attitude is part of a Holocaust syndrome. Well, the Holocaust is, indeed, a very important part of the picture, but not as an isolated interval in history. Rather, the Holocaust is experienced as the culmination of a long history of persecution in which Christian anti-Judaism has played a key role. The "no" to Christian mission has, as it were, been engraved upon the psyche of the Jewish people.

In line with most Jewish leaders, Irving Greenberg, an Orthodox rabbi and, for more than 20 years, president of the National Jewish Center for Learning and Leadership, sees the work of radical Christian scholars as "the most powerful proof of the vitality and the ongoing relevance of Christianity...."[5] But, by the same token, he and his wife Blu Greenberg continue to pursue dialogue with Christians who come to a diametrically opposite conclusion about what constitutes the vitality of Christianity. As far as they are concerned, Greenberg is recommending an essentially reductionist theology, which the church at large will continue to reject. Their interest perks up, however, when, in his *Quarterly Review* article, Greenberg poses this question: "Should not Jewish theology seek to be open to Christian self-understanding, including the remarkable, unbelievable claim of resurrection, incarnation, etc.?"

In the meantime, mission to the Jews is a reality, because, on the opposite pole of those who pronounce an unequivocal "no" to such mission, stand people who voice an unqualified "yes." They, too, see it as a clear-cut case. As a matter of fact, they believe that "Jewish mission" is not just one aspect of the overall mission of the church, but ought to be a priority concern: first and foremost to the Jews. Once again, it must be pointed out that the picture is rather complex. Those who think immediately in this context of Jews for Jesus and right-wing fundamentalists have, I fear, a somewhat distorted image of the situation.

Nevertheless, it is true that the most aggressive "Jewish mission" enterprises are usually sponsored by independent agencies of a conservative theological persuasion and often with a millenialist-dispensationalist orientation. These people are very eager to be counted among the staunchest supporters of the State of Israel, but, because of their theological stance, they encounter much suspicion, both in the American Jewish community and in Israel. For many of these people, this is very painful.

Support for Israel sometimes takes rather extreme forms. For instance, a sample letter published in one ministry newsletter and recommended for mailing to government officials reads in part:

"Dear Mr. President, Senator, Congressman: I wish to express my full support for the nation of Israel. I believe that the Bible gives to God's chosen people all the land of Israel, West Bank, Golan Heights, east bank of Jordan and all of southern Lebanon to Tyre and Sidon as well as southern Syria to Damascus."

Another appeal letter offers "a new ministry for our partners," namely, "a limited genealogical service free for our partners to find out if they have any Jewish ancestry or roots in their family." I am no longer easily surprised by various fundraising gimmicks, but I must confess that this one struck me as a somewhat startling novelty.

Sometimes, the fundraising letters from pro-Israel Christian ministries do not come straight out stating that they seek the conversion of Jews, but they nevertheless want to assure the donor that they are involved in the "real thing." So, they use "hint language" in order to convey to the prospective contributor that great things are happening, while avoiding coming into conflict with Jewish leaders, either in this country or in Israel.

Many donors want to know that true missionary work is being done with their money. I am not suggesting that conservative Christians don't care about human suffering and don't contribute to programs that feed the hungry or heal the sick. They indeed do. But, by the same token, they want to know that the true inspiration behind the mission, the ultimate goal is the "salvation of souls."

But how does an evangelist, let us say after a meeting with the Prime Minister of Israel, get people so excited about what has happened that they will generously contribute to this ministry? "Hint language" is the answer. My files contain numerous examples of this. The reader is told that prophetic Scriptures were discussed (former Israeli Prime Minister Begin loved quoting the prophets of Israel as much as his Christian visitors). Then the letter goes on to describe how there was a sense of the mighty power of the Holy Spirit in the room. That's usually enough to raise the level of expectation and excitement. Who knows what may grow from the seed that has been sown?

But some evangelists do not beat around the bush. They are quite open and honest about their intentions, even if one may sometimes have doubts about their statistics. For instance, one mailing contained the claim that "in the past two months fifty dear Jewish souls were won to the Lord." A newsletter by the same ministry reported that the evangelist had witnessed to several rabbis in Buffalo, New York. Since it did not say that fifty Jews were baptized or what "witness" the rabbis gave in the encounter, the language of the newsletter leaves much room for interpretation.

Fundamentalist-dispensationalist Christians, however, are not the only ones advocating and practicing mission to Jews. There are evangelicals within the so-called mainstream churches who feel a strong commitment to a witness that has, as its aim, the conversion of Jews. For instance, the Episcopal Church, a communion about as mainstream as one can get, has within its fellowship a Christian Ministry among Jewish People (CMJ/USA). It is advertised as "an authorized agent in the Anglican Communion founded in 1809 to work in loving service among the Jewish people." This ministry and similar projects tend to adopt a less aggressive approach than those who operate with a more apocalyptic sense of urgency.

While CMJ/USA is not officially sponsored by the Episcopal Church, it does have a semi-official status within the Anglican communion. Its board of advisors includes a number of bishops. The leadership of this ministry is well aware that the past Christian record *vis-à-vis* Jews and Judaism may not recommend it to its intended audience. The Rev. Philip Bottomley, CMJ/USA's director, wrote in one of the ministry's newsletters that "two thousand years of bad history requires us to be very sensitive in our witness in order that Jewish people may actually hear what we are saying." One folder defines the organization's purpose as follows: "CMJ/USA is an Episcopal organization offering teaching on the Jewish Roots of our Faith and how to witness for Jesus among Jewish people in the United States."

Over against Episcopalian Paul van Buren's position, the Rev. Bottomley quoted Scripture: "There is no scriptural basis for saying that a Jew who believes in Jesus ceases to be a Jew. Peter and the Apostles would have been amazed at such a statement. On the day of Pentecost, Peter addressed the crowd as 'my fellow Jews' [Acts 2:14]. Paul stated emphatically 'I *am* a Jew' [Acts 21:39], not 'I *was* a Jew.'"[6]

It is because of this biblical position that CMJ/USA supporters are often referred to as "a fundamentalist group" by other Episcopalians, who find their presence at General Conventions of the Episcopal Church somewhat of an embarrassment.[7] But, in fact, their broadly evangelical views are shared by millions of Christians who, while perhaps not involved in mission to Jews, defend its legitimacy, if they do not actually advocate its practice.

The results of a poll commissioned by the Anti-Defamation League of B'nai B'rith showed some interesting facts about evangelicals. By and large, Jewish leaders reacted quite positively to the data the poll yielded.[8] For example, 90 percent of those interviewed disagreed with the statement, "Christians are justified in holding negative attitudes towards Jews since the Jews killed Christ."

Two statistics, however, were found to be disturbing: 59 percent of those surveyed agreed that "Jews can never be forgiven for what they did to Jesus until they accept him as the true Savior," and 50 percent said Christians should "actively help lead Jews to accept Jesus Christ as the Savior."

As to the first point, it seems to me that the way the question is posed creates a few problems of its own. The question did not ask: "Do you believe that the Jewish people today are to be held responsible for the death of Jesus?" I wonder whether 59 percent of the respondents would have answered that question in the affirmative. Instead, however, the question as posed simply implied that certain Jews did something to Jesus and then wants to know whether there is forgiveness without faith in Christ. Since, as far as evangelicals are concerned, the source of forgiveness for any misdeed done by anyone is to be found in the atoning sacrifice of Christ, the 59 percent may reflect more their view on forgiveness than their feelings about Jewish culpability. It seems to me that mixed questions like that produce as much confusion as enlightenment.

As to the second point, I was surprised that the percentage was not higher. It is hard to say how the person questioned interpreted the qualifying word "actively" when asked whether one should "help lead Jews to accept Jesus Christ as the Savior." Perhaps it raised in their minds images of an aggressive kind of evangelism that singles out Jews as special targets, an approach they may not feel comfortable with.

The Lausanne Committee for World Evangelization sponsored a Consultation on Jewish Evangelism in Great Britain, attended by 160 delegates from 17 nations. They issued a declaration in which they expressed grief "over the discrimination and suffering that have been inflicted upon the Jewish people in the name of Jesus the Messiah," adding that "these deeds constituted a denial of God's love for his people and a misrepresentation of the person and work of Jesus."

After a denunciation of all forms of anti-Semitism "as contrary to the gospel and to the content of the New Testament," the Lausanne declaration made the following point: "We must protest, however, when past history is used to silence the church in her witness to the Jewish people. To withhold the gospel from the Jewish people would be an act of gross discrimination." My guess is that, if this proposition were to be submitted to the same people surveyed in the A.D.L. poll, more than 50 percent would agree with it.

History makes it imperative that great sensitivity be shown, so the argument goes, but it does not excuse one from the missionary mandate. For many Christians, history, even the horrors of the Holocaust, cannot supersede Holy Writ. That point is made repeatedly in articles promoting "Jewish Evangelism." For instance, *The Banner*, a magazine sponsored by the Christian Reformed Church, published an article on courses taught at Westminster Theological Seminary in Philadelphia to help students witness to Jews. "Christians," we read there, "need to ask forgiveness for many wrongs committed against Jews." Furthermore, "deep sensitivity to Jewish feelings must characterize all evangelistic witness to Jews." But this can never mean that Jews are to be excluded from Christian witness.

It is important to keep in mind that, from the very beginning, the church saw itself as an *apostolic* community, which means that mission was not regarded as an elective, but rather as a divine imperative. Mission was not seen as one of the many activities with which Christians keep themselves busy–it was the church's *raison d'être*. Mission is not done for the sake of the church's well-being; it belongs to her *being*. That notion, in my view, rather than being a Christian invention, grows out of a perspective that is deeply rooted in the Hebrew Scriptures. Furthermore, as some Jewish scholars have pointed out, there were periods in their people's history when that perspective was translated into proselytizing practices.

But here we are talking about the Christian dilemma. Between the "Mission, yes!" proponents on the one side and the "Mission, no!" people on the other, there are multitudes of church members for whom the issue has become a matter of profound moral-spiritual struggle, a genuine dilemma. There are elements in both the "yes" and the "no" positions to which they ascribe a degree of validity, and their sympathies tend to sway back and forth as the debate goes on. For instance, taking the New Testament as a whole, it would seem very difficult, if not impossible, to defend the position that the conversion of a Jew is a bad thing. Such a view would seem to undercut the very foundation of the church's origins. Therefore, Christian adherence to both the New Testament message and its practice would seem to require that the gospel of Christ be shared with all people, none excluded.

Blu Greenberg, in her contribution to the book *Evangelicals and Jews in an Age of Pluralism*, shows great sensitivity in her understanding of the dilemma many Christians face on this issue. "Now I know the dilemma that evangelical Christians face, and I am not trying for the jugular. . . . Scripture says, go convert the Jews. What is a decent Christian to do? I know how it feels. As an orthodox Jew, as one who believes in revelation, who loves Torah, and who tries to live her life according to *Halakah* yet also as a woman of the 20th century who is committed to the new values for women I have experienced the dilemma in my own life many, many times: the tension one feels between faithfulness to Scripture and the need to respond to unfolding religious realities, the conflict one feels about Biblical authority and infallibility when it clashes with historical and social necessity, the tension between absolute and pluralist models, the anxious feeling one has at times that by chipping away a tiny piece, one begins to weaken the whole structure. Yes, I understand the dilemma a well-meaning evangelical faces."[9]

Once again, "evangelical" here has to be taken in a very broad sense, because I meet Christians representing a wide range of Christian theological opinion who feel the tension described here very personally. They have to be honest to their understanding of Scripture. At the same time, they have to be honest to a deeper understanding of history as well. To claim, as some Christians still do, that anti-Judaism and persecution represented the activities of some bad individuals who were not truly reborn Christians, is clearly a dishonest or, at least, a willfully ignorant response to the truth.

Furthermore, Scripture itself contains elements of ambiguity, or of high paradox, if that term is preferred. It is enough to give one pause for reflection. For instance, the mission mandate of Matthew 28:19 tells us to go and make disciples of all nations (*ta ethne* in Greek). But the Jewish people are not to be counted as a nation among the nations. There is a very important difference, because they are the people of the covenant, the people of the promise, the people of the Book *par excellence.* Even the fact that some Jews may not be very familiar with their own heritage does not gainsay the truth that, in addressing them, we are dealing with people whose souls have been stamped, so to speak, by the history of Israel. I have the impression that, of all people, it is perhaps the most difficult for a Jew to become a one hundred-percent secular person, someone who has lost all sense of Jewish history and heritage, a person totally out of touch with Torah.

At any rate, some Christian statements have sought to deal with the element of uniqueness with respect to the Jewish people while at the same time talking about witness. In a policy document developed in the Presbyterian Church, U.S., before its union with the United Presbyterian Church, we read this: "In witnessing to the Jews . . . we encounter a unique reality, namely, that they already worship and serve the One True God. Like the apostle Paul, we are eager to share with them what we believe to be the saving grace of Jesus Christ for us and for all humanity. But at the same time, like Paul in Romans 9:11, we too live with the mystery that God's election of the Jews for salvation is irrevocable."

But, what does it mean to recognize this mystery and to acknowledge the horrors of Christian history? What form of Christian witness remains valid in light of those truths? How does one maintain the integrity of one's faith, the integrity of one's relationship to Jewish neighbors with whom one seeks to engage in dialogue, and the integrity of one's support for Israel? For many Christians, these have become profoundly perplexing questions.

As a starter, it may be helpful to distinguish between witness and proselytizing, but, in the end, that does not really resolve the issue. Take, for instance, the two essays by Vernon Grounds and Blu Greenberg, an Orthodox Christian and an Orthodox Jew. "I draw a sharp distinction between proselytizing and witnessing," writes Dr. Grounds.[10] Ms. Greenberg suggests a distinction between "mission-proselytism" and "mission-witness."[11] So, they seem to agree in substance. But what happens when one turns to specifics?

In his rejection of proselytizing, Dr. Grounds appeals to a WCC report, as well as the writings of the Catholic scholar Tommaso Federici. In both cases, proselytism is defined in terms of illegitimate pressures, coercive actions, and the violation of another human being's personhood. He recognizes potential abuses and the need to let a person make decisions in freedom. Nevertheless, he maintains, none of those considerations would warrant declaring a moratorium on Christian mission, nor the watering down of what we believe about Jesus as the Christ.

Blu Greenberg, on the other hand, holds that "the idea that only through Christ will Jews be saved is out of order ... It is obscene!"[12] In order to appreciate the case she makes for this conclusion, I would urge the reader to turn to the full text of her essay. She writes with passion about her people and their history, but also with a profound understanding of her dialogue partners.

Can Christians meaningfully share their faith in Christ without implying that their Jewish neighbors are separated from the God of redemption? How does a Christian convey his or her convictions and feelings about Jesus, his uniqueness as understood in faith, his ministry of reconciliation, without implying that Jews live in darkness without him?

Witness, at best, is a sharing of one's faith in an atmosphere of love. At worst, it is a drive for mental and spiritual conquest, usually born much more out of the insecurity of the zealous evangelizer than his or her inner peace about personal decisions that have been made. The failure to distinguish clearly between scoring points or pushing another person against the wall with clever arguments and a loving witness to one's faith has frequently led to a spiritual imperialism that has alienated countless people from the Christian community.

The apostle Paul suggested that a basic mission strategy, as far as his Jewish brothers and sisters were concerned, was to provoke them to jealousy. Love, lived out in joy, more than anything else will make others wonder what internal resources produce such results. But, in light of the past two thousand years, Paul's advice, at least to many serious people, sounds like a sick joke. Instead of following the road of love, the church pursued the path of polemics. When that did not work, it applied power and turned to persecution. No wonder Jews pick up negative signals whenever they are made the "object" of Christian witness.

On the other hand, Christians often feel that they are being pushed toward a minimalist position in order to maintain friendship with the Jewish community. Must they deny or leave unmentioned what Jesus means to them in order not to be accused of proselytism? How low-key must Christian witness be in order to be considered legitimate? A take-it-or-leave-it approach, or a hyper-intellectual approach, that does not seem to care about commitment are for many Christians hard to accept as valid witness. And so the arguments–or perhaps it would be better to say the probings–move back and forth.

At its first meeting in Amsterdam in 1948, the WCC reaffirmed its commitment to the missionary mandate, including mission to Jews, but rejected the idea of singling out Jews as special targets for Christian outreach. Rather, witness to Jewish neighbors should, according to the Council, be done "as a normal part of parish work." At that time, Christian-Jewish dialogue was still a function of the Commission on World Mission and Evangelism.

Eventually, as the dialogue proceeded, Christian-Jewish relations became the concern of the Division for Dialogue with People of Living Faiths and Ideologies. Some have suggested that it would signal a further advance if conversations with Israel were conducted in the framework of the Commission on Faith and Order, i.e., as part of the ecumenical rather than the interfaith dialogue. Thus, it would indicate the common roots of Judaism and Christianity plus the idea that the alienation between church and synagogue is to be seen as the original schism.

Obviously, such a move would eliminate the notion of mission altogether, because one does not missionize people with whom one entertains ecumenical relations, although, within an ecumenical context, one could still speak of a mutual witness to one another. But others, both in the Jewish and Christian communities, hold that structuring the dialogue on the principle that Christianity and Judaism are in essence "one faith" is going a bit too far. Some also see a danger that Christians who urge this approach in effect seek to define for Jews how they should understand the dialogue relationship, even though there are leading Jewish scholars as well, like David Flusser, who defend the "one-faith" thesis.

Since 1973, however, the WCC office on Christian-Jewish Relations has been called the "Consultation on the Church and the Jewish People," thus correctly suggesting that dialogue is a matter of mutual exchange, a two-way street. Also, mutual consultation seems very far removed from mission or evangelism. But, on the other hand, consultation sounds so safe, so businesslike, so devoid of deep engagement or even passion.

What is dialogue really all about? Surely, it involves more than the exchange of information. After all, such a function could be handled by a computerized data bank with an "800" number. Because, above all, dialogue has something to do with person-to-person encounter, it belongs in Martin Buber's world of I-thou. As such, it involves risk, on both sides. Without the element of risk, or exposing oneself to the possibility of fundamental change and mutual transformation, dialogue will end up in sheer boredom, or at least in interminable meetings attended by "official" representatives who love consultations as long as their travel expense accounts hold out.

Some Christians become visibly upset, if not actually annoyed, whenever a Jew is grasped by the figure of Jesus to the point of a radical life commitment. Why don't those Jews understand what seems as clear as light of day to the Christian dialogue expert, namely, that they don't need "it." The implication, of course, is that Jesus is for the Gentiles and has no redemptive relevance for Jews. A similar argument can be heard from the Jewish side when certain rabbis assure the world that they discourage people from becoming converts to Judaism because they don't need "it" either, i.e., by simply leading a good life one can gain a place in the world to come without "it."

These assurances sound very well-meaning. But it strikes me as somewhat arrogant, even triumphalistic, when people are so confident telling another person what he or she needs. Who are we really to pontificate on such matters, except in a general and abstract way? Theoretically, people may not need this or that, but life has its own needs and the heart its own reasons. What do we know about the searchings of another's soul, about the hungers of the heart, about the passionate inner struggles?

It is my contention that an honest-to-God encounter with Judaism and Israel could have radical consequences for the life and theology of the church, and that, in the main, that would be a good thing. But it is risky business. And what is true of the corporate entities engaged in dialogue is also true of the individual participants. Dialogue that is totally safe is never very serious, and certainly not very interesting. The same can be said of dialogue that has smoothed out all rough edges and, with the aid of neat phrases, resolved all ambiguities.

Take the Vatican document, "Notes on the correct way to present the Jews and Judaism in preaching and catechesis in the Roman Catholic Church." It contains some very obvious ambiguities. On the one hand, as we have seen earlier, the document reaffirms the words of the late Pope John Paul II to the effect that the Jewish people are "the people of God of the Old Covenant, which has never been revoked . . ." and refers to the "witness–often heroic" that this people has made to the whole world throughout its history.

On the other hand, the "Notes" observe "the sad fact that the majority of the Jewish people and its authorities did not believe in Jesus . . ." In other words, the Vatican does not seem to agree that the Jewish "no" to the church's message should in every respect be appreciated as a positive. Furthermore, the mission of the church is defined in terms of "the all-embracing means of salvation" that leads through Jesus to the Father. It seems an almost explicit rejection of a dual-covenant theology when the document adds: "Church and Judaism cannot then be seen as two parallel ways of salvation and the Church must witness to Christ as the Redeemer for all . . ."

Dr. Eugene Fisher does not read it that way. He still argues that there is a basis in teachings of the Holy See and the popes since Vatican II for the view that "the Jews, in not becoming Christians, were and are following God's will." He maintains that this Jewish response is part of the mystery with which the apostle Paul struggles in Romans 9:11. And he, too, has a point.

Apparently, the "Notes" wish to present a clear claim of the salvific and universal significance of the Catholic Church without denying that Jews can and should draw salvific gifts from their own traditions,[13] but also without denying the apostolic mandate of the church. How to put all of this in a nice, neat formula? Personally, I doubt that this can be done. The paradoxes of faith and life cannot be packaged that easily. I am not plugging for obscurantism; clarity of language is a good and virtuous thing. And, as a tool for educators, the "Notes" could definitely be improved upon. But, even under the best of formulations, the Catholic Church (as well as many other churches) would still be saying both that the Jewish people continue to be the people of the covenant, that throughout history they have given a witness to divine faithfulness (in a sense their very survival is such a witness!), *and* that the church is called to share the message of Christ with all people, including Jews.

Some will insist that this is not a satisfactory arrangement. But ambiguities and inner tensions are part of all historical existence. Geoffrey Wigoder, in commenting on the "Notes," complained that, "despite the discontinuation of mission, an implied conversionist hope is manifest."[14] Absolutely! There is no denying the fact that a certain sense of satisfaction will stir the souls of many Christians, even Christian advocates of dialogue, when someone from another faith or no-faith decides to join their fellowship. The more prominent the convert, the bigger the catch. And I dare say that precisely the same sentiments prevail among Jews when the person turns out to be a convert to Judaism.

How pure are the motives of the various parties involved in such situations? One can only guess or try to play God. But to start complaining about "implied hope" seems to me to ask for interfaith relationships that transcend the boundaries of historical existence. History fully justifies Jewish suspicion about Christian witness. It is, therefore, right that Christians should be needled and pushed to clarify their positions. Do you advocate mission to Jews? That is a fair question. Do you practice such mission and, if so, what form does it take? Another fair question. Can you guarantee me that you have abandoned, not only advocacy of mission, not only the practice of such mission, but all "implied hope" that someone of my community might become committed to the faith of your community? For some Christians the answer will be "yes." But most Christians, I believe, would hope that such a promise would not be made the condition for dialogue or friendly relationships.

Suspicions within the Jewish community usually are especially strong with respect to evangelicals, because, after all, that is where the strongest missionary drive often is to be found. And on their part, many evangelicals who have become sensitized to Jewish concerns are struggling with the mission issue. The International Christian Embassy in Jerusalem has chosen the words of Isaiah 40:1 as its motto: "Comfort ye, comfort ye my people." That, say the Embassy leaders, represents their calling and they remind all who will listen that the text does not say "Preach ye, preach ye to my people." Perhaps others are called to do that. A past director of the U.S. ICEJ branch put it this way in his newsletter: "the purpose, goals and sovereign call of God upon the Embassy is to awaken the Christian community the world over to our responsibility to stand with the Jewish people as God's ancient covenant people. It is not our purpose to evangelize."

Nevertheless, it cannot be taken for granted that those fine distinctions will be accepted and observed by all supporters of the International Christian Embassy or all those who participate in events sponsored by it. When former ICEJ spokesman Jan Willem van der Hoeven was quoted in *The Jerusalem Post* (International Edition), as stating that "Christianity is for the Gentiles" (implying that God himself will take care of his people the Jews, i.e., open their eyes at his appointed time), many ICEJ supporters did more than display a frown. Still, it is my impression that a growing number of evangelicals are prepared–while not denying the missionary mandate, which they in good conscience cannot–to adopt a position "in which the missionary urge to convert Israel is held in check," as Krister Stendahl words it.[15] For some this means that the resolution of the dilemma is simply pushed to the *eschaton*, when God himself will intervene in the history of Israel in such a way that, as Paul stated it, "all Israel will be saved" (Romans 11:26).

In the meantime, I hear some evangelical leaders say that our calling toward the Jewish people is to repent of past sins and to show unconditional love, which includes that one stands in solidarity with the always-beleaguered nation of Israel. To others in the evangelical community, this sounds like compromise, if not outright deception. To them, the priority can never lie in Israel's security, important as that is. It must always be that the gospel be preached to all nations.

For those who cannot, in good conscience, write off the universal claims of the gospel's message, the question of the *form* that Christian witness should take *vis-à-vis* the Jewish people becomes crucial. In light of what the Scriptures teach us about the eternal covenant, and in light of what history teaches us about Christian conduct over almost 2000 years, what can be considered a valid witness to our Jewish neighbors?

Furthermore, how well have we listened to the witness of Israel before we issue our urgent calls to conversion? As J. Coert Rylaarsdam wrote, "For the foreseeable future the primary concern of Christian mission to the Jews must be the redemption of Christians, specifically with respect to their understanding of their relation to the faith of Israel."[16] Markus Barth, makes the point that "Israel is God's chosen missionary to the Gentiles."[17] Hence, he adds, such designations as "Christian mission to the Jews had better be dropped. The way in which it often is carried out alienates more Jews than it wins."[18] The younger brother owes a testimony to the older brother, says Barth, but it must be characterized by modesty, "by his asking for forgiveness." [19]

Then, what shall we still say and do after we have truly listened and confessed? It seems to me that whatever form Gentile witness to Jews takes after that, it will lack all characteristics of ambitious campaigns and triumphalistic "crusades." There is evidence that some of this is already happening. Gentile mission to the Jewish people in the old style is being practiced on a lesser scale than ever before. On the other hand, "Jewish mission" in the sense of aggressive outreach by converts from Judaism to their own people is probably on the increase. Such mission has dimensions all its own. Some thoughts on the phenomenon of "Hebrew Christians" or "Messianic Jews" will follow in the next chapter.

I would like to sum up this one with a quote from an article John S. Conway wrote for the first issue of the journal *Holocaust and Genocide Studies*. Toward the conclusion of the article, Conway writes:

"By its essence the Christian church is mission-oriented and committed to the person of Jesus Christ as the Saviour of the World. For Christians, mission is the sharing of the Good News about God's action in history through Jesus Christ. The church may renounce all claim to exclusive truth or absolute authority, or it may reject the methods of persecution, coercion and enforced proselytism of earlier years. But it cannot deny or obliterate its duty to witness in one way or another. The task for Christians is to attempt to find appropriate forms which will reflect neither the repulsive aspects of triumphalist mission, nor the inadmissible relativism of a conscious or unconscious syncretism. The task for Jews is to be aware that the church's terrible and tragic involvement in the genocidal missions of the past need not represent the only possible pattern of relations between the followers of the Jew Jesus and the people of his original family."[20]

[1] Peter Johnson, "Mainline Churches and United States Middle East Policy," *American Church Politics and the Middle East,* Basheer K. Nijim, ed. (Belmont, MA: Association of American-Arab University Graduates, 1982), p. 65.

[2] *Ibid.,* p. 73.

[3] Peter Grose, *Israel in the Mind of America* (New York: Knopf; Distributed by Random House, 1983), p. 214.

[4] Paul van Buren, quoted in *Religious News Service,* November 26, 1985.

[5] *Quarterly Review,* Winter 1984.

[6] *Shalom,* March 1986.

[7] *New York Times Magazine,* September 1985.

[8] cf. *New York Times,* January 8, 1987.

[9] Blu Greenberg in Marc H. Tanenbaum, et. al., *Evangelicals and Jews in an Age of Pluralism* (Grand Rapids, MI: Baker Book House, 1984), p. 231.

[10] *Ibid.,* p. 220.

[11] *Ibid.,* p. 232.

[12] *Ibid.,* p. 230.

[13] cf. *Midstream,* January 1987, p. 61.

[14] *Midstream,* June/July 1986, p. 12.

[15] Krister Stendahl, *Paul among Jews and Gentiles, and Other Essays* (Minneapolis: Augsburg Fortress Publishers, 1976), p. 4.

[16] *Face to Face,* III/IV, 1977, p. 18.

[17] Markus Barth, *Israel and the Church in Ephesians,* p. 109.

[18] *Ibid.,* p. 110.

[19] *Ibid.,* p. 113.

[20] John S. Conway, "Protestant Missions to the Jews 1810-1980: Ecclesiastical Imperialism or Theological Aberration?", *Holocaust and Genocide Studies,* Vol. 1, No. 1, 1986, pp. 127, 146.

DIALOGUE AND
MESSIANIC JEWS

CHAPTER 18

Messianic Jews:
A Troubling Presence

When it comes to Christian-Jewish relations, particularly Christian-Jewish dialogue, the most sensitive issues of all, of course, are those of mission and conversion. Thus, those of us Christians who are seriously engaged in such dialogue need to be particularly sensitive about conduct on our part that could even remotely be interpreted as being missionary in nature.

At the same time, the question as to what constitutes "authentic Christian witness," particularly *vis-à-vis* our Jewish interlocutors, is as unavoidable as it is unresolved for us. From time to time assemblies of major denominations, in the course of discussing pronouncements about Christian attitudes toward Jews, have come close to concluding that Jews ought to be exempted from any Christian outreach. In the end, however, it would seem that the imperatives of the gospel prohibited them from going so far: the missionary mandate was maintained, albeit–practically speaking–in a state of dormancy.

Michael Kogan proposed that we move toward something called "total dialogue," that is, risk the vulnerability of "expos[ing] one's own community's beliefs to influence by the other in a mutual enrichment process."[1] This proposal inevitably evoked a good deal of debate, raising once again as it does the issues of conversion and mission. Invited by the editor of the newsletter to contribute a few observations on the idea of "total dialogue," I myself decided to up Dr. Kogan's ante by adding a further complication: "To exclude from the dialogue *as a class*," I declared, "all Jews who confess Jesus as Messiah in the Christian sense is wrong, as wrong as any other violation of people's conscience." My comment was accompanied by an editorial stating that such a position would lead to the "overnight destruction of dialogue," because people like Jews for Jesus insist on engaging in proselytizing activities toward their own people.

By coincidence, David Novak's article "When Jews Are Christians" appeared in *First Things* just around the same time. In it, Novak warned that the progress made in Jewish-Christian relationships could be jeopardized because of a "new type of Jewish convert to Christianity," namely, one who claims to remain a Jew while accepting Jesus as the Messiah of Israel and the Savior of the world. Arguing that the views of Messianic Jews are a problem both to the Jewish and the Christian communities, the author pointed out that a sympathetic hearing for these views on the part of church leaders could well cause difficulties for those Jews who have precisely been the strongest supporters of Christian-Jewish dialogue.[2]

The complexities involved in this situation–theological, historical, and psychological–are clearly immense and may not be possible to overcome. In addition, there is often not even a common language in which to discuss the problem. Take, for instance, the terms "a follower of Jesus" and "a convert to Christianity." Some Jewish Christians accept the former designation, but assiduously avoid the latter, because, to them it seems to imply that they embrace all of historic "Christendom." By focusing on Jesus, they can retain a critical stance toward much that goes by the name of "Christianity."

There is also the question as to whether a Messianic Jew is by definition someone who confesses Jesus as Messiah. Some Jewish Christians do not wish to define themselves in those terms; they are content to be known as Christians, period. But what if those same people still claim to remain Jews? Such is clearly the position of Aaron Jean-Marie Lustiger, archbishop of Paris.[3] He is reluctant to discuss his decision to be baptized in the Catholic Church–out of a desire to avoid provocation. However, when pushed by reporters, he is most emphatic about his conviction that he has not ceased to be a Jew. "I am discovering another way of being Jewish," he reports having told his parents, because to him Christianity is "a natural extension of Judaism."

If the status of Cardinal Lustiger presents a problem to Jews, even more problematic, not only to Jews but to many Christians as well, is what could be called "the organized Messianic Jewish community"– Jewish Christians who form separate Messianic congregations, observe the Jewish Sabbath, continue many Jewish practices, and celebrate certain Jewish festivals. Such congregations have also organized themselves into national and international networks, such as the Messianic Jewish Alliance of America, the Union of Messianic Jewish Congregations, etc. Then there is Jews for Jesus, a separate organization with its own agenda and constituency. The same is true of various Hebrew-Christian mission societies. As an increasingly organized community with a strong missionary thrust, such groups are sometimes viewed as a major threat to Jewish-Christian rapprochement.

There have been periods in history when the problem of Christianity for Jews was very much focused on Jesus. He, as the central figure of the Christian faith, became the great symbol of all the evil that had been perpetrated against Jews in his name. It was not uncommon for pious Jews to spit in disgust at the mere mention of that name.

Much has changed in this respect. Jesus, as a Jew who was faithful to Torah, has become a figure with whom many Jews have become quite comfortable. He is seen as "one of ours." As a matter of fact, many students today are gaining profound insights into Jesus through the large and rich body of literature on the subject by Jewish authors. The line, to be sure, is drawn at the Christian belief in Jesus as Son of God.

As it is on the question of conversion. It is always difficult for faith communities to see one of their own convert to another religion. But a Jew converting to Christianity has often been experienced by Jews as particularly painful. Not only has the Jewish community historically had a profound sense of peoplehood, but it has also been a minority community regularly subjected to persecutions in which, one way or another, Christians have played a part. So, in the case of a conversion, there has not only been a painful sense of loss to the community, but a bitter sense of betrayal as well. Moreover, the fact that expediency sometimes played a role in a Jew's decision to convert didn't make things any easier. Assimilated Jews were usually despised because they tried so desperately to be just like Gentiles.

Today, the Jewish community is confronted with a very different kind of conversion problem: namely, that of converts who, having embraced Christianity, seem to feel a greater need than before to accentuate their Jewishness, sometimes even to the point of Judaizing their names. In many cases these people are well-educated and determined to raise their children as Christians with a strong sense of Jewish identity. They appear to want to flaunt what assimilated Jews of previous generations often sought to hide.

Ironically, it is precisely their desire to retain a Jewish identity and to maintain certain aspects of the tradition of their forebears that often is turned against them, leading to accusations that all this is a ploy, part of a covert and deceptive missionary strategy whereby they seek to seduce other Jews to forsake their faith as well. For centuries the Jewish community has had to struggle to maintain its faith in the midst of an often hostile Gentile world or in the face of the church's missionary efforts. But the movement of Messianic Jews must look to many like a fifth-column assault.

Permit me here to introduce my own experience, which has offered me a very special vantage point from which to view some of the perplexities of this most perplexing issue. My wife and I both grew up in Dutch Reformed homes. Our fathers were not only committed church members, but professional workers. Our youthful experiences in life were by and large typical of Dutch Reformed children in the Netherlands, even though my grandfather was an Hasidic rabbi in Poland and my father a convert to Christianity, while her father had been a socialist activist in that same country who had also "converted." We were never really part of the Jewish experience–until the Nazis made us so.

Hitler and his cohorts reminded us constantly about "the blood in our veins." They made us part of one of the most traumatic experiences in all of Jewish history. My father was arrested as a Jew who had written books critical of Nazism and, after spending some time in Buchenwald, he was murdered in Mauthausen. When Jewish children put on a show for International Red Cross executives who came to inspect Adolf Eichmann's "Paradeise ghetto" Terezin (Theresienstadt), my wife was there and her younger sisters were part of the group that so famously performed "The Tales of the Vienna Woods." So you might say some experience of "Jewishness" had come into both our lives, almost in spite of our upbringing–and along with it, a sense of ambiguity about being at the same time part of a people's history but, basically, still "outsiders."

We have never talked much about these experiences, certainly not among the wide circle of our Jewish friends and acquaintances. Not only would it somehow seem an intrusion, but we have no desire, either, to join the ever-growing band of Christian Holocaust specialists. Thus, it has been granted us to live and work at the borderline of the Jewish experience and the Christian encounter with that experience.

This will explain the impulse behind my comment to the *National Dialogue Newsletter*. I have come to feel increasingly uneasy about a certain current tendency to characterize converts from Judaism as people of questionable integrity.

None will deny that the greater the fervor to convert others, the stronger may be the temptation to engage in questionable missionary tactics. Nor can serious Christians oppose the idea that there should be a constant critical evaluation of Christian evangelistic methods and practices. Converts (to almost any kind of movement) tend to be highly aggressive in their attempts to persuade others. The prophetic-apostolic witness, too, knows of an inner imperative to speak, a mandate to proclaim. "If I say, 'I will not mention him, or speak anymore in his name,' there is in my heart as it were a burning fire shut up in my bones, and I am weary with holding it in, and I cannot" (Jeremiah 20:9). "Necessity is laid upon me. Woe to me if I do not preach the gospel" (1 Corinthians 9:16). Sometimes it can be a bit uncomfortable to be confronted by a zealous convert.

Certainly, all of us must be prepared to listen to the critiques of other faith communities, and especially those of our Jewish brothers and sisters. But, critical analysis also requires that we avoid quick and easy answers, particularly if they are motivated more by feelings of guilt about past sins than by faith commitments.

In this connection, the word *proselytizing* ought to be used with some care. It tends to be applied in an indiscriminate fashion, often with an implied negative connotation, so that by simply stating that someone engages in proselytism, one can implicitly be making a moral judgment.

Historically, the word *proselytism* did not necessarily carry such baggage. Highly respected Jewish scholars, like Dr. Bernard Bamberger[4] and Dr. William C. Braude[5] used the term quite unapologetically. Building on their research, Rabbi Ely E. Pilchik felt that he was in the spirit of ancient Jewish tradition when he wrote the following sentences (no doubt controversial to many) "We need numbers. We need more Jews lest we wither and disappear. We need proselytes. We need to win over Christians, Muslims, Hindus, Shintos, and other 'goyim' to Judaism."[6] This was not meant as a threat; it was meant as a call to righteousness and concern about the future of the Jewish people in the post-Holocaust era.

Still, as noted before, in the minds of many, proselytizing has become a code word for unethical missionary practices, implying coercion, deceit, and even bribery. Judging by such a standard, it becomes a bit easier to agree that any kind of evangelization would be unethical.

David Novak, in the aforementioned article, does not confine himself to quick brush-offs with terms like "proselytism" or "deception" as he presents his case for why Messianic Jews could pose a threat to the future of Jewish-Christian dialogue. Rather, he offers a theological analysis in order to explain why these people, although according to normative Judaism would still be considered Jews, are not justified in making their claims. Today's Messianic Jews, says Professor Novak, should be compared to the (heretical) "syncretists of the second and third centuries," not to the first Jewish Christians (with whom they often compare themselves). At one time, it may have been plausible to view Christianity as a form of Judaism, runs this argument, but a long and eventful history, including the history of Christian doctrinal formulations (e.g., "Jesus as the incarnate Son of God, the second person of the Trinity"), makes that now impossible.

Novak is concerned that churches might come to accept the self-definition of Messianic Jews, which in turn would arouse the suspicion among the Jewish partners in dialogue that their Christian counterparts silently condone proselytizing aimed specifically at Jews. Thus, the mission/witness issue which, at least in the mainline churches, had been largely but not entirely dormant, is once again moved to the forefront of Christian-Jewish relations.

One statement in Novak's article is particularly striking. He points out that, according to the Pauline principle that "in Christ there is no Jew or Greek," the church has expected Jews to become what could be called "regular members," just like all the other members. As a matter of fact, he then adds, Jewish converts to Christianity themselves almost always "accepted the church's definition of their new status. They no longer regarded themselves as Jews and were often quite vehement in repudiating their former identity."

Here we remind ourselves that, in the Middle Ages, it was quite common for church authorities to force Jews to publicly renounce their heritage before accepting them into the church. We know the formula: "I do here and now renounce every rite and observance of the Jewish religion, detesting all its solemn ceremonies and tenets that in former days I kept and held." In short, a "good convert" was one who had totally abandoned his/her Jewish identity.

But, in more recent times, it has become recognized in Christian circles, missionary circles in particular, that our blindness to the need for contextualization of the gospel has been one of the biggest mistakes the church has made in its worldwide outreach. The Christian message must be incorporated into the life and culture of the peoples to whom it is addressed, be it in Africa, Asia, or wherever. It has now become clear that the approach followed previously was unfortunately tainted by a certain ecclesiastical imperialism. A "good convert" was often portrayed as a person well acculturated to our Western ways. Missionary success stories were frequently about "native" evangelists who acted, talked, and even dressed like British Methodists or American Southern Baptists. Jews, too, were usually most welcome if they adjusted to our churchly ways.

Today the situation is quite different. The need for contextualization is widely recognized, and, consequently, the development of ethnically oriented churches is not only condoned, but actively encouraged. Even in the United States we see a growing number of Korean Presbyterian churches, Reformed Taiwanese churches, and the like. Each of these Christian communities is recognized as being unique in its own way, and yet all are seen as part of the one body of the church.

As it happens, discussions about the preservation of Jewish identity within the church and the pros and cons of establishing separate Hebrew-Christian congregations have been going on for many years now. In the rather extensive body of literature produced by Jewish converts to Christianity, one finds all sorts of questions raised, including questions about the early formulations of Christian doctrine. As the U.S. Catholic bishops pointed out in one of their pronouncements, a process of de-Judaization of the Christian faith started very early in its history. Elements of the Hellenistic thought-world were introduced, and, in many cases, Christian theological expression became quite dependent on Greek metaphysical categories.

We know why this happened and how it helped communicate the gospel to the Greco-Roman world. But we also know that the process of de-Judaization eventually became a handy tool in the hands of those who advocated an anti-Judaic theology. After all, the biblical revelation came to humanity in Hebrew context; it is important that one be able to enter into Hebrew thought. Yet, for many Jewish converts, the Christian theological climate never seemed very hospitable, nor have they always felt "at home" in our local congregations.

The church, for its part, has its own difficulties with trying to determine what constitutes an "authentic witness" *vis-à-vis* Jewish neighbors. Jews as Jews are not outside the orbit of revelation. Quite the contrary, they are the people of the covenant in whose midst the God of Abraham, Isaac, and Jacob made himself known and revealed his Name. A growing number of denominations have confessed that they were wrong when, over a long history, they taught a replacement form of theology and contributed to the sufferings of the Jewish people. In light of that history, it is no wonder that many church leaders are inclined to pause before proposing ambitious missionary schemes. For most of them, however, this whole situation is experienced as a dilemma, because, with few exceptions, these church leaders also agree with someone like Professor Gabriel Fackre who, in a commentary on a United Church of Christ document on the church and the Jewish people, declared quite unequivocally: "Antisupersessionism does not forbid sharing the Gospel with Jewish people." The question is, how do we do that, while honoring the continuing covenant of God with Israel?

The apostle Paul was not yet burdened by the history that now weighs so heavily upon the churches. But in his missionary outreach, he faced some of the same questions that we must confront today. For instance, he never lost sight of the distinction between those who know Torah and those who do not, even when he argued their equal status before God–as people in need of forgiveness. Jews and Gentiles live in different thought-worlds; they raise different questions, because they do not share the same expectations. Take, for instance, a passage like 1 Corinthians 1:22-23: "Jews demand signs and Greeks seek wisdom, but we preach Christ crucified. . . ." Jews know Torah. Their expectations about future redemption have always been closely related to historical reality. They want to know where the empirical evidence is to be found that the Messianic age has been inaugurated. How can the message of Christ crucified reveal the power of the kingdom? Hence, the challenge to preach the gospel in such a way that it does not preclude a theology of history and culture. The New Testament does that by emphasizing the cosmic dimensions of a biblical Christology.

The Greeks, on the other hand, seek wisdom. Their fundamental vision is one of world harmony. Hence, the message of the cross seemed, from the perspective of their philosophical presuppositions, a rather foolish idea.

But in terms of guilt before God, Paul sees both Jews and Gentiles in need of the same grace. Similar ideas can be found in other passages. Romans 1:18-2:29 is an example. Those who are outside the orbit of revelation of the God of Israel, who do not know Torah, are tempted to deify the cosmos. Instead of glorifying God, who has revealed himself as Creator, they tend to worship their own images (1:23). Jews know better. But, as Paul sees it, they, too, are without excuse (2:1), because their actions do not conform to the demands of the law, and, hence, they stand guilty before God and are in need of redemption. So, in the end, Paul finds the answer for the predicament of both Jew and Gentile in Christ's fulfillment of the law, an obedience he interprets as an act of redemption.

Still, he is deeply aware of the dangers that loom on the horizon as soon as the church loses sight of the mystery of the calling of Israel, a theme he develops in the much-discussed chapters Romans 9-11. Triumphalism takes over; the branches that have been grafted into the tree of God's covenant with the people of Israel forget that they do not support the root, the root supports them (11:18).

Paul could hardly have imagined how his fears would play out on the stage of subsequent history. Now, almost 2,000 years later, we know what that kind of triumphalism has led to. To the inherent offense of the cross were added offenses that were rooted in the sins of the churches. And so, for many Jews, the thought of any Christian witness directed at them is scandalous. The late Rabbi Pinchas Peli raised a protest against missionary activities that was both sharp and direct: "What they are doing is something that cannot be pardoned, cannot be forgiven, especially in Israel, especially after the Holocaust. We have not yet settled our account with Christianity as it is. One doesn't need to add insult to injury, and try to take us away from our religion." And so, we live in the tension field between our own *peccavi* and the gospel imperative to witness to all humankind. The missionary mandate is not denied, but, in practice, the issue is often surrounded by an embarrassed silence.

Enter the Messianic Jews, filled with the missionary elan of new converts, more than vocal in spreading the word about their new-found faith in Jesus, sometimes even taking out full-page advertisements in major newspapers. No closet Christians they. They do not see themselves as "targeting" a special group "out there" for their witness, because for them the confrontation normally starts among their immediate families, relatives, and friends, and then spreads through the broader community of which they still feel themselves a part, albeit perhaps in a state of estrangement.

How to respond to these realities? David Novak undoubtedly speaks for the great majority of Jews when he writes that Christians cannot expect them to accept any notion that Messianic Jews might serve as "a unique link between the Jewish people and the Church."

However, from the Christian point of view it could well be argued that the idea of such a link ought to be explored. If Hebrew Christians were to introduce a more Hebraic mode of thinking into our often Hellenized ways of doing theology, the church could benefit greatly. For decades we have been struggling to develop a prophetic-messianic vision, an eschatology that includes both expectancy and social responsibility, that would help us break out of our sterile either-or theological constructions and ideological preoccupations.

In our search for a vision of the future, we have traveled from fad to fad; from ahistorical existentialist theologies to theologies of revolution; from post-Christian celebrations of the secular city to the establishment of peace, justice, and liberation bureaucracies that are ever itching to be prophetic if denominations will provide secure financial support—even, in some cases, to the point of assessing (i.e., taxing) their membership for the "service." The churches desperately need a theology of the kingdom of God that incorporates the broad historical and cosmic themes of the Hebrew Scriptures and apostolic writings.

Can Messianic Jews serve as a link in such matters? Potentially, I would say, "yes." Still, as of now, there seems to be little reason to be optimistic on that point. In many instances, their thinking seems to be permeated by Christian otherworldliness. Much of their piety is imbued with a "precious Jesus" Messianism that lacks a broad historical vision. The type of fundamentalism that many Messianic Jews have embraced has much to say about the soul (often in very Hellenistic terms), spiritualizing the gospel message so as to virtually empty it of its social-political implications. In short, to me, all this sounds too much like more of the un-Hebraic dualistic mode of thinking that the church needs to overcome. Furthermore, when a historical perspective is presented, it is often so charged with the hype found among some of the television prophecy preachers that a calm discussion of biblical theology becomes almost impossible.

Still, isolation without conversation cannot be the answer. Messianic Jews are part of the church, a fellowship in which many differences coexist within a community of common faith. Potentially, they have something important to contribute to the whole church. Nobody's interest is served by pushing them to become an increasingly sectarian movement. True, some of their present isolation may well be self-imposed. Perhaps there is an element of clannishness involved. Honesty, however, demands that we look deeper than that. The fact that these people often see themselves as "twice exiled," rejected by their old home and not entirely welcome in their new one, requires our serious consideration.

Among evangelicals, who do not experience mission, including mission to Jews, as much of a dilemma, one finds a measure of openness toward Messianic Jews. Since the evangelicals' dialogue with the Jewish community is less developed than that of the Christian mainstream, they also feel less pressure to protect contacts that have been cultivated over a long period of time.

Still, evangelicals who are strong supporters of the State of Israel, even though they may have positive personal feelings toward Messianic Jews, are often inclined to tone down their churches' mission theology and to keep cautiously quiet about any contacts they may have with them. The reason is quite simple: they are eager to maintain their close ties with Jewish leaders, both here and in Israel. Consequently, they are caught between conflicting loves and loyalties.

All in all, one senses a good deal of ambivalence in the evangelical community at large about the Messianic Jewish movement. Theologically, there may be a feeling of kinship, but on the level of community life there often is a hesitation about the otherness of the other. If dialogue is based on "I-thou" relationships, rather than the absorption of one party into the other, if dialogue means expectant openness to mutual transformation, then it would seem that the evangelical and Messianic Jewish movements have a long way to go.

The mainline Christian-Jewish dialogue movement is quite another story. Some of the leading theologians in those circles tend to see a closer link between their faith and traditional Judaism than between them and Messianic Jews. Of course, they also have made a greater effort to develop contacts and exchange views with the Jewish community. Messianic Jews usually are seen as a disturbing, even threatening, element in the mix of Christian-Jewish relations, and, hence, they frequently evoke feelings of hostility.

Participants in the mainstream dialogue have reached a virtual consensus that no true dialogue is possible with anyone who may give even the slightest indication of believing that the answer to life's mysteries in the final analysis is to be found in his/her religious tradition. That, they say, is the true mark of triumphalism and means the death of dialogue. Nevertheless, these same people express a desire to reach out to Islam, even though there is no reason to believe that Jewish-Christian-Muslim conversations presently can be conducted on the basis of a "theology of equality."

No doubt, truth claims can complicate dialogue, but do they necessarily lead to the death of dialogue? All forms of ecumenical and interfaith dialogue were born when, in a general atmosphere of polemics and antithetical positions, some pioneers persisted in listening to each other even though their differences seemed insuperable. On the other hand, the death of dialogue may well be caused by indifference about fundamental beliefs that historically have been seen as touching on people's eternal destiny.

At the moment, we are facing a stand-off. Some of our Jewish part-ners want the issue of Messianic Jews on the agenda under the category of a "threat to dialogue." Some Christian advocates of improved rela-tions with the Jewish community, for a variety of reasons, find avoid-ance (if not rejection) of Messianic Jews an acceptable position, at least until the latter tone down their enthusiasm to share their new-found faith with others. Messianic Jews themselves, while often eager to por-tray themselves as potentially a creative link between Judaism and the Christian faith, may–also for a variety of reasons–prefer to make those claims "from a distance," i.e., without making a real effort to contribute to a climate in which such issues can be explored. So, we end up with the worst of all possible dialogical worlds. All the parties seem stuck in their own peculiar fundamentalism.

Where will new incentives come from? The history of religious bodies shows that new initiatives usually come from pioneers who are prepared to probe the boundaries of establishment positions and estab-lishment politics (including the politics of dialogue), people who are ready to take the risk of utilizing all the valuable lessons that have been learned during the past decades of interfaith encounters.

Issues raised by Messianic Jews today have deep roots in church history, going back to apostolic times. They deserve to be discussed, rather than summarily dismissed as mere repetitions of ancient heresies. Christians engaged in conversations with Messianic Jews ought not to be considered a threat to the ongoing Christian-Jewish dialogue, unless they say or do things that clearly are inimical to the integrity of inter-faith relationships. Whether or not this is the case ought not be deter-mined exclusively in terms of the politics of dialogue, but also, or per-haps even more so, in terms of the moral-spiritual values embedded in our faith.

Religious communities recognize a variety of callings. This is also the case within the context of interfaith dialogue. What we do not need are adversarial postures between people who feel called to explore dif-ferent areas of dialogue. Maintaining links to both the Jewish and the Messianic communities will require a considerable dose of graceful sen-sitivity, as well as a bit of political savvy. Only Christians who have honestly and humbly confronted the history of the Christian-Jewish experience should apply.

Dialogue, by its very nature, is an open process, always prepared to respond to new challenges. All new ventures in ecumenical and inter-faith endeavors tend to start out as impossible dreams. The status quo never is good enough, least of all to those who have had long practice in the often painful process of dialogue and have tasted its fruits.

The original, unedited form of this chapter was first published in the December, 1992, issue of First Things. Reprinted by permission.

[1] Michael Kogan, *National Dialogue Newsletter*, Winter 1990-91.

[2] David Novak, "When Jews Are Christians," *First Things*, November 1991.

[3] Aaron Jean-Marie Lustiger, *Dare to Believe* (New York: Crossroads, 1986).

[4] Bernard Bamberger, *Proselytism in the Talmudic Period* (New York: Ktav Publishing House, 1939).

[5] William C. Braude, *Jewish Proselytizing in the First Five Centuries of the Common Era* (Providence RI: Brown University, 1940).

[6] Ely E.Pilchik, *The Jewish Week*, December 24, 1981.

CHAPTER 19

Israel and Jewish Christianity

Is Israel the key to Christian unity, and should the phenomenon of a Jewish Christianity within the church be judged positively as a potentially stimulating factor in that search for unity? Anyone familiar with the history of Christian-Jewish relations, and particularly developments in the post-Holocaust era, knows that, in raising such issues, we are treading on very hazardous territory. The question, however, is whether, biblically and/or historically, these issues can be avoided. One thing is sure: The sins of the church's past are being visited upon us, confronting the Church with harsh consequences that cannot be resolved without much struggle and pain; and any resolution will require a measure of love and wisdom beyond our purely human capacity.

Father Peter Hocken has suggested that the phenomenon of the so-called Messianic Jewish movement in our day is, as it were, a "first fruit" of the "reintegration of Israel into the one body being formed by the Spirit," and as such should be seen as a major positive in our search for greater catholicity and unity among Christians. That is not the kind of talk we tend to hear in conciliar ecumenical circles, or among mainline denominational dialogue participants. There, rather than being seen as a divinely ordained promise, "Messianic Judaism" is more often viewed as a divisive force and an obstacle to dialogue.

Hocken has said that the olive tree image of Romans 11 suggests that

> a wholly Gentile Christianity was doomed to division. This is implied by Jewish connaturality with the olive tree, which is the one body being formed by the Spirit. Since the gift and call of God are irrevocable, we should expect that the vocation of Israel to be a priestly people will be restored with their reintegration. In this case, Israel's re-grafting into the olive tree will make them mediators of covenant blessing to the churches of the Gentiles. This perspective reinforces the idea that God will use Israel in the restoration of Christian unity.[1]

To those folk, this statement will sound suspiciously like the rapturous hype of certain prophecy preachers. While it is true that the author is someone who is deeply involved in the Pentecostal and charismatic movements, he also happens to be a balanced scholar who is not only well-versed in the theological tradition of his own church, but also remarkably well-informed about and sensitive to Orthodox and Protestant positions. Furthermore, as indicated by the title of his book, *The Glory and the Shame*, he is not afraid to take a critical look at a movement he loves.

Hocken uses an approach that is marked by a broad pneumatological approach which focuses not only on the "baptism in the Spirit," but also sees the Holy Spirit as operative in history, including the various Christian traditions (Catholic, Orthodox, Anglican, and mainline, as well as nondenominational Protestant). Furthermore, he views the work of the Spirit very much in terms of unity. "Israel holds the key to Christian unity . . . there is something unbalanced, literally uncatholic, about a wholly Gentile Church in which Jewish converts have been totally assimilated into Gentile culture," he declares.[2] Hocken relates the contemporary manifestations of the renewing and reuniting power of the Spirit to the rise of a distinctively Jewish form of Christianity for the first time since the patristic period.[3] Others who have entertained such notions have usually thought in terms of an increasing number of conversions to Gentile Christianity, rather than the emergence of "Messianic Judaism" as a dynamic historical movement with the potential of impacting the life and theology of the church.

The Church began as a Jewish Christian movement–or, as some would say, a "sect"–within Judaism. There is little argument among scholars on that point. However, almost anything else having to do with Jewish Christianity tends to be engulfed in controversy. Many factors were involved in the decline and eventual demise of a Judeo-Christian form of the church's faith, as well as the parting of the ways between Judaism and Christianity, which some consider the first schism within the one people of God. Mention should be made of sociocultural differences as a growing number of Gentiles were incorporated into basically Jewish Christian congregations, theological disputes about the law, imperial politics and Jewish nationalism, as well as interreligious rivalries.

Jews who settled in the major cities across Asia Minor, living among Greek-speaking people and often engaged in commercial activities, had become accustomed to, and even comfortable with, Hellenistic thought and culture. But in the earliest and rapidly growing Christian congregations, the integration of Hebraists and Hellenists did not always go that smoothly.

Questions about food and drink or the observance of certain days are subjects of discussion throughout the New Testament. Circumcision became the core issue under dispute; but after a debate at the so-called Jerusalem Council (50 A.D.), a consensus in the Spirit was reached on that particular question (Acts 15). Still, some among the Hebraist segment of the church, people who were deeply devoted to observance of the law, continued to spread suspicions about Paul's outreach to Gentiles. The apostle's letter to the Galatians contains a passionate and uncompromising counter-attack in which the apostle accuses his opponents of preaching "another gospel." In his letter to the Romans, on the one hand, Paul pleads for mutual accommodation and tolerance on similar issues, because in that situation the practices had not been made a precondition for salvation.

Gradually, the base of Jewish Christianity was eroded within both the church and the synagogue. The departure of Jewish Christians from Jerusalem, and their settlement in Pella during the First Jewish Revolt (66-73 A.D.), led to the charge of disloyalty. By the end of the Second Jewish Revolt (132-135 A.D.), the separation between Judaism and Christianity had become virtually complete. The messianic claims of Bar Kochba, supported by the famous Rabbi Akiva, did not help the situation. Jewish Christians were not quite prepared to switch their allegiance to a new Messiah.

Jewish Christians continued to exercise influence within the church well into the fourth century. Anson Laytnew quotes Jerome, for example, who complained as follows in a letter to Augustine: "Take any Jew you please who has been converted to Christianity, and you will see that he practices the rite of circumcision on his newborn son, keeps the Sabbath, abstains from forbidden food, and brings a lamb as offering on the fourteenth of Nissan."[4] As noted before the church father John Chrysostom's viciously anti-Jewish sermons (386 A.D.) were to no small degree motivated by the fact that some of his Sunday morning listeners had been in a synagogue the day before.

By that time, another momentous historical switch had taken place: Emperor Constantine had become a convert to Christianity, and a strong supporter of the church. Now backed by the might of the Empire, the church put its faith less and less in the power of Pentecost and, as it took on the airs of imperial glory, lost the intense anticipation of the *parousia*. Rome promulgated edicts against Jewish proselytizing, and the church became de-Judaized in its theology; anti-Judaic in its attitudes; and, worst of all, anti-Semitic in many of the measures taken at its synods and councils.

After World War II, when the realities of the Holocaust were revealed in all their horrendous truth, some Christians began to confront the fact that a long and dark history of the church had helped create the climate that made this genocidal crime possible. A new readiness emerged to reevaluate the relationship of the church to Judaism and the Jewish people. With the search for greater ecumenicity among the churches also came the desire to enter into dialogue with Jews.

The de-Judaization of the church's life and theology has been acknowledged with sorrow by Catholic and Protestant leaders alike. Nevertheless, Jewish Christians who refuse to become absorbed into a Gentile Christianity, but seek to express their faith and worship in Hebraic forms, are the one group of believers who are absent from the dialogue table. How does one account for this incongruous situation? A complex combination of factors is at work here: fear, indifference, hostility, a sense of ambiguity, and the "politics of dialogue" are all operating against the backdrop of a very troubled history.

The standard Jewish position is that it is impossible for one to be a Jew and a believer in Jesus' messiahship, especially if one's faith is cast in a trinitarian framework. Hence, there is a tendency to characterize the whole Messianic Jewish movement simply as a conspiracy of deception, and to warn Christian dialogue partners that association with such folk could jeopardize future relationships with the Jewish community. Jewish Christians should not become the scapegoat for the church's past anti-Judaism and anti-Semitism. True, it will be extremely difficult to achieve reconciliation with both our Jewish and Jewish Christian brothers and sisters. But it seems to me that the gospel leaves us no other choice.

The church at large needs to return to a more Hebraic mode of thinking with its holistic rather than dualistic approach to issues both theological and "secular." With God's help, may the sons of Zion be aroused against the sons of Greece (Zechariah 9:13).

Judaism's worldview is deeply rooted in the confession of the Oneness of God. That affirmation has little to do with counting (i.e., is there one God or are there many?). Biblical writers were well aware that there is a plethora of gods in the world (Psalm 82:1; 138:1; 1 Corinthians 8:5f). The term *gods* in these passages may refer to human judges or rulers or to ungodly kings or possibly the deities they represent. Deified rulers were very common in the ancient world. In Egypt pharaohs often took the name of deities. Even one king of the Southern Kingdom, Amon, was named for an Egyptian deity.

In Judaism, however, the Oneness of God has everything to do with the divine nature as revealed in the midst of Israel. YHWH is the historically acting God who will reunite all things in the great shalom of the kingdom to come. The Hebrew Scriptures teach us to think holistically *and* historically. Believers are turned into futurists who live according to a vision of the approaching new age.

How do we listen to the voice of Israel, both as it comes to us through dialogue with the Jewish community and through the presence of Jewish Christians within the church? All listening in dialogue needs to be an open listening and, at the same time, a critical listening. Too much sweetness and light is not good for anyone's soul and, in the end, will not promote greater church unity, except perhaps bureaucratically.

As long as dialogue is also a struggle for truth, it will be a painful process. As mainline church members, we need to listen to the critique of our evangelical-charismatic brothers and sisters; but we also need to confront our Messianic Jewish brothers and sisters with whether they do, indeed, represent the rich holistic tradition of Moses and the prophets, or whether they have succumbed to sectarian impulses. Methinks there are some valid questions to be raised on that score.

[1]Peter Hocken, *The Glory and the Shame: Reflections on the 20th Century Outpouring of the Holy Spirit* (Guildford, Surrey, UK: Eagle Press, 1994), p. 139.

[2]*Ibid.*, pp. 151-155.

[3]Eva Fleischner wrote: "It seems that for the first time since the days of early Christianity, one can speak today of a Jewish Christianity within the Church. Whatever one's interpretation of it, attitude toward it, or diversity within it, it exists and is active." (*Judaism in German Christian Theology since 1945* [Metuchen, NJ: Scarecrow Press, 1972], p. 62). Today the movement is more real and more active than when Fleischner wrote these words.

[4]Anson Laytnew, "Christianity and Judaism: Old History, New Beginnings," in *Journal of Ecumenical Studies*, Spring 1996, pp. 187-203.

DIALOGUE AND ISRAEL

CHAPTER 20

Uniting Christians in Support of Israel

A funny thing happened to me on my way up the ecclesiastical ladder. I became deeply involved with issues I had not planned to make central concerns in my life: namely, Christian-Jewish relations and the State of Israel. I am not saying that I had been indifferent about those matters. Far from it! I think it would be fair to say that I had kept myself better informed on those issues than most people. The fact that I had survived the brutalities of Nazism would virtually guarantee that. But I was not personally *involved*. My career plans pointed in a different direction.

The first professional detour occurred in 1968 when my denomination asked me to join the national staff as director of communications. From being a pastor in a local congregation as well as a published author on various theological subjects, I now became a church bureaucrat in New York City. The second surprise came when in 1974 the National Council of Churches decided to open an Office on Christian-Jewish Relations, and I ended up as the first chairperson of its executive committee. Now, this grandson of a Hassidic rabbi in Poland became drawn into the manifold complexities of Jewish-Christian relations, both in terms of "Israel theology" and the "Israel politics" that tends to trouble the waters when mainline churches touch that third rail of interfaith dialogue: Israel, reborn as an independent state in its ancient homeland.

The third unexpected twist in my professional journey occurred when, in 1980, I accepted the position of executive director of the National Christian Leadership Conference for Israel (NCLCI), an ecumenical network of pro-Israel activists. This virtually assured that for almost a decade there would be very little time for me to engage in scholarly research and writing.

I have often referred to Israel as a great ecumenical catalyst. Love and concern for that country have a way of bringing together the most extraordinary combinations of people, persons who would otherwise have little occasion to meet, let alone cooperate with one another. Still, this is not just an ecumenicity of political expediency. It goes much deeper than that. In spite of profound theological and social-political differences, these Christians share certain fundamental perspectives on God's dealings in history and particularly on the nature of the divine covenant with the Jewish people. To say the least, most of them are convinced that this covenant has not been revoked or transferred to the church. Christians enter into a relationship with the God of Abraham, Isaac, and Jacob only by becoming incorporated into the divine and eternal covenant with Israel.

True, bringing people together for dialogue is not the same as establishing an effective network of support, and, on many occasions, Israel has also become a stumbling block to better Christian-Jewish relations. However, I have become increasingly convinced that an encounter with Judaism and with the reality of Israel is of immense significance to the life of the churches, including their search for greater unity among Christians.

The word *ecumenical*, like the word *catholic*, even though commonly used in rather narrow ecclesiastical context, has connotations too rich to be confined to any particular group or organization. Those words seek to reach beyond churchly realities. They aspire to open up vistas of a unity that encompasses humanity and the world in which we live.

In that sense, too, Israel must be seen as the great ecumenical catalyst. In ancient times the Jewish nation and its ethos were formed around a fundamental confession of unity: "Hear, O Israel: the Lord our God is one Lord." This is not just a matter of addition and/or subtraction. Rather, it is an expression of the unitary nature and purpose of the Divine Creator and Lord of history. It was through the history of Israel that a certain kind of vision concerning unity has entered our world. Any ecumenical movement that ignores this fact will eventually become anemic and lose its vitality.

The immediate occasion for the NCLCI's beginning was the 30th anniversary of Israel's independence in 1978. That also happened to be one of those years when the U.S. Congress was debating the sale of sophisticated weaponry to Arab countries. Some 400 Christian leaders, representing a broad spectrum of churches, gathered at the Hyatt Regency Hotel in Washington DC. Those attending felt good about what was happening there. Here they were, Christians of many stripes, united as friends of the Jewish state: members of church hierarchies, evangelists, labor leaders, academicians, people from the art world, prominent politicians from both the Republican and Democratic parties. It is not surprising that the question arose whether there ought not to be a framework wherein such contacts could be maintained and further cultivated on an ongoing basis. A resolution to that effect was proposed and enthusiastically endorsed.

Thus NCLCI was born. In a way something new was being started here, but in another sense it was the beginning of a new chapter in an old story. There were antecedents; forerunners who had laid foundations on which others could build. The immediate predecessor to NCLCI had been Franklin Littell's Christians Concerned for Israel (CCI), formed after the Six Day War. At that moment of agony and trauma for the Jewish community, some of the leaders who had devoted years to improving relations with the churches were looking for signs of support from their dialogue partners. Instead, in most instances, they were met with an ominous silence.

The situation was not that Israel was totally without friends in the Christian community. But so much of the dialogue is conducted through church establishments and, therefore, with people who in the very nature of the case are caught up in all sorts of internal political dynamics, no matter how much they might like to see themselves as officers in the Lord's army at the "prophetic" frontiers. The question had to be raised as to how the voices of the grassroots friends of Israel in the churches can be made more effective and their support more visible. Littell, a professor at Temple University, and his wife almost singlehandedly provided the network through which those Christian efforts might be reinforced. Many of their contacts were with people from academia, but church and community leaders were represented as well.

Christians Concerned for Israel became incorporated into NCLCI. But CCI itself was, in a sense, a revival of a previous endeavor, namely the American Christian Palestine Committee founded in 1946 and disbanded in 1961. And before that, the Christian Council on Palestine had been very active during World War II as the groundwork was being laid for the establishment of the an independent homeland for the Jewish people in Palestine. Earlier yet, during the 1930's, the Pro-Palestine Federation of America, whose membership consisted mainly of Christian clergy and teachers, had vigorously advocated the Zionist cause.

But, in fact, the story goes yet further back. We can point to the 16th century and the teachings of the Restorationists, pious Protestants who were persuaded by their reading of the Scriptures that the God of Abraham, Isaac, and Jacob would eventually restore his people and that this would involve a return to the Holy Land. Restoration and Return, when capitalized, became terms of profound theological meaning, understood as touching on the divine destiny of history. For those people these were issues of world historical significance. God's covenant with Israel was believed to have implications for all creation and all history.

The Restorational Movement has its own list of martyrs to the cause. As early as 1589, Francis Kett, a fellow of Corpus Christi College in Cambridge, was burned alive as a heretic because he taught the eventual return of the Jewish people to their ancient homeland. Some Christian supporters of Israel today may face less-than-friendly treatment in a sometimes hostile ecclesiastical environment, but surely nothing as radical as what happened to poor brother Kett.

The same thread of Restorationist thinking can be traced through 17th century Puritanism as well as through the 18th and 19th centuries. I shall not include the details of that story here. The well-known words of President John Adams sum up some of the basic sentiments, including the less-than-noble undertones that were usually part of the picture:

> I really wish the Jews again in Judea, an independent Nation, for, as I believe, the most enlightened men of it have participated in the amelioration of the philosophy of the age; once restored to an independent government, and no longer persecuted, they would soon wear away some of the asperities and peculiarities of their character. I wish your nation may be admitted all the privileges of citizens in every part of the world.

At times Christian Restorationists caused consternation among Jews who were not at all happy with this emphasis and, for their own reasons, considered those views to be heretical. A case in point was the 1891 petition, composed by the evangelist William Blackstone and signed by more than 400 prominent Americans. It urged President Benjamin Harrison to join them in promoting the return of the Jewish people to *Eretz Yisrael*. This was six years before the first Zionist Congress in Basel, convened by Theodor Herzl. A rabbi named Emil Hirsch felt deeply offended by this Christian evangelist's activities and took to the road himself as a sort of one-man truth squad, assuring everybody who would listen that Jews had no such aspirations whatsoever and only wished to be good citizens in whatever country they resided.

History is so full of ironic as well as tragic twists. The good rabbi, although perhaps not consciously, may have reacted against those who at times have supported the idea of a Jewish homeland from racist motives and as a convenient way of ridding their country of Jews. In 19th century Europe, for instance, we find certain nationalist movements supporting the Return for all the wrong reasons.

One further observation on the Blackstone affair. Peter Grose, in his book *Israel in the Mind of America*, says that it "contained one lesson that would be learned and relearned over the coming half-century of Zionist agitation: the futility of grand public statements unaccompanied by pointed and discreet political pressures."[1] It seems to me that "Christian Zionists" still have a long way to go in learning and relearning that lesson.

The danger I see in the mainline churches is that they are strong on dialogue but weak on solidarity. Among evangelicals, on the other hand, I see a good deal of strength in the area of inspiration, but often a failure to recognize the importance of organization and the kind of mobilization that turns goodwill into action. The end result in both cases tends to be friendly talk but little active support.

I certainly do not mean to disparage dialogue or to suggest that it has failed to produce any concrete results. I consider myself a veteran dialoguer, and I am proud of it. Without that movement, to give one example, many church education materials would still contain the same myths and misinformation about Jews and Judaism that they did some years ago. Dialogue has definitely made a difference.

But dialogue can become somewhat seductive, and it easily becomes a substitute for action. When dialogue becomes an end in itself, we produce talk without end (it goes on and on, but it doesn't go anywhere). During the crisis of 1967, during the Yom Kippur war in 1973 and at other critical moments in Israel's history, the question of solidarity became an increasingly urgent one. If dialogue means that people enter into each other's historical experiences, how then can one party be left so isolated during moments of deep suffering? One is reminded of the old rabbinic question: "How can you love me [or even care for me] if you do not know what hurts me?"

A classic illustration of what I am talking about occurred during the Sixth National Workshop on Christian-Jewish Relations, held in Milwaukee during October 1981. I think there were about 1400 of us attending that conference, a multitude of eager dialoguers buzzing about the hotel, listening to speeches, meeting in small groups and all in all feeling excited about it all. In the meantime, the U.S. Senate was in the final stages of a debate on the sale of AWACS to Saudi Arabia.

I had the eerie feeling that in our Milwaukee hotel we were living in a world all by ourselves, totally detached from the world of Washington DC and AWACS. Finally, on Wednesday–the day of the Senate vote–Father Robert F. Drinan broke the spell during a speech in which he reminded the solemn assembly that the Senate vote that afternoon could have more far-reaching consequences for Jewish-Christian relations than anything we had done that week. Because of the intervention by a few activists, a drive was started immediately to raise funds and send telegrams to the members of the Senate urging them to vote down the AWACS proposal. In order to avoid conflict, it was emphasized that this action was not part of the Workshop's official agenda and that participation was entirely voluntary.

For me personally, the issue of solidarity and, therefore, the need for a network like NCLCI became an increasingly urgent matter. I am not talking about knee-jerk support for anything Israel does. Solidarity does not preclude criticism. It does, however, lend credibility to whatever critiques one may feel compelled to utter.

As to the question of inspiration versus organization, it must be said that some of the most exciting gatherings in support of Israel in recent years have been organized by evangelicals. Many of them have a real gift to put on a good show. I see nothing wrong with that, except when the "proclamations" issued become exuberant to the point of embarrassment and people go home feeling good but not inspired to do good works where it really counts. I am not implying that prayer does not count or that praising the Lord does not count. But there are moments when a letter to the President or members of Congress can make a crucial difference and therefore, may be *the* Christian thing to do.

In the meantime, a little caution in language may help enhance Christian credibility. For instance, I have seen an evangelical statement assuring the Jewish people that if–God forbid–another Holocaust were to occur, Bible-believing Christians would be marching with Jews to the crematoria. I do not say that certain individuals might not act that way, but I do believe that those who behave heroically and commit acts of supreme sacrifice are not necessarily the same people who have signed statements. The truth is that none of us can be quite sure how we might behave in moments of extreme crisis. It behooves us all to exercise a measure of humility in our public pronouncements, while prayerfully hoping that in the moment of decision we shall not compromise our conscience and betray our principles.

A remarkable Dutch woman, Etty Hillesum, not yet 30 years old, wrote in her diary as she was preparing to depart on the journey that would lead her to Auschwitz and death: "I don't fool myself about the reality of my situation and I even let go of the pretension that I will be a help to others. I will always be motivated by the desire to help God as much as possible, and if I succeed in doing that, well, then I'll be there for others as well. But one shouldn't entertain heroic illusions about such things." Indeed, and least of all those of us who have not had to travel that kind of *via dolorosa*.

As to support for Israel in the rather safe surroundings of the USA, I have come to the conclusion that the trouble with Christian supporters of Israel is not that there are so few, but that they are often so ineffective. Again, I do not claim that nothing has been achieved, but, rather, that in a country where the public at large tends to be sympathetic to the Israeli cause, Christians rarely play a role as a distinctive force on critical issues.

A noteworthy exception has been the Unity Coalition for Israel, organized in the early 1990s by Esther Levens, a Jewish political conservative from Kansas who happened to notice that polls at that time indicated that 67% of U.S. citizens supported Israel in the ongoing conflict with the Palestinians. She calculated that less than 2% of those were Jewish, so she set out to find the other 65%. Her Unity Coalition for Israel brought together various factions of Christian Zionists and produced press briefings, seminars, and prayer breakfasts in Washington DC, designed to demonstrate to the national political powers joint Jewish-Christian support for Israel. The Unity Coalition continues to be a strong force in promoting Jewish-Christian solidarity in supporting the nation of Israel.

Another emerging effort that has considerable promise is the Knesset Christian Allies Caucus, which was initiated in 2003 and represented the first time that the Knesset (the Israeli parliament) as an institution had officially acknowledged and engaged with the growing Christian pro-Israel movement worldwide. This organized effort has produced more than warm mutual greetings: it has provided a framework for rare and unusually frank dialogue between Jews and Christians.

Among the Christian organizations that have been a part of this effort are the International Christian Embassy, Jerusalem, Bridges for Peace, Christian Friends of Israel, The Ebenezer Fund, and the International Fellowship of Christians and Jews. All of these organizations have formally committed their constituencies to mobilizing Christians around the world to support the security of the State of Israel and the welfare of the Jewish people, to helping the Israeli public and Jews internationally to understand the strength of Christian support for Jewish aspirations in the land of Israel, and to providing Christian and Israeli leaders with a Knesset forum for face-to-face encounters and enhanced cooperation.

Many of these Christian Zionist organizations have a history of significant contributions to support of Israel. The International Christian Embassy, Jerusalem, founded in 1980, has conducted large conferences in Jerusalem to demonstrate Christian solidarity with Israel. Bridges for Peace, organized in 1976 by Dr. G. Douglas Young, initiated a continuing humanitarian service in 1991 that has featured food distribution to needy Israelis and support for the mass immigration of Jews from Russia, in addition to an annual Solidarity Mission to Israel and educational programs in many nations.

Christian Friends of Israel has also sponsored conferences and extensive humanitarian efforts. The International Fellowship of Christians and Jews, organized by Rabbi Yechiel Eckstein, since 1983 has enlisted major support largely from the evangelical Christian community to support Jewish *aliyah* from the former Soviet Union and various humanitarian causes in Israel.

Still, with all of these strong and commendable efforts, support for Israel from the Christian community has not been nearly as effective as it could have been had greater cooperation and coordination of activities been maintained, especially in the political arena where focused efforts can produce significant results.

A major source of our ineffectiveness lies, I believe, in our fragmentation. I am realistic enough to recognize that the answer to that problem is not to be found in centralization. It could not be done, and even if it were achievable it would, in my judgment, not be desirable. There are many mavericks in pro-Israel Christian circles, and there is immense diversity, not only in theology, but also in programs and general approach. That's fine! But some consultation, plus at least a minimum of coordination and cooperation, would surely benefit the common cause. It could be achieved without compromising anyone's integrity or independence.

This is where a vision like that of the National Christian Leadership Conference for Israel could be very fruitful. Founded on the principle of inclusiveness, NCLCI sought from its very beginning to be a forum where people who share this particular concern could interact with each other and reinforce each other's efforts. To cultivate such a network, one that is considerably more inclusive than existing ecumenical councils, takes tact and much patience.

Networking is a hard item to sell to the faithful, however. People may agree that it is a good idea, but in order to raise money one needs more than that. Hunger, earthquakes, and other assorted calamities tend to bring forth a flood of donations as I well know from my denominational leadership days. The whole notion of "networking" lacks romance and will always be hard to finance.

Then there is the problem of bringing together both "conservative" and "liberal" Christians in the common cause of support for Israel. Some of our conservative Christian friends are concerned that these efforts seem to lack even a modicum of missionary motivation. For them, it all sounds a bit too political. Language is so important when dealing with various forms of spirituality. Such efforts must address a very broad spectrum of the Christian community, casting promotions in a "tongue" that to some conservative Christian believers often find rather flat, yes, even "secular."

On the other hand, for many of our more liberal Christian friends are concerned that these efforts sound a bit too partisan. They much prefer an "evenhandedness," forever dealing in "moral equivalencies" in an attempt to assure everybody that they stand above all parties. There is something to be said for keeping one's lines of communication open and, to be sure, in no dispute will one find all truth or righteousness on one side of the issue. But the never-ending balancing act that somehow seeks to press everything into a neat system of symmetry strikes me as resting on either intellectual laziness or a lack of moral nerve. For instance, I see a qualitative difference between the Irgun's actions during the British Mandate against predominantly military targets and attacks on schoolchildren, athletes, and civilian air travelers in the name of Palestinian rights. Hence, as is common practice in some church circles, to call Israeli leaders who at one time served in the resistance movement terrorists, in the same sense that Osama bin Laden is a terrorist, strikes me as moral subterfuge.

It is important, then, that the Christian-Jewish dialogue be undergirded with communication and collaboration among Christians as to ways in which they can be mutually supportive and tolerant of diverse viewpoints among themselves as to proper and effective strategies for support of Israel and the international Jewish community. Such efforts can undoubtedly strengthen the efforts of fragmented groups of Christian Zionists and friends of Israel and make their commitment to the Jewish people far more effective in the public and private arenas that generate significant results. Great opportunities await true activists as the stage of world events changes.

The death of Yassir Arafat has introduced new dynamics into the Israeli-Palestinian negotiations. U.S. involvement in Afghanistan and Iraq may have consequences, either for good or ill, that are hard to foresee. Finally, the emergence of a militant and violent Islamist movement within the Muslim world poses a threat to cities across the globe.

When Adolph Hitler wrote outrageous things in *Mein Kampf*, few people took his rantings seriously. The same was true when Osama bin Laden wrote years before September 11, 2001, that "there are two parties to the conflict: World Christianity which is allied with Jews and Zionism, led by the United States, Britain and Israel" and the Islamic world.

In the midst of these cataclysmic events, millions of Christians continue to demonstrate solidarity with Israel and the Jewish people. Large sums are being raised to aid new immigrants from Russia and North Africa to *Eretz Yisrael*. The missionary impulse among Gentile Christians has turned decisively toward converting churches which for centuries have lost contact with the Judaic roots of their faith. A tremendous blessing awaits both church and Israel if, through a process of re-education, a transformation were to take place within the world Christian community that has once again reclaimed its Hebraic heritage. Signs of such a new and radical reformation can be discerned on different continents.

While these positive developments are occurring in the midst of a dangerous world, the adversaries of the State of Israel do not lie still and, unfortunately, some of them are to be found right in the Christian community. Leaders of major ecclesiastical and ecumenical bodies, advocates of dialogue and evenhandedness all, have initiated a campaign designed to hurt the Israeli economy. For instance, in July, 2004, the General Assembly of the Presbyterian Church USA voted to begin a process of selective divestment from companies doing business with Israel. In 2005 the United Church of Christ followed suit and officials of the WCC are singing the same song. This goes far beyond legitimate criticism of certain Israeli policies: this is a direct attack on the wellbeing of a whole people. In the name of promoting justice and peace for the Palestinians, Israel must be punished as if it is solely responsible for the conflict that has lasted since the first moment the state of Israel was born and then immediately attacked by the surrounding Arab states. In order to justify this one-sided stance, Israel is portrayed as if it were the equivalent of the South Africa of yesteryear.

Even now NCLCI is setting a strong example of the kind of cooperation that can make a difference. With its many supporters in mainline Christian circles, it has become a voice of fairness in defense of the Jewish people as well as of the multitudes of church members who do not agree with what denominational officials are saying in their name. David Blewett, the organization's national director, is making sure that countervoices among pastors and their congregants are heard. For instance, the pastor of Bel Air Presbyterian Church in Los Angeles did not mince words when he addressed his congregation as follows: "The [General Assembly] fell out of the stupid tree and hit every branch coming down. The idea that withholding funds is going to make peace between the Israelis and Palestinians is ridiculous."

In a "Backgrounder," Blewett put it well: "Christian arrogance has caught up with the dialogue and is threatening to end one of the most dynamic and enriching experiences of church history, one that had opened exciting new vistas for understanding who we Christians are and how we should be reading our Bible." Dialogue without solidarity is like preaching without love, little more than "a noisy gong or a clanging cymbal" (1 Corinthians 13:1).

May the work of NCLCI, the Christian Embassy, Bridges for Peace, Christian Friends of Israel, and all other similar organizations encourage fellow Christians to work together to impact world opinion and public policy and generate sustained moral and material support for Israel and the international Jewish community. May organizations like the International Fellowship of Christians and Jews and the Unity Coalition for Israel serve as examples of ways in which Christians and Jews can interact to promote mutual understanding and affirmation.

Finally, as we pray and work for the peace and security of Israel, it should be clear that we do so without prejudice or malice toward the Palestinians and the Arab people in general. We fervently hope for reconciliation and *shalom* for that whole region, which plays such a crucial role in history.

[1]Peter Grose, *Israel in the Mind of America* (New York: Knopf, 1983), p. 37.

CHAPTER 21

Dialogue: Dream and Reality

It was an exciting day in our home during my early teen-age years when Willem Visser 't Hooft came to visit. He was known in church circles as a dreamer, a pioneer in the not-yet organized ecumenical movement. There were those who believed that the dream would never become a reality. But it did, namely in the form of the WCC. Visser 't Hooft would become that organization's first General Secretary, a world-renowned leader in the interfaith movement and the author of important theological works. As a youngster who had no intention of entering the field of Christian ministry, I learned to admire the visionaries who pursued the path of unity among the people of God.

As I stated, the dream did become a reality. For many of us, however, it eventually developed into a reality that was far removed from our dreams. I do not take pleasure in telling that tale. Some of my most spiritually enriching experiences have been as a participant in WCC affairs, including the writing of some of the documents that have come out of this organization's assemblies. As the saying goes, I write more in sadness than in anger. But this is the story as I see it.

The WCC came into being during an Assembly held in Amsterdam, August 22-September 4, 1948, just a few months after the establishment of the State of Israel. That was a great year for those in the church who loved the Jewish people and longed for greater unity among Christians. For a decade prior to the Amsterdam gathering, the organization had existed in embryonic form, listing itself as "the World Council of Churches in process of formation." The long interim period was caused by the fact that World War II had forced a postponement of the official founding of the Council.

The heart of the WCC agenda has always been "unity," and the basic approach whereby it hopes to achieve this goal is "dialogue." Active attempts to bring about greater unity between the churches, which for centuries displayed not only great diversity, but often considerable mutual hostility as well, had been going on for at least half a century. As usual, the initiatives for this visionary movement were taken outside the "official" church establishment: in the Bible societies, the YMCA/YWCA organizations, the World Student Christian Federation, etc.

Major Ecumenical Missionary Conferences held in Edinburgh (1910), Jerusalem (1928), and Tambaram, India (1938) had established the basic framework of cooperation and the network of interdenominational contacts, which eventually would lead to the founding of the WCC. These were all predominantly Protestant enterprises. The Roman Catholic Church was not much involved in unity efforts during the pre-Vatican II era.

The Christian world mission movement, which had undergone tremendous expansion during the 19th century, gave a powerful impetus to the search for greater unity. Western church divisions, often more determined by history and culture than by theology, were being exported to other continents and were increasingly becoming cause for confusion (certainly among the "natives" to whom love was being preached), frustration, and embarrassment. Members of ancient tribes who began to look and act like Scottish Presbyterians or American Baptists often came across more like comic figures than like people who might have an impact on their own culture.

World War II and the sufferings it caused contributed in a somewhat ironic fashion to the breakdown of Christian divisions. For instance, missionaries from countries occupied by the Nazis were left stranded in various parts of the world and, in many instances, received support from church agencies in the free world. Prison camps also played a role as catalytic agents toward greater Christian unity, as Catholic and Protestant leaders, thrown into forced association, often discovered that they were united not only through their common resistance to Nazism, but also by spiritual bonds, which had been left unexplored before.

In addition the Nazi war against the Jews introduced a wholly new dimension into the ecumenical agenda, namely Christian-Jewish relations. The churches could not ignore the fact that during this period of great suffering and pain among the general populace of occupied and war-torn lands, a horror of incredible proportions had occurred in the Holocaust: the systematic murder of six million Jewish men, women, and children.

For instance, less than one year after the liberation of Holland from Nazi rule, leaders of the Netherlands Reformed Church, convinced they would "have to come to a renewed confession against the false gods and temptations of this century, both those around us and within us," appointed a special committee charged to explore the feasibility of a new confessional statement. The document resulting from this church's reflection on its experience during the Nazi era was entitled *Foundations and Perspectives of Confession*. It contained two features not commonly found in Christian credal statements: an article on "history" and another one on "Israel." As already pointed out, once people begin to focus on the faith of Israel, they inevitably begin to reflect more seriously on the meaning of history.

Through the centuries, the most common Christian response to Jewish suffering has been that it was the logical result of the Jews' rejection and crucifixion of Jesus. The argument in essence was a straight and simple one: the Jews have rejected Jesus; God in return has rejected them, has cast them off as his covenant people and has chosen the church in their stead. The Dutch Reformed confessional statement sounded a very different note, however, claiming that the divine covenant with the Jewish people had never been revoked. It affirmed that the Jews "remain the people of the promise" and that those who are offended at this "take offense at God's sovereign action, to which they themselves owe their salvation."

Forty years later, I regret to report, that same Reformed Church in the Netherlands refused to renew the contract of its "theological advisor" in Israel. The *Jerusalem Post* (August 8, 1986) quoted Dutch ecclesiastical sources as stating that this person had identified too closely with Jewish concerns and had failed to comply with instructions that he meet with PLO representatives. Eventually he was offered an extension of his contract if he was prepared to accept severe limitations on what he would be allowed to say publicly. This incident is symptomatic of what has been happening in the Protestant ecumenical world elsewhere.

One can detect so many examples in history of movements that were started by visionaries turning into institutions with bureaucratic establishments that are more concerned about self-preservation than a prophetic witness. The visionaries are then replaced by functionaries and the dreams by ideological dogma. I know this is a severe judgment, and I also know that many wonderful and dedicated Christians continue to be involved in the ecumenical councils. But, from my personal experiences I would say that there is enough truth in my observation for the remaining dreamers to be concerned and work for radical reform.

Dialogue is the holy ground on which the ecumenical movement stands or falls. For instance, once the dialogue approach is exchanged for an ideological approach, the ecumenical movement has lost its soul. After all, dialogue is not just one among many techniques; it is a way of ecumenical life. It calls for nothing less than a new way of relating to one another. Dialogue implies that one has not only an open mind, but also a heart that is responsive to overtures of understanding from people with whom one has, perhaps, profound theological or social-political differences. True dialogue embodies in a very special way the art of listening as an expression of loving other human beings. As Bishop Krister Stendahl has so often pointed out, one of its first fruits is that one refuses to bear false witness against other believers by portraying one's own position in the most positive light and the other person's faith fellowship according to its most questionable features.

From the vantage point of the 21st century it is sometimes difficult to recall the sad estrangement, even enmity, that existed between Baptists and Methodists, Presbyterians, and Episcopalians and–above all–Protestants and Roman Catholics only a few decades ago. The dialogue with Jews was in sadder shape yet, having hardly advanced beyond the situation in the second century when the church father Justin Martyr wrote his famous *Dialogue with Trypho the Jew.* As we have noted, historian Adolph von Harnack called this book "the victor's monologue," for Justin accused his Jewish "partner" of "obstinacy of heart" as well as "feebleness of mind." In sum, Jews who could not be argued into becoming Christians were not only dumb; they clearly had a character defect as well. Thus began the process whereby Christians increasingly defined themselves in anti-Judaic terms. Dialogue became polemics, and polemics derailed into diatribe and, further along the road, pogroms.

The ecumenical movement sought to change all that, and it must be said that the dream of moving from confrontation to new forms of relationships has at least partially been fulfilled. Much re-thinking has been going on in certain Christian circles with respect to Jews, Judaism, and Israel. Helga Croner's two volumes of ecumenical documents entitled *Stepping Stones to Further Jewish-Christian Relations* demonstrate the considerable progress that has been made in redefining Christian positions. The critical observations on certain ecumenical policies and practices that I will be presenting are in no way meant as a denial that the Christian-Jewish dialogue has often made a difference for the better.

As one studies various ecclesiastical and ecumenical pronouncements on the church and the Jewish People, several themes stand out. A central point in many of those documents has been the rejection of so-called "supersession" or "displacement theology," the teaching on which millions of Christians have been nurtured over many centuries: that the Jews stand eternally condemned and that the church is the "New Israel" that has replaced the old and discarded covenant people.

We have already referred to the new confessional statement of the Netherlands Reformed Church. In 1967, the WCC's Commission on Faith and Order issued an important study document on the relationship between the church and the Jewish people. This statement, usually referred to as the Bristol Declaration, affirms the following: "We believe that God formed the people of Israel. There are certainly many factors of common history, ethnic background and religion, which can explain its coming into existence, but to Old Testament faith as a whole, it was God's own will and decision that made this one distinct people with its special place in history."

The document goes on to say that God "chose this particular people to be the bearer of a particular promise and to act as his covenant partner and special instrument." It finally expresses the conviction "that the Jewish people still have a significance of their own for the Church." These sentences have the flavor of the kind of compromise that is so often characteristic of ecclesiastical (and particularly ecumenical) documents. Some would have wished a stronger affirmation, like the one in the Dutch Reformed statement declaring that the Jewish people "remain the people of the promise" because "the gracious gifts and calling of God are irrevocable." However, for some representatives, those from the Orthodox churches in particular, such a clear-cut anti-supersessionist position was unacceptable.

A number of later ecclesiastical pronouncements, on the other hand, were much more explicit in their affirmation of God's continued covenant with Israel. One illustration is the famous document adopted in 1980 by the Synod of the Rhineland in Germany, stating simply: "We believe in the continuing election of the Jewish people as the people of God . . ." Another example is "A Declaration of Faith" in the Book of Confessions of the Former Presbyterian Church, U. S., which puts it in very plain language: "We can never lay exclusive claim to being God's people, as though we had replaced those to whom the covenant, the law and the promises belong. We affirm that God does not take back his promises. We Christians have rejected Jews throughout our history with shameful prejudice and cruelty."

This particular declaration of faith does not only condemn anti-Semitism, as numerous ecclesiastical and ecumenical bodies have done, (including most major assemblies of the WCC) but it also confesses Christian complicity in the persecution of Jews throughout the Church's history. As it was put by a Lutheran World Federation body some years ago: "We confess our peculiar guilt and we lament with shame the responsibility our church and her people bear for this sin (of anti-Semitism)," adding "we can only ask God's pardon and that of the Jewish people." In 1987, a United Church of Christ statement that studiously avoided any reference to the people of Israel, asked "for God's forgiveness through our Lord Jesus Christ," because of the church's history of anti-Jewish theology and actions.

There can then be no doubt that through dialogue, which was conducted on a world scale through such bodies as the WCC, many Christians have been induced to rethink traditional theological positions on Jews and Judaism and to face with greater honesty than ever before the historical role of the churches in the teaching of contempt. However, once it is accepted that the covenant with Israel has not been revoked, new questions arise, such as, what does the covenant encompass? Or, to put it quite specifically, what about the land dimensions of biblical covenant promises?

We read in Genesis 17:7: "I will establish my covenant between me and you and your descendants after you throughout their generations for an everlasting covenant . . ." If we accept that promise as still valid in our day, what then about the next verse: "And I will give to you, and to your descendants after you, the land of your sojournings, all the land of Canaan, for an everlasting possession . . . ?" Has that promise been invalidated? Many evangelicals answer, "Of course not!", without any equivocation whatsoever. Some even see scriptural grounds for speaking about "biblical boundaries," claiming that "all the land of Canaan" definitely included today's West Bank plus quite a bit more.

In mainline ecumenical circles, even those where anti-Semitism is repeatedly and vehemently denounced, that issue is usually considered a bit more problematical. Critics of any kind of covenant/land position scornfully speak of "theological tribalism" and "real estate theology." Such primitive particularism, they insist, has been transcended by a more universalist message that comes to us through the gospel of Jesus Christ. Nevertheless, some documents that have been the product of ecumenical dialogue do indeed affirm that the divine promise of the land is part of the covenant message still valid today.

In 1970 the General Synod of the Reformed Church in the Netherlands once again assumed a pioneer role by issuing a statement entitled "Israel: People, Land and State." This expresses the hope that their efforts at theological reflection on those issues would "start a broad discussion, which up till now has sorely been lacking in our church, in the sister churches abroad and in the WCC." They not only declared the land to be "a vital aspect of the election of Israel" and proclaimed their joy in the "reunion of people and land," but also stated that "in the present situation a state gives greater opportunity to the Jews to fulfill their vocation than any alternative can offer." In short, the State of Israel, too, receives a positive place within the realm of theological reflection.

Subsequent ecclesiastical documents have made the same point, sometimes referring to the State of Israel as "a sign of the mercy and faithfulness of God to the Jewish people." However, the hope of the Dutch church leaders that the WCC would place those issues on its dialogue agenda has hardly been fulfilled. Quite the contrary, Israel has increasingly become a topic of controversy. As the ecumenical processes became more and more politicized, this issue was moved from the realm of dialogue into the sphere of ideological dogma and diatribe. A brief survey of what happened at the six major WCC assemblies following the organization's founding in 1948 gives an interesting picture of how things have evolved and to what extent the dialogue has degenerated into politics of self-righteousness.

In 1948, the Council declared that "to the Jews our God has bound us in a special solidarity linking our destinies together in His design." Anti-Semitism was condemned as a sin against God and man. With regard to the Middle East situation, the Council appealed to the nations to deal with the problem not as one of expediency, but as a moral and spiritual question that touches a nerve center of the world's religious life. That latter statement was sufficiently vague as not to offend anyone.

The next assembly was held in Evanston, Illinois, in 1954. This time when theologies of hope were stirring in the ecclesiastical air, the theme was "Jesus Christ, the Hope of the World." A group of prominent theologians concluded that this would be an appropriate occasion to say something about Israel as a sign of God's faithfulness in history and, therefore, in some sense, a source of hope. Their proposal was voted down after the Assembly had received a telegram from the Christian statesman Charles Malik in Lebanon, urging the delegates to say and do nothing that might give offense to Arab Christians. In later years, Charles Malik found plenty to criticize in the ideological preoccupations of the WCC. No doubt, at that time, his desire was to de-politicize the Council's voice on Middle East issues. In fact, he helped de-theologize the Council's approach to the question of Israel.

The next Assembly, held in New Delhi in 1961, dealt with the theme "Jesus Christ, the Light of the World." Questions pertaining to the relationship of the Christian faith to other (particularly Eastern) religions were predominant at this conference. The issues of anti-Semitism and Israel did not come into sharp focus in India. As a matter of fact, the section under "I" in the index of the assembly's reports ends with "Investment Portfolios."

By the time the WCC met in Uppsala, Sweden in 1968, the theological climate was undergoing rapid and radical changes. The theology of hope was being replaced by "a theology of revolution." The so-called Third World agenda, dealing with issues of poverty and oppression, became increasingly central to the ecumenical movement's concerns. That in itself, it seems to me, should be no cause for complaint. Poverty and oppression, too, are issues with profound theological implications. But, unfortunately, the dialogical approach was more and more replaced by an ideological rhetoric with a distinctly anti-imperialist slant. More unfortunately yet, it became fashionable to refer to Israel as an outpost of Western imperialism in the Middle East. As church historian Martin Marty put it in the jouranl *In Context* (March 1, 1971), "being anti-Israel has become part of the anti-Establishment gospel, the trademark of those who purport to identify with masses, the down trodden and the Third World."

During the 1960's various radical theologies were much in vogue.

For some Christians the basic questions had to do with the need for a radical reinterpretation of traditional beliefs. They posed the challenges: What can a person still believe in this modern age, and how does one speak about God in a secular era? For others, the fundamental issue was not how to adapt to modernity, but rather how to counter the forces of conformity. They asked, what is a Christian lifestyle? Instead of emphasizing radical theological criticism, this movement advocated radical biblical obedience. Its basic stance was more counter-culture than contra-orthodoxy.

Among radical Christians of the second type, the United States was sometimes referred to as "the great whore of Babylon" mentioned in the book of Revelation. There was a tendency to use apocalyptic terminology when describing what were perceived to be the crises of our age, particularly the sins of the West. The radical evangelical paper *Sojourners,* first called the *Post-American*, was started during the days of anti-Vietnam war protests. History was frequently analyzed in somewhat Manichaean terms as the struggle between the forces of Light and Darkness. The imagery is always one of sharp demarcations.

At the same time, the New Left was falling more and more in love with the language of excess, an intellectual climate in which some Christian radicals seemed to feel right at home. Radical Christian journals, like *Témoignage Chrétienne* in France, felt free once again to engage in explicitly anti-Judaic writings. In this country people like Father Daniel Berrigan certainly did not go that far, but in his astonishing October 1973 speech to the Association of Arab University Graduates, in which he referred to himself as "a Jew in resistance to Israel," he proceeded to attack the Jewish state in such vitriolic language that one wondered whether any boundaries of restraint were left.

All those cultural-ideological ingredients were already brewing as the WCC met in Uppsala. But something else was part of the picture as well. The Six Day War had been fought in the Middle East only one year earlier. That same year, the WCC's own Faith and Order Commission had issued the so-called "Bristol Declaration" on the church's relationship to the Jewish people. Politically that document was now considered an ecumenical hot potato, even though its authors had very carefully avoided all explicitly political issues.

So what did the Uppsala Assembly do? It simply ignored the whole question, including the work of its Faith and Order Commission. Once again, the ability or inability to engage in dialogue was determined more by current events than by the Christian faith and the vision that had inspired the founding of the Council. Thus one further step was taken in the process of de-theologizing the question of Israel, as well as in the decline of ecumenical dialogue.

By 1975, when the Council held its fifth Assembly in Nairobi, the politicization of its agenda had grown apace. During the early years of the ecumenical movement the slogan most often cited had been "Let the Church be the Church!" The church was seen as a unique fellowship of faith, full of human frailties and follies, but nevertheless empowered by the presence of the divine Spirit and living under a divine mandate. In short, it was claimed that the church is more than one of the many voluntary associations in the world, at least for those who have committed themselves to Jesus Christ as Lord. Hence it was felt that the church must present its own kind of witness to the world.

As the years went by, however, a new slogan emerged: "Let the world set the agenda!" The central idea here was that the church, rather than being isolated from worldly concerns, should be sensitive to the sufferings and aspirations of humanity. In other words, a claim of uniqueness may never be turned into a form of escapism and social irresponsibility.

As valid as the basic intention may have been, in practice the slogan came to mean that the churches issued an endless stream of statements on every conceivable social issue and that somehow the churches, instead of sounding a voice of their own, seemed to be able to express themselves only in a language that was both bland and bombastic. Someone has appropriately characterized this style of communication as United Nations English.

In 1975, it will be recalled, the UN spent months in a rhetorical orgy on the question about whether Zionism is a form of racism, ending up with the predictable, albeit absurd, conclusion that indeed it is. That organization too, one recalls with sadness, at one time was inspired by dreams about dialogue and reconciliation. Fearing a "Zionism-equals-racism" resolution at the Nairobi meeting, the WCC's General Secretary summoned a group of us to Geneva for a strategy session. No Jewish observers were invited, but Clovis Madsoud, who did not belong to a member church and later became the Arab League's representative at the UN, was present as a full participant in the deliberations. He used the occasion to propagate a shameless anti-Israel rhetoric that made it very difficult for a fair and balanced discussion to take place. In 1983, as the sixth WCC Assembly, scheduled to meet in Vancouver, Canada, approached, the anti-Israel forces within the WCC decided once again to hold a meeting in Geneva. This time it was not under the official sponsorship of the Council, to make sure that no dissenting voices could be present. This self-appointed group of partisans, financed by the Middle East Council of Churches, came to Vancouver carrying a draft statement that no longer even gave the appearance of being fair. In short, they came, not for dialogue, but to pull off a political coup. The climate they found was sympathetic (or, at least, indifferent) enough for them to succeed.

I will not dignify the document by presenting details of its content. *The Christian Century*, hardly a rabid pro-Israel periodical, observed in an editorial (August 17-24, 1983) that the Vancouver resolutions could just as well have been formulated at the UN and indicated "a total lack of concern for Christian-Jewish relations." That about says it.

As was stated before, it is a sorry but not unusual story. A movement started by dreamers and visionaries was step-by-step undermined by people who knew how to manipulate the bureaucratic machinery. There are still many wonderful, decent and idealistic people around. But they are not into playing that sort of game, and the top leadership is either unable or unwilling to put a stop to the nonsense. It happens in politics, in labor unions, and also in churches.

At a press conference during the Vancouver meeting WCC General Secretary Philip Potter was asked about the obvious biases and imbalances in the document on the Middle East. According to press reports his response went as follows: "The Jews have other voices speaking on their behalf." In other words, through our imbalance we balance the scale for the poor Palestinians and the PLO. Having no other voice, they, therefore, deserve the compassionate concern of the WCC. If that means partisanship instead of rapprochement, well, so be it. But why then, one wonders, did the Council reject every proposal to say something about the plight of people in Afghanistan who were being murdered *en masse* by Russian troops? The truth, of course, is that power plays, not compassion, determine the agenda. The officially recognized Russian churches, having declined the invitation to participate in the founding assembly of the WCC in 1948 because they feared that the Council would become a platform for critics of totalitarianism, later decided that the potential rewards might justify the risk of joining. And so they became members. However, every time a position was recommended that would displease the Soviet rulers, the Russian Orthodox churches forced its removal from the agenda by threatening to withdraw from the Council.

Most pathetic of all was the inability at Vancouver to respond with fervor and conviction to the plaintive cry of the Russian priest Vladimir Rusak who, living under the cross of Communism, wrote in an open letter to the Council: "It is difficult to reach you, so very difficult, much more difficult than to reach God, yet I cannot remain silent." Selective indignation, the endless quest for "moral equivalencies" and political deals, eventually blur the vision and quench the inner fires of the soul.

References to Israel in WCC documents were cast increasingly in the form of questions rather than affirmations. On that issue, ambiguity became the mark of ecumenical witness, while on other,–particularly political–topics, the "prophetic" witness became ever more apodictic and audacious. For instance, in 1974 tens of thousands of dollars were spent to convene an International Consultation on "Biblical Interpretation and the Middle East." Did they talk about the divine covenant promises in the Bible, touch perhaps on the question of covenant and land? No, such issues were now too hot to handle and the delegates decided early in the proceedings that they ought to focus on the question of justice in the Middle East.

Jews and Israel are still mentioned in the minutes of the meeting, but in the form of questions. "Does the New Testament nullify the theological meaning of the Jewish people and its continuing existence?" "Can we evaluate and decide questions of the promise of the land, the election of Israel, etc. on the basis of the New Testament, and from a Christian perspective?" "In what sense can Christians identify with the right of the Jewish people to Statehood?" It should not be hard to guess what kind of answers some of the participants in such a consultation would give to those questions.

Every once in awhile people within the Council, like the members of its Consultation on the Church and the Jewish People, would address the questions and seek to provide some answers. One would think that those efforts were welcomed as an open invitation to engage in dialogue. But in fact such ecumenical endeavors were handled with a good deal of hesitation, even embarrassment. Whenever such a situation arose, the issues were put on the bureaucratic escalator from committees to sub-committees, then to sub-sub-committees where behind-the-scenes maneuvers could apply the proper revisions and corrections.

Take, for instance, the "Guidelines for Christian-Jewish Dialogue" on which the WCC's Consultation on the Church and the Jewish People; worked for a number of years. It all started in 1977 when the Consultation group met in Jerusalem. I thought the choice of meeting place was excellent; it afforded me my first opportunity to visit Israel. But some people within the Council were infuriated. They saw it as damaging to Arab interests, and never forgave Dr. Franz von Hammerstein, the Consultation's executive director, for this "trespass." In fact, he did not survive very long as a WCC employee after that Jerusalem meeting.

Still, a draft document was finally produced and approved on several top levels of the Council's bureaucracy, including in January 1982 by the Division of Dialogue with People of Living Faiths and Ideologies, the overarching agency of which the Consultation was a sub-division. The draft contained some helpful and hopeful statements.

Then, at the last minute, came the denouement. The democratic process came to a sudden halt. A small inner group of the bureaucratic elite announced that they would further "revise and reorder" the text before the document became official. As a result, a separate section on "the Land" was taken out and, after being eviscerated, subsumed under the section entitled "Towards a Christian Understanding of Jews and

Judaism." Furthermore, the phrase "the indissoluble bond between the land of Israel and the Jewish people" was deleted, while the phrase "the need for Palestinians for self-determination and expression of their national identity" became "the quest for statehood by Palestinians." Silence on the bond between Israel and the Jewish people but a strong endorsement of statehood for the Palestinians. Surely, some of the Jewish partners must have wondered whether this was the best they could get after years of dialogue with church representatives.

There has, of course, never been unanimous enthusiasm in the Jewish community for dialogue with Christians. There are those who, as a principle of faith, oppose any form of theological dialogue. To them, as to some conservative Christians, the very idea of dialogue seems to imply a relativizing of the faith and betrayal of the truth. As recently as 1986 the Rabbinical Council of America reaffirmed its position that theological discussions, as distinguished from conversations on social and human welfare issues, ought to be avoided.

Others remain skeptical about Christian motives and are particularly concerned that the dialogue process might be manipulated for missionary purposes. The fear of proselytizing is also extremely strong in the Jewish community.

Then there are people who feel that, in general, the dialogue is overloaded with friendliness and tends to lack honest confrontation. Eliezer Berkovits, in a 1966 article in the periodical *Judaism*, put it quite sharply when he raised the question about who the people are who are so eager to engage in dialogue. Scornfully, he provided his own answer: "They are either Jews without memories or Jews for whom Judaism is exclusively a matter of public relations, or confused or spineless Jews unable to appreciate the meaning of confrontation in full freedom."

No doubt, public relations play a role in the interfaith enterprise, as do political calculations. And, I would think, quite understandably so. There is no need to romanticize all that goes on in the name of Christian-Jewish relations. On the other hand, sometimes the politics and P.R. may be a bit overdone. There have been times when Jewish leaders seemed excessively eager to show gratitude to church officials for little favors. For instance, after the slaughter of innocent worshippers in the Istanbul synagogue in 1986, several church bureaucrats spoke out in protest, and Jewish organizations cited their words in mailings across the land. But some of those same leaders had been silent at times when it was much less safe to speak out, when nothing less than Jewish survival was at stake. In some cases, as during the 1967 and 1973 wars, a few of those same leaders had called for cut-off of U.S. arms shipments to Israel when it was in a life-and-death struggle with enemies who were heavily armed by the Soviet Union.

Still, it seems unfair to me to accuse staff members of Jewish organizations who are professionally involved in relations with the Christian community of avoiding confrontation at all cost. I know from personal experience that this simply is not so. We all live with dilemmas and ambiguities, except perhaps some inhabitants of academia, professors who dwell within the certainties of their own theories. So, yes, Jewish bureaucrats, too, play games, and sometimes it is done under the large umbrella of dialogue and defense of Jewish interests. But that is not the whole story.

Of course, the whole story of Christian-Jewish relations is quite complex. One of the major mistakes we tend to make is to overestimate the role of national establishments. They are part of the picture, even an important part, but in the final analysis perhaps only a small part. It is certainly not the only game in town. In numerous local communities all sorts of activities go on that never hit the headlines. Men and women of goodwill, Jews and Christians, join together in a common search for better understanding as well as for ways to serve the community in which they live.

So, in spite of the noises that sometimes emanate from solemn ecclesiastical assemblies, and at times seem to jeopardize progress that has been made, the dream is kept alive by people who may never be in the limelight but who quietly seek to obey the biblical injunction: do justice, love kindness, and walk humbly with your God.

CHAPTER 22

Vatican Affirmations and Vacillations

"The big, the inevitable, question to the Church is that of the permanent election of the Jewish people and its meaning for Christians." Thus spoke Cardinal Roger Etchegary of Marseille, France, during an "intervention" at the 1983 Synod of Roman Catholic Bishops. "So long as Judaism remains exterior to our history of salvation," he added, "we shall be at the mercy of anti-Semitic reflections." Then followed this expression of penitence: "May we learn how to ask pardon of the Lord and our brothers who have so often been nurtured on 'the teaching of contempt' and plunged into horror and holocaust."

If the permanent election of the Jewish people is indeed the big and inevitable question to the church, it has to be admitted that the addressee has succeeded in avoiding that question for many centuries. One even wonders how many members of the hierarchy present during Cardinal Etchegary's speech would have wholeheartedly endorse the sentiments he voiced, not to mention the millions of priests and local church members around the world.

Still, the Cardinal spoke from an historical context in which his affirmations make sense, and that context is the Second Vatican Council and subsequent official pronouncements from Rome. We are talking about an extremely short historical period. Before that, there was a very different history, covering many centuries which, according to the U.S. Catholic Bishops' declaration in 1975, were "replete with alienation, misunderstanding and hostility between Jews and Christians."

To state things a bit more explicitly, it was the era of the "Jew badge," instituted and enforced by the church. Those were also the days, not only of anti-Jewish fulminations, but also of forced conversions and forced baptisms, surely among the worst violations against the human spirit. Later, powerful figures within the Vatican, motivated by strong anti-Communist impulses, put their hopes in Hitler's forces and, after World War II, even became involved in helping Nazis escape from Europe and hence from justice.

Vatican II, the basic context of Cardinal Etchegary's remarks, meant a decisive turning point in the history of Catholic-Jewish relations. Perhaps we should say in a more direct way that it was an encounter between Pope John XXIII and the French historian Jules Isaac, the man who coined the now famous phrase "teaching of contempt," that began to bring about change in Catholic attitudes toward Jews and Judaism.

From all accounts, the Jewish historian did have quite an impact on Pope John XXIII, who already was preparing to open up the windows of the church to the world in order to let the breezes of new insights and inspirations refresh the stodgy atmosphere in the Catholic establishment. Some people, among them the pope's confidant, Loris Capovilla, have intimated that the thought of making the Jewish question and anti-Semitism central concerns at his upcoming Council had not occurred to the Holy Father until his meeting with Isaac on June 13, 1960, just one week after he had created the Secretariat for Promoting Christian Unity.

In my own life as a young, recently ordained pastor, Pope John XXIII became an important figure. I was deeply impressed by his diary, *Journal of a Soul*, which tells us so much about the spiritual formation of this humble giant among the saints. "The whole world is my family," he wrote in 1959. Drawing on "a strength of daring simplicity," he declared himself "ready for the Lord's surprise moves." Not only did he put the "Jewish question" (as a *Christian* problem!) on the Council's agenda, but together with Cardinal Bea, he made sure that it stayed there, despite the efforts of some within the hierarchy to get it removed or, at least, to have its impact weakened.

One of the most moving prayers of Pope John XXIII was not published in *Journal of a Soul*, but one he is reported to have written on June 4, 1963, a few days before his death.

> We realize now that for many, many centuries our eyes were so blind that we were no longer able to see the glory of your chosen people, nor to distinguish on their faces the signs of the special status of our brothers. We have come to see that the sign of Cain is on our foreheads. Century after century our brother Abel lived in blood and tears on account of our trespasses because we had forgotten your love. Forgive us the curse which we have so unjustly inflicted upon their flesh. We have crucified you for a second time, because we did not know what we were doing. Lord, help us turn from the evil way we have gone in history and church history. Let our conversion consist of a concrete renewal. May the peace of God, which guards our lives and thoughts, fill our hearts in Christ Jesus our Lord.

Two and a half years later, the Vatican Council promulgated *Nostra Aetate*, a declaration on the Relationship of the Church to the Non-

Christian Religions. Containing a special section on the church's relationship with the Jewish people, the declaration speaks about "the spiritual bond linking the people of the New Covenant with Abraham's stock." It reminds the faithful that it was through the people of Israel that the Church received divine revelation. It advocated "fraternal dialogues" and affirmed that Christ's death "cannot be blamed upon all the Jews then living, without distinction, nor upon the Jews of today." Finally, it deplored "displays of anti-Semitism directed against the Jews at any time and from any source."

The use of the (in this context) rather weak verb *deplore* seemed more than a little surprising to many readers of the document. One explanation given for this word choice was that "condemn" in a Council document should be reserved for matters of formal heresy, and Pope John explicitly had expressed that this Council not engage in such condemnations. Nevertheless, an exception on this particular point would have seemed most appropriate. Anti-Semitism often did develop within the churches as a form of heresy; in this case, the Council would not just have condemned the aberration of some individual, but a most grievous error of the Christian world at large.

The statement declaring that neither all Jews living in the time of Jesus nor those who have lived since that day should be blamed for his death was also considerably weaker than an earlier proposed version, which had expressed the hope that Christians "may never again present the Jewish people as one rejected, cursed, or guilty of deicide." Quite understandably, such revisions in proposed drafts caused great disappointment in many circles. But it was also generally recognized that this was the best that could be achieved in the theological/political climate of that moment.

Dr. Eugene J. Fisher, Executive Secretary of the Secretariat for Catholic-Jewish Relations, National Conference of Catholic Bishops (U.S.A.), frequently has pointed out that he finds the real breakthrough in *Nostra Aetate*, not in the rejection of collective guilt, important as that was, but in the paraphrase of Romans 11, "the Jews still remain most dear to God because of their fathers, for He does not repent of the gifts He makes nor of the calls He issues." With those words, Rome sought to transcend a long tradition of supersession theology. A people that remains most dear to God cannot at the same time be a cursed people, replaced in the divine covenant by the church. Vatican II constituted a definite shift in 1900 years of Catholic-Jewish relations, or rather, the lack thereof. It meant the beginning of what some Catholic scholars have called an "irreversible movement" that, step by step, would produce radical change of perspective within Catholicism.

Fisher has claimed that *Nostra Aetate* was, for all practical purposes, the beginning of Catholic Tradition (as distinguished from tradition with a small "t," summed up in the phrase "teaching of contempt") on the relationship between the church as "People of God" and "God's People, Israel." Never before had the church really dealt with those issues as a matter of *doctrinal* concern. Previous Councils, like the Fourth Lateran Council (1215), had plenty to say about Jews, but the mean-spirited and discriminatory canons issued at that time were not of a doctrinal nature. I realize, of course, that that fact gave little comfort to the victims of those laws and in no way alleviated the sufferings of all who were subjected to them. Nevertheless, in view of the way things work in Christian theological tradition, I think that Fisher's observations about the theological significance of the developments started at Vatican II have a good deal of validity.

In my opinion, a graphic portrayal of post-Vatican II developments would, while showing up-and-down movements, exhibit a gradually ascending line. In analyzing developments within the WCC from Amsterdam (1948) to Vancouver (1983) we unfortunately were forced to draw the opposite conclusion. It was a downhill process. Although, as we shall see, things turn less positive within the Catholic community as well, once the "Israel factor" becomes part of the equation. In that respect, the Protestant and Catholic dialogue movements share a common weakness.

But first, let us trace the line of progress in Catholic-Jewish relations. On December 1, 1975, the Holy See issued "Guidelines and Suggestions for Implementing the Conciliar Declaration, *Nostra Aetate*, paragraph 4." In comparing the various Catholic documents, I have been helped by materials that arrive regularly from Dr. Fisher's office and particularly from a paper he wrote entitled, "The Evolution of a Tradition: From Nostra Aetate to the 'Notes.' "

By the time the Guidelines were issued, Rome had overcome its reluctance to use the word *condemned*. Now, all forms of anti-Semitism and discrimination are, indeed, condemned "as opposed to the very spirit of Christianity." Also, there is a specific reference to contemporary Judaism, something that had been lacking in *Nostra Aetate*, although it was there by implication. The need for an explicit emphasis on this point is so important, however, because many people viewed Judaism, in essence, as a fossilized relic of something that had died soon after the death of Jesus and the rise of Christianity. When, in recent years, the fossil proved to be very much alive–when history refused to comply with the theory–and the State of Israel, as well as the Hebrew language, were revived, some proponents of the Judaism-is-dead theory had a hard time concealing their resentment.

Over against the historical fiction of the fossil, the Guidelines put the unmistakable teaching of the Catholic Church that Judaism has continued to evolve as a vital reality: "The history of Judaism did not end with the destruction of Jerusalem but, rather, went on to develop a religious tradition." Throughout the 1975 document the Jewish people, who in 1965 were still mainly defined in terms of biblical categories, are portrayed as a living, neighborly reality; as a people of faith whom Christians, also a people of faith, must learn to understand through open dialogue; as two communities of faith, drawing in part on a common prophetic tradition, that will be a blessing to humanity by cooperating in the areas of justice and peace.

In 1985, after one more decade of internal discussions, as well as dialogues with people of other faith-perspectives, the Vatican came out with "Notes on the correct way to present the Jews and Judaism in preaching and catechesis in the Roman Catholic Church." The use of the term "Notes" would seem to suggest that the document is perceived as one further step in a process of development, not as final dogma, much less as *summa theologica*. The "Notes" are meant to give some assistance to those who are charged with teaching responsibilities in the church. Above all, they seek to serve as an authoritative educational tool in an effort to portray Jews and Judaism in a fairer and, hence, more positive way than has often been done in the past.

Before discussing the content of this 1985 document, a few parenthetical observations may be in order. When we read the best in recent ecumenical literature on Jews and Judaism, we may be inclined to conclude that we have come a long way, especially when the present situation is compared with a very bad past. Upon visiting theological seminaries, however, one soon discovers that, in many instances, that literature is not being studied or assigned for reading. Numerous pastors continue to be trained without any clear understanding of the long tradition of the teaching of contempt, both in Catholic and Protestant churches.

If pastors are ignorant of the past, one can imagine what happens at the level of the local parish, especially in church schools where millions of children receive their knowledge about the Bible and the story of Jesus from mostly untrained teachers. The gap between the best of what is being published "up there" among the relatively small group of people who are preoccupied with these matters and what goes on in local churches and Sunday schools is immense. At that level many myths and misinterpretations, repudiated by reputable scholars, are still being disseminated as gospel truths.

I personally have little doubt, however, that, on the whole, the Catholic community has tried harder to correct the situation and has done a better job in revising educational materials, than either mainline Protestants or evangelicals. People like Dr. Fisher and Sister Rose Thering, Professor Emeritus of Education at Seton Hall University, have done pioneer research in this field that has led to numerous changes, often brought about with the eagerly sought assistance of Jewish scholars. True, not all Catholic teachers use the materials available to them, and perhaps some do not use them very well, but the overall movement is in the right direction.

It seems to me that it is in that context that the "Notes" must be viewed. As the introduction points out, Pope John Paul II himself set the tone when, in 1982, he told delegates of episcopal conferences and other experts who were meeting in Rome to study relations between the church and Judaism: "We should aim, in this field, that Catholic teaching at its different levels, in catechesis to children and young people, presents Jews and Judaism, not only in an honest and objective manner, free from prejudices and without any offenses, but also with the full awareness of the heritage common [to Jews and Christians]."

Once more, the "Notes" seek to move a few steps beyond what was affirmed in the preceding Vatican pronouncements. New areas are opened up for exploration, such as positive elements in the contribution of the Pharisees, who traditionally have been treated with almost total negativity in Christian teachings. Other emphases are reinforced and, in some cases, reformulated in light of what has been learned during the preceding years. For instance, the danger of anti-Semitism is pointed out with renewed urgency as an evil that is "always ready to reappear under different guises."

Citing Pope John Paul II who, in an address to the Jewish community of Mainz, West Germany, in 1980, referred to "the people of God of the Old Covenant, which has never been revoked," the "Notes" also present a strongly anti-supersessionist message. But beyond that, there is a very positive assessment of Jewish history which, as the 1975 document stressed, did not end with the destruction of the Temple in 70 A.D. This history, we are now told, "continued, especially in a numerous Diaspora which allowed Israel to carry to the whole world a witness, often heroic in its fidelity to the one God and 'to exalt him in the presence of all the living' " (Tobit 13:4).

In the Catholic community, the voice of final authority obviously resides in the Holy See. But the role of the various national conferences of Catholic bishops should not be underestimated. Some of the statements they have issued represent dramatic breakthroughs in Christian-Jewish dialogue and, in turn, influenced subsequent Vatican documents.

Then there are the words and actions of the Holy Father as he travels around the globe, particularly important in the case of someone like Pope John Paul II, who operated on the world scene with such a well-attuned sense of symbolic drama. One year before his address to Jewish leaders in Mainz, during a very dramatic visit to his native Poland, the pope visited Auschwitz and there spoke movingly about the millions of murdered Jews.

Even more dramatic was the pope's visit to the Great Synagogue in Rome during the Spring of 1986. His very positive message on that occasion was all the more welcome because several Lenten homilies, delivered by him only a few weeks earlier, had raised serious questions among Jews as well as concerned Christians, including some prominent Catholics, whether supersession theology really was a thing of the past. In the Great Synagogue the pope once again affirmed that "the Jews are beloved of God, who has called them with an irrevocable calling." The homilies, I suspect, reflected a long-standing past that is dying only slowly, while the message in the Great Synagogue represents the wave of the future. At least I fervently hope that this will prove to be the case.

Speaking of hope, we have already noted that the 1985 Vatican document spoke of the Jews who, throughout their history, have preserved "the memory of the land of their forefathers as the heart of their hope." But what about our faith and our hope as Christians? Or, to repeat the question raised when discussing the Protestant ecumenical world: If the covenant promises are still valid today–if as the Holy Father has said, these have never been revoked–does that include the "promised land," and does the answer to that question affect our faith and our hope?

Where does the Catholic Church stand on that question, which also encompasses the issue of the status of Jerusalem? In the midst of much ambiguity and ecclesiastical/political gamesmanship, it could with certainty be said that the Catholic Church has moved beyond the position of Pope Pius X, who, in 1904, held a meeting with Theodor Herzl shortly before the latter's death. The founder of the modern Zionist movement was looking for the "goodwill" that was lacking during his visit to the Vatican. A statement made by the pope on that occasion ranks among those famous unfortunate remarks to which the world is treated with sad regularity by religious and secular leaders alike. "We cannot approve of the Zionist movement," declared the Holy Father. "We cannot prevent the Hebrews from going to Jerusalem, but we could never sanction it. The Hebrews have not recognized our Lord; therefore, we cannot recognize the Hebrew people . . ."

Two weeks later, a mild spirit of charity had apparently taken over as the Vatican Secretary of State, Cardinal Merry del Val, wrote in a letter to Herzl,: "If the Jews believe they might greatly ease their lot by being admitted to the land of their ancestors, then we would regard that as a humanitarian question. We shall never forget that without Judaism, we would have been nothing." The first sentence in this quote seems to imply some goodwill toward, or at least a toleration of, a non-political type of Zionism (the Jews are allowed to live in the land as a favor, a humanitarian gesture). The second sentence seems to appreciate Judaism mainly as a *preparatio evangelii*, an instrument to bring forth Christ and the Christian church.

In 1917, Pope Benedict XV, protesting the Balfour Declaration, had still manifested a spirit of Catholic imperialism when he wrote, "Our apostolic charge makes it a duty to demand that the rights of the Catholic Church in Palestine, when they are so manifestly superior to the rights of others involved, should be respected and safeguarded prior to all others; not only the claims of Jews and infidels, but those of members of non-Catholic confessions, no matter what their race and country."

As Father John F. Morley so clearly showed in his book, *Vatican Diplomacy and the Jews during the Holocaust 1939-1943*, the Vatican suffered from a longstanding phobia about a Jewish majority in Palestine, convinced that this would be very much opposed to Catholic interests. Still, in 1943, while debating the feasibility of sending rescued Slovakian children to Palestine, Monsignor Domenico Tardini, a principal assistant to the Vatican Secretary of State wrote, "The Holy See has never approved the project of making Palestine a Jewish home. . . . And the question of the Holy Places? Palestine is by this time more sacred for Catholics than . . . for Jews." The words spoken in the Rome synagogue in 1986 were indeed a world removed from the remarks by these papal predecessors.

Still, the question of Israel is far from resolved. It continues to haunt Catholic-Jewish dialogue. In *Nostra Aetate* the whole subject was treated with silence. That was not an oversight during the early stages of dialogue. In fact, it represented a clear defeat for those who had attempted to raise the issue. A first-draft document proposed at Vatican II was rejected precisely because it hinted at the possibility of extending diplomatic recognition to Israel. This defeat led to a withdrawal into safer territory, and *Nostra Aetate* ended up focusing mainly on what, in a fondly condescending fashion, is often referred to as "the Israel of old." Later Vatican pronouncements sought to correct this by making positive statements about Jewish history since the destruction of the Temple in 70 A.D.

But the question of Israel could not be silenced that easily. In 1966, one year after the promulgation of *Nostra Aetate*, Father Cornilius Rijk, a Dutch biblical scholar, was assigned the task of follow-up and implementation. Once again, he and associates sympathetic to his views went to work on a draft document designed to attribute a certain theological significance to the rebirth of the State of Israel. However, in 1969 this preliminary draft was leaked and published in *The Catholic Review* of Baltimore. This raised the level of internal Vatican politics to a feverish pitch, showing that church politics and bureaucratic infighting are by no means a Protestant monopoly, least of all when the issue of Israel is at stake.

Father Thomas F. Stransky, a founding staff member of the Vatican

Secretariat for Promoting Christian unity, wrote in *America*[1] that "politics should not be allowed to place theology in chains,"[2] while knowing full well the dynamics of church discussions when the Middle East is involved. So, according to Father Stransky, "no matter how purely theological and pastoral the conciliar intentions might be, any positive development in Catholic-Jewish relations would have political implications in the Middle East, saturated with Christian, Moslem and Jewish conflict. Beleaguered minority Catholic communities would express that anxiety through their bishops. And Arab diplomats to the Holy See would bluntly state their disquiet." A little later he mentions his surprise "that, while over the past two decades, the results of the dialogue have been changing, the theological and pastoral horizons, the political pressure, subtle or not so subtle, has stubbornly refused to subside."[3]

Some progress has been made. The 1975 Vatican "Guidelines" once again remained silent on the question of Israel. But conferences of bishops in several countries began to speak out, some of them even before 1975. For instance, the French bishops, in their Declaration of 1973, stated: "It is at present, more than ever, difficult to pronounce a serene theological judgment on the movement of return of the Jewish people on its land. In this context, we cannot forget as Christians the gift once made by God to the People of Israel of a land where it was called to reunite."

In 1975, the U.S. Catholic bishops declared that "an overwhelming majority of Jews see themselves bound in one way or another to the land of Israel. Most Jews see this tie to the land as essential to their Jewishness." They went on to make the point that "whatever difficulties Christians may experience in sharing this vision, they should strive to understand this link between land and people which Jews have expressed in their writings and worship throughout two millennia as a longing for the homeland, holy Zion." They added that this in no way implied agreement with specific policies or political positions.

In this statement the U.S. Catholic bishops seemed to be practicing what the "Guidelines" preached, namely to take into consideration "by what essential traits the Jews define themselves in the light of their own religious tradition." Finally, in a 1983 message, the Brazilian bishops spoke of "the right of the Jews to a calm political existence in their country of origin, the State of Israel."

Encouraged no doubt by such collective efforts on the part of conferences of bishops, some members of the hierarchy have also taken individual initiatives. In the case of Archbishop Peter L. Geraty, then Archbishop of Newark, New Jersey, this took the form of a pastoral letter which received wide distribution. Picking up on what had already been stated in the "Guidelines" and the Declaration of the U. S. Bishops, it affirmed the following: "Dialogue demands respect for the other in his or her self-understanding. For most Jews, an essential component of this self-understanding is a point of focus on the Land of Israel and the city of Jerusalem. Leaving political issues in their myriad details to be solved in the context of the Near East and its peoples, we Christians rejoice with the Jewish people that a representative portion has come to the land promised to the patriarchs, and hope that they will find there a continuing abode of peace for the creative response of Judaism to the call of God." Now, even Jerusalem comes into view as an essential and authentic component of Jewish self-understanding.

But what about the Bishop of Rome? Pope John Paul II also began to make explicit references to the State of Israel. For instance, in his 1984 Easter message he stated, "For the Jewish people who live in the State of Israel and who preserve in that land such precious testimonies to their history and faith, we must ask for the desired security and due tranquility that is the prerogative of every nation and condition of life and of progress for every society."

All this brings us to the "Notes," the Vatican document of 1985, in which the silence on Israel was finally broken. The "Notes" refer to the "often heroic" witness of the Jewish people to the whole world, to their "fidelity to the one God . . . while preserving the memory of the land of their forefathers at the heart of their hope." Then follow these sentences:

> Christians are invited to understand this religious attachment which finds its roots in Biblical tradition, without however making their own any particular religious interpretation of this relationship. . . . The existence of the State of Israel and its political options should be envisaged not in a perspective which is in itself religious, but in their reference to the common principles of international law. . . . The permanence of Israel (while so many ancient peoples have disappeared without trace) is a historic fact and a sign to be interpreted within God's design.

What exactly does all this mean? Does the statement fail to affirm the right of Israel to exist, as some Jewish leaders read it? Does it empty modern Israel of any possible religious significance for Christians? In short, is the document essentially supersessionist in outlook, regarding the promises of the "old covenant" as having been abrogated? Or, as Dr. Fisher explained it, does the pronouncement, when read against the backdrop of papal statements about Israel, support that country's right to exist, but sound a warning against a fundamentalist-biblicist approach to Middle East problems? Is the Vatican reacting against evangelicals who talk, not only about a theological basis for affirming the rebirth of Israel as a sign of God's faithfulness to the prophetic witness, but also about "biblical boundaries" and the like?

The reference to the principles of international law seems to contain an implicit recognition of the right of Israel to exist. After all, international law is not a bad foundation on which to base a country's legitimacy. But is that all Christian believers have to say on the matter? The document tells us that Jewish attachment to the land "finds its roots in Biblical tradition." Of course, that could mean "old covenant" tradition, no longer valid or authoritative for Christians. But there is more. The permanence of Israel, including, one assumes, the most remarkable (miraculous, some of us would say) rebirth of this ancient nation, is not only a fact of history, but as such also "a sign to be interpreted within God's design." Is that another way of talking about the divine covenant promises which are coming true today?

So many questions come to mind. The problem with this particular section of the "Notes" is that it lacks clarity. And clarity on this issue is precisely what is so desperately needed. In the midst of so much confusion, how are Catholic teachers going to use these "Notes" in a constructive way? The great danger is that they will take the text and fill the gaps with entrenched biases with respect to the biblical message concerning Jews and their destiny.

If the covenant with the Jewish people has not been revoked, why does it seem so difficult to apply it in a clear way to the promises of the land, without thereby giving the church's imprimatur on specific Israeli policies? The answer might be summed up in one word: politics. I refer to both Vatican political infighting and the peculiar dimension that is added by the fact that the Vatican also functions as a state, which means involvement in all sorts of diplomatic entanglements.

Protestants, too, have minority groups in Arab countries. They, too, have often felt constraints on what they can say and do, because they fear for the safety of their people and the survival of their missions. For the Vatican, with its diplomatic *nuncios* across the world, the situation becomes even more complex. For instance, it introduces the question of formal recognition of certain countries but not of others. When it comes to the formal recognition of Israel, Catholic leaders are obviously very much divided.

The Vatican, like the National and World Councils of Churches, is eager to keep the line of communication open to both the Arab and the Jewish worlds. That is understandable, even laudable, as it could cast the churches into a reconciling role in the Middle East. By and large, however, they have not functioned that way at all. Their search for even-handedness has tended to tie them up in awkward theories about "moral equivalencies," leading to more questions than trust. Such questions were raised, for instance when, in 1982, Yassir Arafat was received by the Pope, a gesture that may have produced some political benefits for both parties involved, but was incomprehensible to most Jews, since it seemed to give credibility to the murderers of Jewish men, women, and children.

Diplomatic intricacies and the requirements of *Realpolitik* are no doubt part of the picture here. They sometimes raise troublesome questions about the meaning of Christian integrity in the midst of all this international gamesmanship. The pope's reception of Kurt Waldheim in 1987, praising the man's alleged achievements while ignoring the serious questions that were being raised about his character and his actions during the Nazi period, did little to enhance the Vatican's credibility. On the other hand, it is very easy to become overly self-righteous in condemning the accommodations that others make while demanding understanding for one's own dilemmas. None of us functions in an atmosphere of purity that transcends politics. To put it quite bluntly, I can honestly come to no other conclusion than that the sin of theological triumphalism continues to influence Christian attitudes towards Jews, Judaism and the State of Israel.

This sin has been confessed over the past decades by a number of ecclesiastical and ecumenical bodies. It has been admitted that such triumphalism has meant untold suffering for the Jewish people over many centuries. It is a sin from which many Christians have sought to repent. But this sin, like all other sins, is never totally overcome. To claim, for instance, that one is free of all pride would be one of the most boastful statements a person could make. There is a constant need for self-critical honesty, to confess ever anew that continued change is called for. It will not be a painless process. Healing usually is not.

The topics of the State of Israel and Jerusalem are among the most touchy and troublesome in Christian-Jewish relations. We tend to handle them with utmost care, because we do not want to shatter the precious treasures that dialogue has yielded thus far. However, what can be worked out rather neatly during programs of the National Workshop on Christian-Jewish Relations, avoiding confrontations that might cause a measure of discomfort, usually becomes a more knotty problem when real or imagined Christian "interests" in Jerusalem are at stake.

In a letter dated December 1, 1986, the NCLCI addressed an "open letter" to the sponsors of the National Workshop on Christian-Jewish Relations, by all counts the major regular gathering point for people who are concerned about such issues. The letter expressed some disquiet about how the topics of Israel and Zionism were being handled in the dialogue movement. Everybody knows that the "Israel dynamic" is stirring constantly just below the surface, occasionally bursting into the open with explosive force. Nevertheless, these issues are rarely confronted with the sense of urgency that one would expect such an obstacle to candid dialogue to receive. "We are aware," the letter stated, "that in most National Workshop programs something has appeared on Israel and Zionism and that in a few instances those issues have been dealt with in a rather tangential fashion. In most cases those topics were included somewhat hesitantly and mainly as a concession to those who raised questions about the matter."

In essence, the leadership of the National Workshop was being asked to live a little more dangerously, to stop avoiding certain issues by dealing with them in a context that made them relatively safe and domesticated. For those in charge of designing conferences, that is not a very difficult thing to do. But the problems keep on festering, from time to time exploding in ways that threaten to set back the progress that has been made in building bridges of understanding and mutual trust.

An example of that happened a few weeks after the "open letter" was sent out. Cardinal John O'Connor of New York went on a post-Christmas visit to the Middle East. He very much wanted this to be a journey of reconciliation and, in the spirit of even-handedness, made arrangements to meet with King Hussein in Amman, Jordan, and with Israeli officials in Jerusalem. That seemed fair enough. But, as the good Cardinal learned just before he was to leave the U.S., such an arrangement was in conflict with Vatican policy. Once again, even-handedness turned out to be a weapon against Israel, or at least an item on the ecclesiastical agenda where the principle of "moral equivalency" did not apply. For the Cardinal to meet with Israeli leaders in their offices located in the capital of their country would accord a recognition to the authority of the Jewish government that Rome was not prepared to concede. In the end, a compromise arrangement was negotiated and meetings took place. But, instead of reconciliation, the incident led to recriminations and renewed distrust.

There is no argument about the fact that Jerusalem is very special, not only to Jews but to Christians and Muslims as well. The real issue is what we say and do after we have cited the familiar formula that Jerusalem is a Holy City for the monotheistic religions: Judaism, Christianity, and Islam. Having said that, are we as Christians willing to acknowledge that Jerusalem, the city where Jesus walked, ministered, and died, the city of David, is essentially a Jewish city? And, having said that, are we prepared to accept the legitimacy of Jewish sovereignty over the land of Israel and its capital, Jerusalem? The letter from the NCLCI to the National Workshop leadership was basically an invitation to have serious conversations on those issues.

The WCC issued a warning at its 1983 meeting in Vancouver, to the effect that "the tendency to minimize Jerusalem's importance for any of these three religions should be avoided." Fine! I, for one, have no desire to belittle the intensity of anyone's spiritual attachment to Jerusalem or anything else. But it seems to me that there is something else that ought to be avoided: namely, a tendency to equalize the position of the three monotheistic faiths to the point of ignoring basic historical facts in order to deny the Jewish people sovereignty over their capital city.

Centuries before the birth of Christianity or Islam, the Jewish people had established Jerusalem as the capital of its commonwealth. They have maintained a presence there ever since. It has been a "trimillenial love affair" (Lelyveld). Jerusalem is "home" to the Jewish people in a way that it is to no other people. Honesty requires that we not minimize such facts.

Christians and Muslims have genuine and legitimate concerns about open and free access to the sites that are holy to their faith. But for the Jewish people, the very land of Israel lies at the heart of their covenant faith. That is the way it has been from time immemorial and it is something that ought not to be minimized. When the Vancouver Assembly of the WCC expressed an interest in becoming involved in a dialogue with Jews and Muslims that "can contribute towards political processes that would lead to a mutually acceptable agreement for sharing the city," one suspects that those political processes would be *à priori* designed to deny Jews sovereignty over Jerusalem and, therefore, the gesture would have to be considered basically insincere. A charade really.

At one time, the Vatican favored internationalization of Jerusalem, which would also, in effect, deny the Jewish people sovereignty over their capital city. In recent years, the Holy See has advocated "international guarantees" or "a special internationally guaranteed status" for Jerusalem assuring that there will be no discrimination against any faith. Only the most biased observers deny that there is freedom of worship whenever Israel has authority of the united city. Therefore, one becomes a little uncomfortable when Christians, who declare themselves to be pilgrims in the world, find it so hard to take chances with their Jewish brothers and sisters who have given no indication whatsoever that they wish to do to Christians and Muslims what the latter have done to them, in Jerusalem or anywhere else.

It seems to me that it ought to be stated candidly that Vatican diplomacy needs to catch up with Catholic theology, if the former is not to undermine the credibility of the latter. We Christians simply must come clean on the question of Jerusalem. A clear-cut position in favor of full Israeli authority may well involve a certain sense of vulnerability. The Catholic Church, more than some other Christian communions, feels that there is much at stake in protecting its interests in the Holy Land. Furthermore, concerns about minority Catholic communities in Arab lands are quite real. There are no easy answers. But that was also true when Pope John XXIII, in "daring simplicity," ventured forth into the Second Vatican Council.

Once again, a certain kind of "daring simplicity" is called for. The Servant Church is rightfully concerned about the requirements of spiritual devotion; it has a right to expect that, in that respect, its needs shall be met. But a truly Servant Church also dares to be vulnerable and is certainly not preoccupied with prestige or property claims. The Holy Sites, instead of serving as centers of reconciliation and common devotion, have often been the cause of the most unedifying intra-Christian conflicts. They must not now also become a stumbling block in Christian-Jewish relations.

In May 1983, the NCLCI issued a "Christian Affirmation on Jerusalem." It stated in part: "We believe that the essentially Jewish character of Jerusalem must be accepted by Christians, not grudgingly but gratefully. We see here a sign of God's providential grace in history and eternal faithfulness, a source of hope to all." It is not just a matter of the mystique of the Holy City, as real and alluring as that is; it is also very much a matter of the mystery of the divine covenant of grace.

Pressures on Vatican diplomacy *vis-à-vis* Israel and Jerusalem are bound to continue, because to a considerable degree they are being propelled by the expectations that have been raised by Catholic theology. The big and inevitable question with respect to the meaning of Israel has been raised within the Catholic community. Some daring answers have been evolving over the past decades.

But other big questions still remain. And one of them goes like this: "Will the Catholic Church be able to draw the political consequences from the theological truths it has been advocating about Jews and Judaism since Vatican II?" Or, referring to the prayer by Pope John XXIII a few days before his death, will our conversion consist of a renewal so real and so concrete that it will encompass new Catholic attitudes and policies toward the State of Israel and Jerusalem?

[1] Father Thomas F. Stransky, *America,* February 8, 1986.
[2] *Ibid.,* p. 92.
[3] *Ibid.,* p. 93.

CHAPTER 23

Evangelical Activism and Israel

"We, representatives of Bible-believing Christianity, gather . . . to affirm the importance of the State of Israel, and to unite with the Jewish people against those who wickedly assail them and their beloved State." This we read in a proclamation issued during a National Prayer Breakfast in Honor of Israel in Washington DC. The question that arises (in addition to whether a Prayer Breakfast should not always be in honor of God) is this: Who can legitimately be categorized as a representative of Bible-believing Christianity?

There has been a lot of talk about evangelical Christians, and–particularly in the Jewish community–there is a tendency to identify evangelicals with that segment of Christianity that sponsors events like the National Prayer Breakfast and is very vocal in its support for Israel. The impression is created, often with the active encouragement of certain evangelical spokespersons, that evangelicals constitute a clearly definable and identifiable group within the Christian community. But do they?

Merrill Simon distinguished between two groups of Christians who each are supposed to have a distinct attitude toward Israel. "While the Evangelical Church has strengthened its ties with Israel," wrote Simon, "the Liberal Church has taken an opposite stand."[1] But, such simplistic schemes hardly bear any semblance of reality. In the end, a total lack of sophistication is bound to lead to more harm than good. Certainly, Israel and its need for friends are poorly served by policy decisions based on this sort of fiction.

There is no such thing as "the Evangelical Church." There is, however, an organization called the National Association of Evangelicals to which many denominations identifying themselves as "evangelical" belong. All of them hold a high view of the inspiration of the Holy Scriptures and in that sense are Bible-believing. But many would not endorse positions expressed in the proclamations issued by the organizers of National Prayer Breakfasts in Honor of Israel. That is one complicating factor. Another one is that millions of people who hold membership in so-called mainline churches also identify themselves as "evangelicals" because they represent the (often large) conservative wing within the more liberal denominations.

If the word *evangelical* proves to be less clear and simple than it at first may appear, would it help if we add the term *fundamentalist*? In other words, in order to be considered a Bible-believing Christian must one give assent to the theory of "biblical inerrancy," implying the infallibility, not of the Scriptures as we have them, but of the original manuscripts? There are those who seem to believe that, as long as a person is a biblical literalist, he or she will automatically join the pro-Israel forces who sponsor Prayer Breakfast-type events. But that, too, is an overly simplistic way of looking at things.

First of all, not all people who agree on the theory of "biblical inerrancy" reach the same conclusions as to what the message of a literally interpreted Bible is. That is especially true with respect to the question of Israel. There are extremely orthodox theological seminaries that require of everyone who is appointed to their faculties that they sign a statement declaring their strict adherence to a literal view of the Bible, but who do not accept the views on Israel embodied in various proclamations, such as that of the Prayer Breakfast.

What does the latter group affirm with respect to Israel? A central element in their beliefs is the conviction that the God of Abraham, Isaac, and Jacob has never revoked the covenant once made with the Jewish people. They remain the chosen people. The term *Bible-believing* in this context implies, as a minimum, that one does not hold to a supersessionist theology, that one rejects the claim that the church is the "true Israel" that has replaced the Jewish people.

Premillenialist and so-called dispensationalist theology tends to view the Christian church as a "parenthesis in history," an emergency measure necessitated by the fact that Israel did not accept the kingdom as it was revealed and offered in Jesus the Messiah (or the Christ). Since a human "no" can never cancel out the divine "yes," the eternal covenant with Israel remains valid. For a while, the divine plan may move on a side track, but eventually, the detours of history will come to an end. Everything will return to the main track, which runs via the Jewish people and the city of Jerusalem.

Thus, divine faithfulness to the promises made through the prophets of Israel is seen as the sure and firm foundation on which not only the future of Israel rests, but also the destiny of the world. According to most dispensationalist theology, history will soon come to its cataclysmic conclusion, and Israel plays a key role in these end-time developments that, it is believed, we are witnessing today. All this is happening according to the scenario foretold by the prophets.

The idea of the church as parenthesis is, it seems to me, much to be preferred over the notion of the church as replacement of Israel. It is, I believe, also much closer to the teachings of the Bible.

Much of the recent prominence of pro-Israel Christian millennialists is due to the fact that this view has been held by prominent television and radio ministers. It is, therefore, not surprising that the Prayer Breakfasts have been held in conjunction with the annual meetings of the National Religious Broadcasters, an organization that for many years was headed by Dr. Ben Armstrong, a kindly and capable gentleman who is also a fervent "lover of Zion."

The Christian Right's hegemony over the airwaves contains one of the truly ironic stories of recent church history. It is so ironic because it is, at least in part, the result of attitudes prevalent some decades ago among the more liberal Protestant establishment, which did everything in its power to keep the views of conservative evangelicals off the radio. The control liberal Christians exercised over such matters had come to them without any cost or great effort on their part.

The Communications Act of 1934 sought to bring a measure of order to the rapidly growing broadcasting industry. Since the airwaves belong to the public at large, and since only certain people are licensed to use them, fairness seemed to dictate that some time be allocated to serve "the public convenience, interest and necessity." And who would make the decision for the religious–or more specifically the Protestant–community? In order to take advantage of this opportunity, mainstream denominations formed broadcasting units as part of existing Councils of Churches. Stations were quite happy to keep their noses out of the hornet's nest of inter-church rivalries. They were more than willing to leave the decision about which Christian voices were to be heard free of charge to such Councils, even though the more conservative churches were not represented in them (partly because they could not join in good conscience, partly because they were not welcome).

Those who were locked out were left only one choice: buy time whenever possible, put on a show that would attract listeners, and develop fundraising techniques to secure the money to pay the bills. By and large, this was a business for mavericks, entrepreneurs in the Lord's business. Step by step, these people built what today is known as the Electronic Church. If the liberal establishment had shown a greater spirit of generosity toward their more conservative brothers and sisters, the latter might never have moved so far ahead of them in the use of media. The mainline churches got a free ride, but they also became lazy and their programs often lacked imagination. In the end, they were poorly prepared for the age of new media technology.

Most Christian mission projects were started by mavericks, often without the blessing of (or even in opposition to the wishes of) the church establishment, who feared competition with their own fundraising efforts. Eventually, many of these independent ventures were co-opted by the denominational bureaucracies, but sometimes it was too late for such a takeover to succeed.

One day, during my tenure as director of communications of the Reformed Church in America, a proposal for the funding of a TV program arrived in our office. Accompanied by an appropriate memo, the package was sent off to the media department of my staff. After a few months an opinion was rendered that the kind of program suggested was not feasible and simply would not do. The man submitting the idea was a somewhat maverick preacher in our denomination by the name of Robert H. Schuller. The proposed program is known today as *The Hour of Power*, for decades one of the top-rated religious programs on the air.

Beware of the experts! In this connection I cannot resist sharing a story I once read. A would-be farmer bought 4000 chickens, but by the end of the first week, 1000 of them had died. In a mood of desperation the farmer called his rabbi for advice. "Feed them rye," the rabbi said, "and all will be well."

During the following week another 1000 chickens died and once again the unfortunate farmer called his rabbi. "Feed them wheat," was the advice received this time. After another 1000 chickens had died, the farmer was told to feed them rice.

Finally, the farmer found himself without any chickens left. "What shall I do now," he lamented to the rabbi. "I have lost all my chickens and don't know what to do next."

"That's a pity," the rabbi replied, "for I have a lot more excellent advice to give."

Evangelicals sometimes blunder. Because of their innate enthusiasm (one could almost characterize it as a quality of "bubbliness") and because of the maverick mentality that is often so strong among them, they tend to do their blundering in a big way. It certainly cannot be denied that evangelicals have come up with their share of quixotic ideas. There are, without a doubt, charlatans and opportunists among them.

But, as far as I have been able to detect, a predilection for folly and fantasy has not infected them to any greater degree than some of the liberal groups I have worked with, particularly the radical wings of the latter. I am not unique in finding that people inclined toward extreme positions, be it on the Left or the Right, tend to be rather similar in psychological make-up.

Mainline leaders, in my judgment, tend to underestimate the mavericks on the Christian Right and to write them off as an irrelevant factor in the larger social context. The latter, in the meantime, aided by sophisticated media technology and wise in the ways of computerized mass mailings, developed their brand of evangelicalism into an increasingly powerful voice both in the religious and political arenas.

In the words of Lionel Trilling, "Liberalism is always being surprised." Liberals tend to keep on hoping for the best, expecting that, in the end, the more noble impulses of human nature will yet prevail. They are often not only surprised but angered when, instead of awakening to our utopian dreams, we are forced to deal with the world of hard and ugly realities. Furthermore, like most of us, liberals often find it difficult to remain true to that most basic ingredient of all genuine liberalism, namely, openness to new directions as dictated by ongoing critical inquiry and historical experience.

In light of the pendulum principle so often operative in historical movements, one might have expected that mainline church leaders would be somewhat prepared for the new challenge. However, in many instances they themselves had become so solidly identified with the countercultural movements of the preceding decades that they lacked the critical insight which is such an indispensable tool for picking up signals about future developments.

Some movements have arisen that have been, in essence, a reaction (revolt, we should perhaps call it) against the radical challenges being posed to what many Americans considered to be traditional religious and cultural values. My own guess is that millions of people who did not have a fanatical bone in their bodies, but who feared a devaluation of all values, have felt sympathetic toward certain positions of the New Right.

There were people who were perhaps incapable of articulating their concerns but intuitively sensed that a moral-spiritual vacuum might eventually be filled by forces that were basically nihilistic in nature and might lead to a normless society. They looked upon the New Right, not as the inauguration of the Kingdom of Righteousness, but as a possible corrective toward values that seemed worth preserving. In short, they saw themselves as part of a traditionalist movement rather than as agents of a right-wing revolution.

As James Neucherlain put it in a *Commentary* article: "One need not be crazy or a sectarian zealot to be unhappy with prevailing trends in our society: in the arts, family life, religion, or public morality. It does not require a true believer's mentality to conclude that moral decay is far advanced in our common social life; it requires only a normally developed awareness of the way things are."[2] Within the mainline church bureaucracies, including within the National Council staff, there were a few individuals, like Dean Kelley, director of the office on Religious and Civil Rights, who dared to state publicly that, just possibly, the New Right, with all its faults and foibles, might yet produce a positive plus as a counterforce to the continued atomization and deterioration of our culture. But theirs were minority voices.

Back in 1660, Blaise Pascal wrote in *Pensées* that "people never do evil so completely and cheerfully as when they do it from religious conviction." Since both the Christian Right and the Christian Left, in their own selective ways, feel quite free to appeal to divine authority, it would seem advisable that we maintain a measure of healthy skepticism toward both.

For many Jewish leaders, particularly in the United States, the emergence of the New Right has posed something of a dilemma, because some of the most prominent leaders of that movement have been outspoken and unapologetic supporters of Israel. Some Israelis–for instance a politician like Menachem Begin or a scholar like David Flusser, who were less concerned about complexities concerning the social agenda on the American scene–have fewer qualms about establishing ties with the evangelical Right. Furthermore, they have been inclined to feel that whatever moralizing on the part of the New Right might offend certain Jewish leaders in the U.S., they in Israel have suffered much more from the sanctimonious moralizing by liberal religious and political figures.

The American Jewish Congress, on the other hand, issued a declaration on the New Right entitled "Where We Stand." It found the New Right a "deeply disquieting" development, and deplored the "violent rhetoric" and "imperious self-righteousness" which, we are told, seems determined to "straight-jacket our minds." In response, the Congress called for an "aggressive advocacy of the classic agenda of democracy." But isn't that precisely the point at issue? What exactly is the classic agenda of democracy? Is it the American Jewish Congress' agenda? The National Council of Churches' agenda? The agenda of the U.S. Catholic Bishops? Or does the real agenda of democracy evolve out of the free and at times fiery debate between all those agendas plus many more, including the views of an organization that somewhat arrogantly called itself the Moral Majority?

Frankly, I found all the talk about a New Inquisition, the ominous threat to the Bill of Rights, and evangelical leaders aspiring to be America's *ayatollahs* a bit overdone. True, the aim of the New Right is nothing less than the reshaping of American culture. There is no doubt in my mind that when religionists enter the social arena as activist reformers, the danger of the politics of self-righteousness lurks right around the corner. But, it seemed to me that the New Right has been merely a latecomer in a game that some other religious leaders have been playing for a long time.

Social concern is hardly an innovation among revivalist Christians. Pietist movements in the 18th and 19th centuries frequently pioneered Christian social ministries: care for unwed mothers, prison work, programs to alleviate the sufferings caused by the industrial revolution. Evangelicals were in the forefront of the war against King Rum and in the defense of Prohibition. However, in their day they also played a significant role in the anti-slavery movement.

But fundamentalism, as it developed during the first decades of the 20th century, was a different story. These were days of bitter polemics and sharp polarization within Protestantism. Higher biblical criticism was in its heyday. Science, particularly the theory of evolution, reigned supreme and in some church circles became an inclusive principle of interpretation. Accommodation to modernity was the order of the day. In some extreme cases, theologians applied those new ideas to issues of faith in ways that led to a virtual naturalization and humanization of the biblical text.

The forces of orthodoxy fought back, organizing themselves under the banner of the fundamentalist movement. Reacting to the relativism of the modernists, they often displayed a rigidity that bordered on obscurantism. Separatism became the watchword and protective shield against the wicked heresies prevalent in both the church and the world.

After the Scopes trial in 1925 and the repeal of Prohibition in 1933, the fundamentalist movement became increasingly isolationist, anti-intellectualist, and socially irrelevant. The movement also became basically apolitical. The children and grandchildren of the first-generation fundamentalists did not always feel comfortable in an environment that they found excessively confining. Instead of attending one of the proliferating Bible colleges, where they felt education had taken the form of indoctrination, some of those young adults once again applied to major universities. They began to avoid the designation *fundamentalist*, preferring to be called "evangelicals," a term that retained the warmth of a gospel movement but lacked the connotation of rigidity.

Eventually, in true pendulum-swing fashion, a reaction movement set in again. Questions about the evangelicalism of some evangelicals began to be raised. Professors teaching in evangelical institutions, especially, were accused of not being evangelical enough, of not sticking firmly to "the fundamentals," with the issue of accommodation to modernity being raised once again. Leaders in the movement added to such old concerns as liquor, tobacco, theater and dance, the issues of abortion, prayer in the schools, pornography, homosexuality, and support for Israel.

Some aggressive dispensationalists made no secret of the fact that they considered the new evangelical activism a sell-out to secular ideas and a betrayal of the fundamental nonconformity, which they believed the gospel demands. Political action, they protested, had become a substitute for the lost power of holiness and those who thought they could use the political system would soon discover that they were consumed by it.

In the meantime, evangelical supporters of Israel extended their activities to the Holy Land itself. In 1980, a group of premillennial Christians with a strongly "charismatic" orientation established the International Christian Embassy, Jerusalem (ICEJ) and initiated the annual Feast of Tabernacles celebration, which brought thousands of Christians from all over the world to Jerusalem. The 13 last remaining nations with embassies in Jerusalem had just moved their staffs to Tel Aviv so the ICEJ was to be a concrete demonstration of continued and worldwide Christian solidarity with Israel.

"Getting high on prophecy is not enough," proclaimed the embassy organizers to their co-millennialists. "Just keeping busy with prophetic charts and theologizing about Israel" will not do. Isaiah 40:1: "Comfort ye, comfort ye my people!" became the embassy's motto, as well as its call to action. They realized that they were speaking to a community where there seems to be an insatiable hunger for new prophetic interpretations, sometimes of a highly sensational nature. Without sacrificing their eschatological beliefs, the embassy staff was determined not to let eschatology become an escape from history. No more paralysis through endless and speculative prophetic analysis.

Some evangelicals then began to discover Israel not just as a theological idea or as a Holy Land where Christians go to walk where Jesus walked, but as a country inhabited by flesh-and-blood Jews, struggling with issues of economic survival and national security.

From early childhood, many of these leaders had been admonished to "love the Jewish people" and to pray daily "for the peace of Jerusalem." But, by and large, it tended to be a love affair with an abstraction or, at least, with eschatological visions. The ICEJ is to be commended for its efforts to put some concreteness into the picture and to encourage Christians to become involved in activities that have practical implications: buy Israel bonds, travel to Jerusalem, write letters to Congress and the White House, etc.

Evangelical statements were usually composed by lesser figures and, by and large, lacked the drabness so characteristic of the United Nations English in which many ecumenical pronouncements are cast. But sometimes they seemed to be overburdened with bombast and excessive claims, thus helping to create a reality-rhetoric gap which is not healthy for intergroup relationships. For instance, in 1982, the Jewish Telegraphic Agency quoted a leading evangelical to the effect that "millions of evangelicals who support Israel will demonstrate this through meetings and demonstrations in order to change the shift in American foreign policy away from support of Israel back to the support Israel enjoyed in the past." If there has been a strengthening of U.S.-Israeli ties, it has surely not come about because millions of evangelical Christians have been bombarding the powers that be in Washington with letters, telegrams, and telephone calls.

Such statements are premised on a romantic notion about a past that never was. Arabists have been entrenched in the State Department for many years, seeking (sometimes with more, sometimes with less success) to steer U.S. Middle East policy toward less of a pro-Israel stance. They also overlook the fact that evangelicals simply have not been organized well enough to sustain an effort of such magnitude. Furthermore, the intensity of feelings on this issue among evangelicals is often exaggerated. For the vast majority of them, Israel is at best a secondary agenda item. The priorities lie clearly with the moral agenda of the New Right: abortion, homosexuality, etc. Mobilization of evangelicals on a policy dealing with such matters is much easier and can be pulled off much faster than marshalling the forces in defense of Israel's security when the United States government proposes to sell arms to Israel's enemies.

In no way am I suggesting that evangelical activism is irrelevant to the cause of Christian support for Israel. Far from it! I would submit, however, that flurries of enthusiasm from time to time and an occasional inspirational mass meeting to honor Israel will have very little lasting effect.

Evangelical eschatologists tend to be people in a hurry. They also, in somewhat paradoxical fashion, frequently lack a sense of history. This can lead to impatience, which, in turn, sometimes produces the kind of resentment which Nietzsche claimed to be a key element in much religion. As Solomon said, "Hope deferred makes the heart sick" (Proverbs 13:12).

It would be wrong to conclude that blunders on the part of some evangelicals mean that no progress is being made. Many evangelicals are establishing increasingly mature relationships with the Jewish community. Nevertheless, it is my impression that evangelical activism on behalf of Israel is not growing; I rather suspect that it is waning. Whatever happens, we can be sure that the subject of Israel will keep on stirring the souls and the theologies of evangelical Christians. It is at the heart of their theology of history and at the center of their eternal hope.

[1] Merrill Simon, *Jerry Falwell and the Jews*, (Middle Village, NY: Jonathan David Publishers, 1984), p. 87.

[2] James Neucherlain, *Commentary*, January, 1983, p. 19.

DIALOGUE AND THE FUTURE

CHAPTER 24

History: Horror and the Challenge of Hope

Is the glass of Christian-Jewish dialogue half full or half empty? Sometimes I am inclined to answer one way, sometimes the other. One thing can be said with certainty: our cup is far from running over.

Nevertheless, some historical dynamics have been set into motion. More people are engaged in a more honest quest for open dialogue. An increasing number of Christians are raising growing numbers of questions about missionary practices. Some education curricula have been revised for the better. Christians join with Jews for *Yom HaShoah* (or Holocaust memorial) services, and so forth and so on.

What has all this accomplished? I agree with Howard Singer that the movement has achieved more than was conceivable 50 years ago but less than many people had hoped for. However, when he then adds that "there seems little prospect that their hopes will be more fully realized in the future,"[1] one has to wonder how long or how short a view of the future he holds. After all, the dialogue as we know it today can so far be measured only in decades.

Some will no doubt say that I myself, while pointing to positive development, have put the emphasis too heavily on the side of pessimism. Well, I hardly consider myself an optimist about human nature or about historical movements. But I am basically a hopeful person. I agree with Pierre Teilhard de Chardin that people of faith are "pilgrims of the future." There is a biblical futurism that cannot be captured by such categories as optimism or pessimism. So, I conclude this book with a few reflections on history, memory, and human responsibility.

Martin Buber stated that "the world of prophetic faith is, in fact, historic reality seen in the bold and penetrating glance of the man who dares to believe."[2] People who live in this world as those who dare to believe–as for example prophets–cannot adequately be described either as optimists or pessimists. Their faith, however, does tend to have a quality about it that gives them courage to face today and hope to move toward tomorrow.

According to Thomas Carlyle, history is, at bottom, "the biography of great men," the story of heroes. But recent history has taught us once again with unmistakable clarity that an Adolph Hitler, hailed by multitudes of people as a great and heroic deliverer, can inflict horror and death upon millions. In this connection we are reminded of the fact that, in Christian tradition, suffering rather than heroism has often been seen as the interpretive principle of history. Therefore, the symbol of the cross has become central to many Christian philosophies of history.

To someone like Nicolas Berdyaev, with little interest in theology in the traditional sense, the historical process itself became a basic source of suffering. His constant complaint was that man is nailed to the cross of time. To him, time as measured by the clock and the calendar represented transitoriness, tragedy, and failure. What he called "common time," as distinguished from the creative existential moment, condemns people to live in what he considered to be an unreal world. History must be transcended, and the way that is done is through ecstasy. Thus, we can be saved from the real world and touch eternity in the midst of fallen time.

For most Christian theologians the problem is not history as such, but human sin. Not "fallen time" but "fallen humanity" has distorted the reality of the good creation. The cross of Christ became the central symbol of human sin, but also of divine love. In his 1949 study *Meaning in History* (note, not the meaning *of* history), Karl Löwith wrote that "nothing else than the life and death of Jesus Christ, the 'Suffering Servant,' who was deserted and crucified, can be the standard of a Christian understanding of the world's history." The scandal of the cross becomes a central interpretive principle of "the way things are."

Others do not wish to focus so exclusively on the cross in their interpretation of history. They emphasize a message of the cross and the resurrection. The cross is not only the symbol of human sin and the horrors of history; it is also the source of healing and a new kind of power. The power of the cross lies in the triumph of love. In such a context we are introduced to a new kind of hero, the person who (in analogy to the Divine Being) enters into the suffering of others.

After attending a preview of the film "The Courage to Care," which is a movie about people who risked their own lives in order to rescue Jews from the horror of the Holocaust, I mentioned to a guest from Holland that the film featured a Dutch woman. When asked for her name and I told him, he replied, "I can tell you that she is a big unknown." But that, it seems to me, is precisely the point. Here we are talking about the heroism of the non-famous, the non-celebrities. I like to call it "the heroism of the common life," of men and women who, in the midst of a grabbing and greedy world, have the courage to do the decent thing. They do not achieve high standing, like General Secretary of the United Nations for example; nor do they worry too much about their *curricula vitae*, neither to hide their past nor to be honored. These people, in a not-very-conscious fashion, live lives that are a true expression of a theology of the cross and the resurrection.

But now we face a new horror, one that is closely related to the horrors of the Holocaust. Because the simple fact is that, in the course of Christian history, the norm (certainly as far as the Jews were concerned) has been the exact opposite of such demonstrations of love. The cross, rather than becoming the symbol of Christian identification with the sufferings of others, became a weapon to hurt others, a symbol of hatred against those accused of being Christ-killers. It all sounds so incredible, almost like the ultimate absurdity, but such is the truth. When people tell us from personal experience how, in certain countries during their childhood years, they would cross the street rather than pass in front of a church because Jewish children often were beaten up, they are not making up a story. They are telling us the crazy truth about certain aspects of Christian history. The most incredible thing about it all is that the beatings usually increased during the Christmas and Lenten seasons.

It is relevant that I quote somewhat extensively from an article I wrote some time ago for the *Reformed Journal*.[3]

When it came to their relationship with God, Christians have usually interpreted the cross in terms of reconciliation, unmerited love for sinful human beings, and divine identification with the needs of the world. Its message became one of comfort to people who knew themselves to be unworthy. But, what happened when it came to Christians' encounters with Jews? In that case, in a spirit of incredible self-righteousness and cruel malice, the cross was frequently turned into a crusader's sword–a curse against the people who were called Christ-killers, an instrument of scapegoating that has set the stage for persecutions, pogroms, and holocausts.

In the novel *The Last of the Just*, by Andre Schwartz-Bart, Golda asks Ernie, "Tell me, why do Christians hate us the way they do? They seem so nice when I can look at them without my star." "It's very mysterious," replies Ernie. "They don't know exactly why themselves. . . . Do you know who Christ was? A simple Jew like your father. A kind of Hasid . . . He was really a good Jew, you know sort of like the Baal Shem Tov–a merciful man, and gentle. The Christians say they love him, but I think they hate him without knowing it. So they take the cross by the other end and make a sword out of it and strike us with it! You understand, Golda," he cried suddenly, strangely excited, "they take the cross and they turn it around, they turn it around, my God. . ."

Still, it took me a long time to discover the true dimensions of Christian culpability with respect to anti-Jewish measures throughout the centuries. It is not the kind of thing most students are taught in theological seminaries. Some have heard about the 4ᵗʰ century church father, John Chrysostom, who was known as "the golden-tongued preacher," but whose mouth spewed venom when he spoke about the Jews. There is, in general, vague familiarity with the fact that Martin Luther in his later years said some vicious things about Jews. But, by and large, there is little awareness that we are dealing, not with unfortunate "incidents" in Christian history, aberrations from the norm, but rather with a continuous saga that goes from generation to generation, from century to century. The moments of respite and tolerance, not persecution, were the exception.

Even for a person with my background it takes a profound reeducation to discover what the true story is. The lack is not historical data, nor is the problem a shortage of sound and solid research. The crisis of the Christian community lies much deeper than that. It has to do with our refusal to deal with memory as a moral issue. In Christian theological terms, the problem lies in our reluctance to engage in genuine confession, our resistance to repentance, and hence our failure to find new freedom though forgiveness.

Alan Ecclestone was right when he observed that "the Holocaust has not been felt in the marrow bones of contemporary Christian life."[4] True, what is being asked of us is a very hard thing to do. Father Flannery has described his well-known study, *The Anguish of the Jews,* as "an invitation to Christian heritage, to undergo what might be called a historical psychoanalysis. . . ."[5] That means that we are being asked to enter into an experience that is bound to be extremely painful.

Remembrance is a moral, even a divine, imperative. Abraham Joshua Heschel has taught us that what the Bible requires can be compressed into one word: *remember.* Even if that might be considered an overstatement, that would not invalidate the central truth that this remark contains. For instance, the repeated and urgent admonitions in Deuteronomy that the people should not forget are rooted in the view that forgetfulness can be a form of unfaithfulness and that memory is not just a matter of the mind, but a moral issue.

There is such a thing as a slip of the mind. But that is a wholly different matter from what concerns us here. When the one-time General Secretary of the United Nations with a hidden Nazi past, Kurt Waldheim, had a hard time putting his biography together, then we are not dealing with a problem of recollection, but rather with a flaw of character, a failure of moral nerve.

In George Orwell's book, *1984*, we find described a world in which three basic principles prevail: newspeak, doublethink, and the mutability of the past. Whenever the past does not suit the purposes of the powers that be, they simply discard it, declare it inoperative and a non-happening. There is no memory in that world. Statues, inscriptions, memorial stones, and monuments–anything that might shed light on the past–have been systematically altered. Such a world is every dictator's dream. Sometimes such dictators receive support from professors who have degrees from highly respectable academic institutions. They are in fact propagandists who disguise themselves as educators. For instance, the work of pseudo-scholars, like the historical revisionists in our day who deny that the Holocaust ever happened, is so dangerous because it has a basically totalitarian impulse behind it.

The burden of memory is at heart the burden of our humanity. There is something glorious about our ability to come to terms with the past–our national, church, and family histories. By facing history, we face ourselves. But this is precisely the freedom of the human spirit from which we all too frequently seek to escape.

In the words of the poet Percy Bysshe Shelley, "the world is weary of the past, oh might it die or rest at last!" It is that sentiment that causes people to say they are tired of hearing about the Holocaust. Let bygones be bygones! Some people anxiously warn that no good will come from rehashing history; it will provoke annoyance and anger among those who do not wish to hear. But as Elie Wiesel has pointed out with never-ceasing passion: If this generation does not remember, will there be a next generation? After all, in the final analysis, it is not the past but the future that is at stake.

For the sake of the future it is so crucial that we cultivate a sense of history. It is troublesome when Johnny cannot read or if Mary doesn't know how to count. But equally troublesome is how many of our young people lack a sense of historical consciousness and context. I recall a letter to the *New York Times* a few years ago, written by Jean Mayer, the President of Tufts University, in which he claimed that a lack of a sense of history is the single biggest deficiency in otherwise bright high school students who apply to our top colleges.

This is an age of immediacy. We live in the era of the TV image. Every day millions of people view the world through the eye of a camera lens, controlled in many instances by people who are more interested in emotional impact than in historical context. Complex situations like the Middle East are dealt with in 30-second commentaries by celebrities for whom ratings, rather than remembrance, are a survival issue.

My point is not that the emotional dimensions of life should be ignored or that the media are to be blamed for all our problems. Modern technology simply tends to expose our weaknesses on a larger scale. Historical amnesia was a well-known phenomenon before the invention of television. It is as old as our natural tendency toward intellectual laziness, reinforced at times by ulterior motives and a nastiness of spirit.

Henry Ford II, who did not achieve fame because of his philosophical insights, is known to have pontificated on the subject of history. His views can be summed up in his somewhat philistine conclusion that history is "mostly bunk." Now let us remember that this same man, who held such a low view of history, used the *Dearborn Independent*, a paper totally dependent on the Ford fortunes, to propagate anti-Semitic forgeries like the *Protocols of the Learned Elders of Zion* as historical fact. Thus we have a classic illustration of George Santayana's dictum that "those who cannot remember the past are condemned to repeat it." Unfortunately, when we repeat the past, we tend to repeat its worst features.

Elie Wiesel has played a key role in making the Holocaust a subject of conscious reflection and extensive research. He was one of the first to break the silence that had prevailed for some decades after World War II. I think this silent interval was needed, especially by the victims who were facing the task of rebuilding their lives. The silence did not mean that those people were not dealing with the experiences of the hell through which they had passed. It was precisely their daily struggles with the horrendous realities of the Holocaust that gave their daily decisions about starting anew, establishing families, and assuming social-political responsibilities such a quality of courage.

But eventually, the memories were vocalized more and more. The Holocaust also became a central concern in Christian circles, especially among those who recognized that this period of horrors was, in a very real sense, a chapter in Christian history. For some theologians the Holocaust was to be a preoccupation in their moral, spiritual, and intellectual pursuits. Theirs was often a lonely journey because there was an inclination among many scholars to give their research little serious consideration.

Nevertheless, because of the perseverance of the few, we now see a growing interest in Holocaust studies, the establishment of Holocaust institutes and museums, the development of Holocaust curricula, annual Holocaust observances, and the like.

At first, I must confess, I felt ambivalent about this persistent emphasis upon the Holocaust and concerned that we might become captives of our preoccupations with the past. For many, especially those of us who lived under Nazi rule as young people, the experience had been one of intense immediacy and concreteness. We knew precisely who the enemy was and what needed to be done. They needed to be killed through acts of underground sabotage; their armies needed to be defeated by the allies and their reign of terror brought to an end. There was little reflection about it all.

After the war, not least for the sake of our own emotional and spiritual health, we needed to come to terms with the hatreds that had been so unquestionably nurtured in our souls. When does the moment come that one concludes that enough is enough? When, in a world where new horrors were being perpetrated, did one make a commitment to work for the future? I wasn't sure that such a strong focus on the Holocaust would be helpful in the task humanity was facing.

However, the more I learned to view the Holocaust in terms of a broader history, the more I became persuaded that the intense reflections and the persistent research on the Holocaust might indeed help us to work for a better future with new insights and wisdom. As Rabbi Nachman of Bratslav has said, "In remembering lies the secret of redemption." Without memory we will have a hard time discovering our destiny. Historical amnesia can so easily become a way of life, a way of living in dishonesty and thus in escape from responsibility.

I have become convinced that Holocaust studies and Holocaust observances can indeed serve a redeeming purpose in our society. At the same time, I have also developed new ambivalences. Holocaust concerns are themselves in danger of becoming poisoned by elements of commercialism or even hucksterism. The endless Holocaust conferences circuit, the never-ending fundraising efforts, the grantmanship, the rivalries between Holocaust bureaucracies, the career seekers, the hunger for publicity: these and similar factors become the seeds of a Holocaust politics that is the more distasteful because it is done in the name of defending holy ground.

When I first heard a Jewish Federation executive use the phrase "there is no business like Shoah business," I was shocked. But the more sacred the cause, the greater is the need that we face up to the danger signals. The U.S. Holocaust Memorial Council, established by an act of Congress in order that a museum might be built in Washington DC, to keep alive the memory of the martyrs and to hold before future generations the lessons we have learned about the nature and consequences of bigotry, became itself the battlefield of clashing interests and egos. The January 16, 1987 issue of the *Jewish World* in New York carried the following headline: "Holocaust Museum tangled in its own barbed wire." The story that followed gave the unedifying account of bitter infighting among Council members and staff, a situation that had been the subject of rumors for months.

The theology department of the university featured in John

Updike's novel *Roger's Version* has among its faculty members a specialist in "holocaustics." It is sad to see the Holocaust associated with tongue-in-cheek descriptions of vanity and pomposity. On the other hand, we need to recognize that we ourselves invite ridicule when we treat the Holocaust as if it were another fad to be manipulated for professional and financial interests.

It is a sin to use the Holocaust in ways that will breed cynicism. It is a betrayal of the memory of those who have died, many of them hoping that humanity would yet come to its senses. Cynicism, like forgetfulness, poses a threat to our future. It undermines faith, dims the sparks of hope that are still aglow in the world and weakens people's motivation to engage in loving and responsible actions.

Through memory, we can shape destiny. "Life can only be understood backwards; but it must be lived forwards," wrote Sören Kierkegaard. Even in the darkest moments of history we can discover glimmers of hope. For instance, the Holocaust has its endless horror stories. They must be told. But there are also stories of human decency and responsibility. They, too, must be told, because they constitute signposts of hope. They speak of character, courage, and self-sacrifice.

What turns people into haters? We need to try and find out. On the other hand, what makes people do the humane thing, even in some instances when it endangers them and their families? We need to research that as well. Dr. Samuel P. Oliver, a sociologist at Humboldt University and himself a survivor who was helped by non-Jewish friends, apparently did precisely that in what he called the "Altruistic Personality Project."

We need memory, and we need vision. Memory without vision can easily turn into a state of morbidity. Vision without memory will eventually lead either to utopian fantasies or to a nostalgia that pursues a past that never was. None of these can serve as a sound basis for moral-spiritual renewal. They are not motivating forces that give hope for the future.

One of the most inspiring stories of memory and vision is the history of the Jewish people and their love affair with the land of Israel. Few have written about that story with greater poetic fervor than the late Abraham Joshua Heschel in his book *Israel: An Echo of Eternity.* Let me cite a few passages:

> Why did our hearts and minds throughout the ages turn to Eretz Israel, to the Holy Land? Because of memory, because of hope, because of distress.
>
> Because of memory. There is a slow and silent stream, a stream not of oblivion but of memory, from which we must constantly drink before entering the realm of faith. To be-

lieve is to remember. The substance of our very being is memory, our way of living is retaining the reminders, articulating memory.

Jewish memory, far from turning into a collection of stale reminiscences, was kept alive by the power of hope and imagination, transcending the limits of believing . . .[6]

Perhaps the most characteristic quality of Jewish existence is *bittahon* ("hope"). Believing and hoping are one. It is part of our very existence to be faithful to the future, to keep alive the beginning by nursing the vision of the end. Hope is the creative articulation of faith[7] . . .

What lends meaning to history? The promise of the future. If there is no promise, there is no meaningful history. Significance is contingent on vision and anticipation, on living the future in the present tense.

This is one of the gifts of the Bible to the world: a promise, a vision, a hope.[8]

The story of Zion is a story of repeated destruction, suffering, and the shedding of tears in many strange lands. It is also a story of hope kept alive through some of the darkest moments of history. Zionism represents a historical movement through which that hope was translated into actions that laid the foundation for a new future. The Zionist pioneers in the end convinced a people who might well have succumbed to a total sense of powerlessness that it is not the will of God that we be victims, but rather that we should be partners in fulfilling the divine plan for humanity.

And so Israel was reborn. It is not the ideal society. Far from it. But it is one of the great signs of hope in modern history. Israel represents a triumph of the human spirit in the post-Holocaust era.

Christians who seek dialogue with Jews but avoid the subject of Israel deprive the churches of one of the most hopeful potentials that such a dialogue can produce. On the other hand, Christians who romanticize Israel in the name of love for the Jewish people may also miss an opportunity to learn important lessons from the Jewish experience. Together we are "pilgrims of the future." In spite of horrendous disasters and failures, the future beckons us to dare to believe and, trusting in the faithfulness of God, to choose life and not death. *L'Chayim!*

[1]Howard Singer, "The Rise and Fall of Interfaith Dialogue," *Commentary*, May 1987, p. 55.

[2]Martin Buber, *Prophetic Faith* (New York: Harper & Row, 1960), p. 135.

[3]Rottenberg, *Reformed Journal*, May, 1982.

[4]Alan Ecclestone *The Night Sky of the Lord* (New York: Schocken Books, 1982), p. 99.

[5]Father Edward H. Flannery, *The Anguish of the Jews* (New York: Paulist Press, 1985), p. 3.

⁶Abraham Joshua Heschel, *Israel: An Echo of Eternity* (New York: Farrar, Straus and Giroux, 1969), pp. 60-61.

⁷*Ibid.,* p. 94.

⁸*Ibid.,* p. 127.

POSTSCRIPT

Christian-Jewish dialogue is mostly a post-World War II and post-Holocaust phenomenon. In other words, from a historical perspective it is a growing but nevertheless young and still developing movement. Can it also be said that it is showing signs of increased maturity?

The first and somewhat hesitant initiatives came from the Christian side. European churches had come face to face with the evils of a Nazi neo-pagan idolatry and its totalitarian claims, its pre-Christian Teutonic deities, and its anti-Semitic ideology of *Blut und Boden* (race and fatherland). During Hitler's reign of terror, the German Evangelical Church had courageously spoken out in the Barmen Declaration, proclaiming the God of the Bible versus the gods of this age.

In May 1946, exactly one year after Holland's liberation from Nazi occupation, the Netherlands Reformed Church set in motion a process that four years later would lead to the adoption of a new confessional statement which sought to express the historic faith in terms of contemporary issues. That document contained an element never before found in Christian creeds, namely an article on Israel's continued role in God's redemptive dealings with the world. The Jewish people, the statement declared, remain God's covenant people because the divine promises to them have never been revoked (Romans 11:29). A Council for *"Gesprek"* (conversation, dialogue) with Israel was established and a sea change in Christian-Jewish relations had begun.

Prominent themes in the early stages of the dialogue were Christian anti-Judaism, theological supersessionism, and the Holocaust. In 1964, the Second Vatican Council gave new and worldwide impetus to the movement with its declaration *Nostra Aetate*. The Catholic Church boldly affirmed "the spiritual bond linking the people of the New Covenant with Abraham's stock," condemned all forms of anti-Semitism, and rejected the notion that all Jews then or now are to be blamed for the death of Jesus Christ. The Council also called for "fraternal dialogues."

Over the past decades, the dialogue has had its ups and downs. In the preceding pages we have looked at a number of the issues: the dynamics involved, the doctrinal disputes, the mission issue, the growing phenomenon of "Messianic Jews," and the theological as well as political controversies surrounding the State of Israel. Few issues have found a final resolution. One can speak, however, of a growing consensus among Christians that supersessionism represented a triumphalistic distortion of the gospel and contributed to Jewish suffering throughout the centuries. Many ecclesiastical bodies have by now asked forgiveness from the Jewish people for those grievous sins.

Slowly but surely, trust relationships have developed between Jewish and Christian dialogue partners. In the section on dialogue dynamics we raised the question: What can we talk about, and how do we go about it? Practice has not made perfect–some issues remain painful to discuss; but just the fact that people are conversing with each other on a faith-to-faith level, and in the process are developing friendships, creates conditions that are conducive to dealing honestly with conflicting views.

Debates on doctrinal matters have, it seems to me, been mostly an internal Christian affair, although our Jewish interlocutors may follow them with intense interest and from time to time even display a distinct preference, particularly when christological questions are involved. The church's historic confession of Jesus as Messiah and Savior of the world continues to pose a serious stumbling-block for our Jewish dialogue partners.

Yet, in recent years we have begun to see more probing and less reflexive reactions to this crucial issue on the part of some Jewish thinkers. As we have noted, Michael Kogan's call for "total dialogue" included such subjects as incarnation, atonement, and the Christian belief in Jesus' resurrection. Some Jewish leaders are less than enthusiastic about such suggestions, but the book *Christianity in Jewish Terms*[1] ventures more deeply into theological questions than would have been conceivable only a few decades ago. The chapters on "embodiment" (incarnation), redemption, sin and repentance offer insights that were not found on the dialogue menu in its early stages. We have repeatedly referred to the sometimes unconventional views of Irving Greenberg and Michael Wyschogrod, both prominent Jewish scholars in the orthodox tradition. They have both produced these recent works: Greenberg's *For the Sake of Heaven and Earth: The New Encounter between Judaism and Christianity*[2] and Wyschogrod's *Abraham's Promise: Judaism and Jewish-Christian Relations.*[3] They offer some challenging reflections on such topics as incarnation, Jesus' messiahship, and "Messianic Jews," which are not always appreciated by their co-religionists.

Rabbi Greenberg, a man of irenic spirit and sharp mind, has been a pioneer in Jewish-Christian relations for many years. In contrast to his earlier thesis that Jesus might be considered a "failed" rather than a "false messiah," he has come to use a less harsh sounding term, namely "unfinished messiah." He now sees Jesus as being one in a line of great Jewish spiritual leaders of Israel who did not live to see their dreams fulfilled but who, nevertheless, may have rendered a great service to both Judaism and the cause of God's kingdom.

Greenberg recognizes that Jews and Christians have a common

covenantal relationship to the God of Israel and therefore the members of the two faith communities are at heart one people in the service of the Holy One–that is, as long as Christians do not perceive of themselves as a "replacement" of Israel. In short, divine election can involve "multiple choice," two covenantal communities working side by side, and sometimes jointly, for *tikkun olam* ("repairing" the world, making it a better place). While differences concerning Jesus' messiahship continue to be fundamental, one can see how Greenberg's daring approach to key issues in the dialogue opens up new perspectives about possible future cooperative ventures in addressing societal issues of common concern.

As we have already learned from his book, *The Body of Faith: Judaism as Corporeal Election*, Michael Wyschogrod is a proponent of a biblical "incarnational theology."[4] Israel, on the basis of God's free and sovereign decision, is God's first and special love. Therefore, Gentiles are the real proselytes–those who were added by incorporation into the divine covenant with Israel in order to serve the redemptive purpose of God for the world.

As to the Christian doctrine of incarnation, Wyschogrod is not inclined to dismiss it out of hand–as long as the church's christological claims do not imply that God has repudiated the promises made to Israel. As a matter of fact, Wyschogrod makes the stunning suggestion that God's incarnation in Jesus could be seen as a kind of intensification of God's presence in the people of Israel. While he would see that as one event among potentially others in the chain of historical phenomena, most Christians would interpret the incarnation in Jesus as the once-for-all redemptive event and therefore the center of history.

The differences here are more than significant; they are decisive for one's confession of faith. Nevertheless, the dialogue now reaches a level of exciting intensity that certainly can be interpreted as a growth in maturity.[5] We can now begin to converse on the basis of commonalities that could have far-reaching consequences for our mutual and, perhaps, joint approaches to world conditions.

The anti-supersessionist stance affirmed by many denominations in recent decades has also, according to Wyschogrod, profound implications for their attitude toward baptized Jews. No longer do we hear the usual mantra that a baptized Jew *ipso facto* ceases to be a Jew. No, the churches must show that they mean it when they proclaim the eternal covenant with the Jewish people by encouraging baptized Jews to observe Torah teachings and maintain a distinct identity within the church. Prohibiting them from doing so would in effect mean a denial of God's special, but not exclusive, covenant with Israel "according to the flesh." These are explosive statements for which many Jews and Christians may not be quite ready, while to others they may be very welcome indeed.

No doubt, there will be those who will respond to Greenberg and Wyschogrod by emphasizing that these are maverick and minority voices. But that can be said of many Christian participants in the dialogue as well, no matter what particular theological viewpoint they may advance. Such voices may either be so out of step with their communities that they become totally ineffective, or they can become the *avant garde* for a new and fruitful thrust in the dialogue. One thing seems certain, at least to this author: if those views are taken seriously even by a minority of believers, they could have a significant impact not only on the life and ministry of our respective communities, but on the social-political and cultural world around them as well. For that reason "Spengler," who regularly writes insightful columns for the *Asia Times*, has called *Abraham's Promise* perhaps "one of the most important books of the 21st century."[6] "The intellectual resources of US evangelicals have not," he asserts, "grown in step with their membership, and the movement is ripe for a re-examination." He then adds that Wyschogrod provides "evangelicalism" with a biblical (as opposed to a philosophical) frame-work "to understand itself . . . [by] coming to terms with the Judaism within it." Hopefully many Christians beyond the evangelical community will come to terms with that reality as well.

Does the dialogue here presented offer an agenda for the future? George Lindbeck expresses the hope that as supersessionism is eliminated the understanding of the church as Israel will be regained, but this time not as a replacement theology that threatens Judaism and the Jewish community.[7] Rather, the church as an implant into the body of Israel receives nurture from that body. Then Jewish believers will no longer be pressured to cut themselves off from their heritage, and the "Old Testament" will once again be deemed as essential for the life and ministry of the churches as the "New Testament." The major challenge Judaism and Christianity face today is, according to Lindbeck, "a pervasive pluralistic consumerism destructive of all enduring traditions and communities. Christians no less than Jews are engulfed by this assimilationist wave, and the best resistance Christians can offer is the reappropriation without expropriation of the church's roots in Israel and Israel's Scriptures."[8]

Of course, any attempt to pattern the life of the church after "Old Testament Israel" may pose dangers all of its own, as some strains in United States history may already have taught us. Till this day we are hotly debating the interaction between religion and politics (church and state) and the word *theocracy* is often bandied about with reckless abandon. Thus we enter the realm of conflicting worldviews and ideologies. Is that the way to go? It is this author's belief that, for the sake of *tikkun olam* and in light of the church's proclamation of the "gospel of the Kingdom," this path will prove to be unavoidable if we do not want to become socially irresponsible and consequently irrelevant to the health of the commonwealth. But that will have to be the subject for another volume.

[1] *Christianity in Jewish Terms*, Tikva Frymer-Kensky, et. al., eds. (Boulder, Colorado: Westview Press, 2000).

[2] Irving Greenberg, *For the Sake of Heaven and Earth: The New Encounter between Judaism and Christianity* (Jewish Publication Society, 2004).

[3] Michael Wyschogrod, *Abraham's Promise: Judaism and Jewish-Christian Relations* (Grand Rapids: Eerdmans, 2004).

[4] Wyschogrod, *The Body of Faith: Judaism as Corporeal Election* (New York: Seabury Press, 1983).

[5] There are other areas where one might discern signs of a growing maturity. On the subject of "mission" I would refer particularly to Yaakov Ariel's book, *Evangelizing the Chosen People* (Chapel Hill, NC: University of North Carolina Press, 2000) and on the topic of "Messianic Jews" to Carol Harris Shapiro's *Messianic Judaism: A Rabbi's Journey through Religious Change in America* (Boston: Beacon Press, 1999) and Dan Cohn-Sherbok's *Messianic Judaism: The First Study of Messianic Judaism by a Non-adherent* (London: Continuum Publishing Group, 2000).

[6] Spengler, *Asia Times Online*, February 8, 2005.

[7] George Lindbeck, quoted in *Christianity in Jewish Terms*, p. 358ff.

[8] *Ibid.*, p. 365.

TEN COMMANDMENTS
FOR CHRISTIAN-JEWISH DIALOGUE

1) THOU SHALT MEET THE "OTHER" AS A "THOU."

Martin Buber noted that "all true living is meeting" in a classic "I-thou" encounter. This is not just going to meetings but is meeting as encounter with each entering into other's experience. It is treating others as persons, endowed with divine image, not as prospects to advance one's own purposes.

2) THOU SHALT LEARN TO LISTEN.

The natural human urge is to talk, to argue, to jump in before someone else does. One needs to listen, to hear not only the words, but also what is behind the words. Douglas Steere said, "Genuine listening is a form of loving."

3) THOU SHALT CONFESS THE SINS OF THY CHURCH.

Christians must face the dark sides of "Christian" history, especially historic Christian anti-Judaism. This takes the form of confession, which is the opposite of a "guilt trip." The former is liberating; the latter is destructive and leads to more negativity. This is true repentance, forgiveness, and the new freedom in Christ.

4) THOU SHALT SPEAK THE TRUTH IN LOVE.

Dialogue cannot escape the "truth question." There must be no compromise, no seeking the lowest common denominator. At the same time, there must also be no spirit of conquest. God's truth is bigger than our truths. Past disputation that turned into diatribe must be avoided.

5) THOU SHALT LOOK FOR COMMONALITIES WITHOUT IGNORING DIFFERENCES.

Either side can be overdrawn, as if Christianity and Judaism are two totally different religions, which have nothing fundamental in common, or as if we are similar "ethical" religions. A good illustration might be our different views of sin.

6) THOU SHALT AFFIRM THE TRIUMPHANT MESSAGE ABOUT THE RISEN CHRIST WITHOUT FALLING INTO TRIUMPHALISM.

Remember the Apostle Paul's warnings about "boasting" against the Jewish people. This will help avoid repeating the mistake in history in which the church virtually identified itself as the kingdom of God and came to view Israel an eternally rejected people. Dialogue demands honesty, but also humility. The church and Israel both play a role in God's eschatological dealings with the world.

7) THOU SHALT NOT FEAR CHANGE.

Dialogue involves various degrees of risk. We need openness to a change of mind *and* heart. Dialogue is not, however, a platform for evangelistic crusades. It is important to hold things in a healthy tension. Both sides may be threatened at times but sensitivity to each other's struggles and pain is essential.

8) THOU SHALT AFFIRM PLURALISM, BUT REJECT RELATIVISM.

Our contemporary cultural context insists that all religion be relativised. "It's all the same: you have your opinion, and I have mine." The reality of pluralism must be recognized; however, we must deal with it, but not by succumbing to either a rigid dogmatism or a spirit of relativism.

9) THOU SHALT MAINTAIN A SENSE OF HUMOR.

"Humor has a touch of holiness" if we recognize that God is God and we are not. "Humor keeps hope alive" (Rubem Alves). And hope keeps people alive. Humor must be maintained in the context of faith, hope, and love. In moments of tension, a little laughter can be so liberating. Christian-Jewish dialogue is serious business, but watch out if a mood of bitter seriousness begins to take over.

10) THOU SHALT ABOVE ALL, PRAY FOR DIVINE GRACE.

Dialogue that is honest to God, to each other, and to ourselves is beyond our human capabilities. The temptations and missteps mentioned above are only a small sample of the forces that militate against "the mind of Christ" in us. Dialogue, while not an evangelistic "technique," can still be a way of witnessing to the Good News that entered the world through *Yeshua HaMashiach*.

INDEX OF TOPICS

INDEX OF PROPER NAMES